Charles S. Gleed

From River to Sea

A Tourist's and Miner's Guide from the Missouri River to the Pacific Ocean via

Kansas, Colorado, New Mexico, and California

Charles S. Gleed

From River to Sea

A Tourist's and Miner's Guide from the Missouri River to the Pacific Ocean via Kansas, Colorado, New Mexico, and California

ISBN/EAN: 9783337242428

Printed in Europe, USA, Canada, Australia, Japan

Cover: Foto ©Andreas Hilbeck / pixelio.de

More available books at **www.hansebooks.com**

FROM RIVER TO SEA;

A TOURISTS' AND MINERS' GUIDE

FROM THE MISSOURI RIVER

— TO THE —

PACIFIC OCEAN

— VIA —

KANSAS, COLORADO, NEW MEXICO, ARIZONA AND CALIFORNIA.

CHAS. S. GLEED, EDITOR.

CHICAGO:
RAND, McNALLY & CO.
1882.

IN THE BEGINNING.

I T should be clearly understood that this little book has but one purpose. This purpose is to give people a good general idea of the vast territory which is tributary to the new line of rail communication between the Missouri river and the Pacific ocean. The subject is too long and too broad to admit of an exhaustive treatment within the allotted space; but the space is, nevertheless, sufficient for the telling of all which the general reader cares to know or can ever remember. On this subject no single publication could be a real authority as to details. The greater portion of the country is so new, and its development is so rapid, that none but the more general geographical specifications would, for any considerable time, hold good. Wherever practicable, however, details have been given; in all cases with the greatest possible accuracy. If future editions of the book do not suffer such misfortunes as have, so far, followed this one, they will bring to the reader more of fact, more of fancy, more of art, more of everything which enters into the composition of a complete volume. Until then, with becoming modesty, this little book recommends itself simply as being the best book in print on the subjects discussed. To Mr. W. H. Hollabird, the well-known expert in the matter of field sports, and to others whose valuable assistance has not otherwise been acknowledged, hearty thanks are hereby returned.

THE EDITOR.

CATHEDRAL ROCK, GARDEN OF THE GODS.

(5)

FROM RIVER TO SEA.

THE SOUTHERN ROUTE.

ATCHISON, TOPEKA & SANTA FÉ RAILROAD — DENVER & RIO GRANDE RAIL-
ROAD — ATLANTIC & PACIFIC RAILROAD — SOUTHERN PACIFIC
RAILROAD — CALIFORNIA ROADS.

HE traveler who contemplates a journey from "River to Sea" first desires to know as much as possible concerning the system of railway lines over all or part of which he is about to pass. The Atchison, Topeka & Santa Fé system of roads is one of the newest, yet one of the most complete and important in the world. It has three eastern termini, viz.: Atchison, Kansas City and Pleasant Hill. The two former places are situated on the Missouri river, Kansas City being at about the middle of the eastern boundary of Kansas, and Atchison being north of it, a distance of forty-seven miles. Pleasant Hill is thirty-four miles southeast of Kansas City. The Atchison and Kansas City lines unite at Topeka—fifty miles from Atchison and sixty-six miles from Kansas City. The Pleasant Hill line unites with the Kansas City line at Cedar Junction, forty-four miles from Pleasant Hill. From Kansas City the road passes along the south bank of the Kansas river, occasionally deserting the river in order to take a more direct course across the incomparably rich farming lands of the beautiful Kansas valley. At Topeka the line turns from its western course to one

(7)

south by west, and maintains that direction as far as Newton, where its western course is resumed to Pueblo. Twenty-six miles beyond Topeka, at Burlingame, the Manhattan branch, known as the Manhattan, Alma & Burlingame Railway—a line operated by the Atchison, Topeka & Santa Fé Company—diverges toward the northwest to Manhattan, a distance of fifty-seven miles. At Emporia Junction, thirty-five miles from Burlingame, the Howard branch diverges to Howard, a distance of seventy-six miles. At Florence, forty-five miles from Emporia Junction, the Marion Center and McPherson branch takes a more directly westward course than the main line, to Ellinwood, a distance of ninety-nine miles. From Florence, also, the Eldorado branch runs south to Douglas. At Newton, twenty-nine miles from Florence, the Caldwell and Arkansas City branches run to Caldwell, eighty miles, and Arkansas City, seventy-eight miles. The line has no other branches until La Junta is reached, in Colorado, 555 miles from Atchison. From La Junta one double band of steel spans the prairie between that point and Pueblo, while the other runs south through New Mexico. The Colorado line, sixty-three miles beyond La Junta, reaches Pueblo, making connection with the Denver & Rio Grande Railway, the principal railway of Colorado. One portion of this road runs directly north, through Colorado Springs and Manitou, to Denver, 120 miles. Another strikes out west by north through the Grand Cañon of the Arkansas to Leadville, 159 miles. The line at Leadville branches to Kokomo, nineteen miles, and to Mitchell's Pass, eleven miles. At Cañon City, forty-one miles from Pueblo, a line is run northwest to West Cliff, thirty-five miles distant. Fifty-six miles northwest of Cañon City the Gunnison branch leaves the main line and runs southwest to Gunnison, seventy-three miles, forming a triangle enclosed on two sides. Short branches to Maysville and Alpine complete the Leadville division. Starting again from Pueblo, the Denver & Rio Grande Railroad proceeds due south for fifty miles to Cuchara, where it divides, one portion extending in the same direction to El Moro, nearly thirty-seven miles south, and the other bearing southwest to Antonito, near the New Mexican northern border line, a distance of just 100 miles, and crossing in the meantime the famous Veta Pass, in the Sangre de Christo range. At Antonito the iron horse plunges westward again, bound for the San Juan region, of which Silverton is a leading point, though the rails have been laid but a little distance beyond Durango, which is 172 miles from Antonito. Again starting from Antonito and heading toward the south, the line is operated in Northern New Mexico as far as Espanola, ninety-one miles from the former place and twenty from Santa Fé. Back again to La Junta, the Atchison, Topeka & Santa Fé road is resumed. The way leads west of south, eighty-two miles to Trinidad, there crosses the Raton range, thence to Las Vegas, 133 miles further on. At that point it bends to the west, sending a twenty-mile branch to

Santa Fé from Lamy, and shortly afterwards, striking the Rio Grande valley, leads due south to El Paso, where connection is made with the Mexican extension. The road from El Paso north to Rincon is merely a branch, seventy-seven miles in length. The line proper proceeds to Deming, at which point it is 1,149 miles from its starting place at Kansas City. The road passes from Deming west to Benson, 173 miles, this stretch of track

THE "BED GROUNDS."

being owned jointly by the Atchison, Topeka & Santa Fé and Southern Pacific Railroad companies. From Benson, the western terminus of the joint track, the Southern Pacific Railroad passes north toward San Francisco. Between Benson and Guaymas, on the western Mexican coast, a line is being built. Mention should also be made of the Atlantic & Pacific Railroad, which, starting at Albuquerque, 230 miles north of Deming, has penetrated Arizona for a distance of 300 miles, and is being extended west toward the Pacific coast. Proceeding from Benson, the Southern Pacific Railroad traverses Southern Arizona and Southern California in a direction west by north, without branches as far as Los Angeles, 710 miles from Deming. At Los Angeles, branches extend to the coast at Santa Ana, thirty-three miles, and Wilmington, twenty-two miles. From Goshen, 907 miles from Deming and 241 from San Francisco, a branch runs to Huron, forty miles distant. At Madera, fifty-six miles further on, connection is made with the stage lines to the Yosemite, about seventy miles distant. From Lathrop one line leads north to Sacramento, and two others, by slightly different routes, to San Francisco, 2,347 miles west of Kansas City. The actual terminus of the Southern Pacific Railroad is at Oakland, but transfers are made to San Francisco proper by ferry. Leading out from San Francisco are the following important lines of railway and steam navigation, by which the Southern tourist is enabled to reach any desired destination: The Central Pacific system, leading north and east; the North Pacific Coast Railway, leading northward along the coast, through magnificent scenery, as far as Duncan's Mills in the Russian river country; the San Francisco and North Pacific Railway, running north to Gurneyville and Cloverdale—the latter point being only twelve miles from the celebrated geyser springs; the South Pacific Coast Railway, leading to Santa Cruz; the Southern Pacific Railroad, northern division, running south to Monterey; the Pacific Coast Steamship Company's lines to all points north and south; the Oregon Railway & Navigation Company's lines to all points in Oregon; the Occidental & Oriental line; the Pacific Mail line, and others of less importance to transpacific ports.

KANSAS IN GENERAL.

GEOGRAPHY — CLIMATE — SENATOR INGALLS QUOTED — POPULATION OF
ORGANIZED AND UNORGANIZED COUNTIES, AND SEVENTY-
TWO TOWNS — DEVELOPMENT.

KANSAS is 404 miles long; 208½ miles wide; lies between the 37th and 40th parallels north latitude, and the 17th and 25th degrees of longitude west of Washington. Its area is 84,000 square miles, equal to 53,000,000 acres.

Its altitude on the eastern border is from 700 to 800 feet above sea level, and on the western border about 3,500 feet. The general trend of the rivers is from west to east. The principal river of the State is the Kansas, called, locally, the "Kaw." It is formed by the confluence of the Smoky Hill and Republican rivers, which unite at Junction City, Davis county. From Junction City to Kansas City, Missouri, the Kansas river passes directly through the middle of the State.

The geographical position of Kansas is such as to exempt it from the extreme and protracted cold of the North, as well as the intense summer heat of the South. The average temperature of the State is about 53° Fahrenheit. There is little wind in winter, but in summer time there is a prevailing breeze from the south, usually a cool, dry wind. The comparatively high altitude of the State, together with its perfect system of river drainage, and the entire absence of swamps, or marshy land, renders the atmosphere at all times electrically dry and invigorating. So far as considerations of health are concerned, therefore, Kansas is not inferior, all things considered, to any section of the United States. It is emphatically a country of clear skies and pure air. There is also, in the climate of Kansas, a certain sort of poetical passionateness which is plainly recognized in the following

TUCSON.

extracts from Senator John J. Ingalls' contributions to the pages of the brief but brilliant *Kansas Magazine*. In his article on "Blue Grass," the Senator says:

"Kansas is all antithesis. It is the hottest, coldest, dryest, wettest, thickest, thinnest country of the world. The stranger who crossed our borders for the first time at Wyandotte and traveled by rail to White Cloud would, with consternation, contrast that uninterrupted sierra of rugged and oak-clad crags with the placid prairies of his imagination. Let him ride along the spine of any of those lateral 'divides' or water sheds whose

'Level leagues forsaken lie
A grassy waste, extending to the sky,'

and he would be oppressed by the same melancholy monotony which broods over those who pursue the receding horizon over the fluctuating plains of the sea. And let this discursion be whither it would, if he listened to the voice of experience he would not start upon his pilgrimage at any season of the year without an overcoat, a fan, a lightning rod and an umbrella.

"But his apprehensions are relieved by the unheralded appearance of a cloud, no bigger than a man's hand, in the northwest. A huge bulk of purple and ebony vapor, preceded by a wave of pallid smoke, blots out the sky. Birds and insects disappear, and cattle abruptly stand agazed. An appalling silence, an ominous darkness, fill the atmosphere. A continuous roll of muffled thunder, increasing in volume, shakes the solid earth. The air suddenly grows chill, and smells like an unused cellar. A fume of yellow dust conceals the base of the meteor. The jagged scimetar of the lightning, drawn from its cloudy scabbard, is brandished for a terrible instant in the abyss, and thrust into the affrighted city, with a crash as if the rafters of the world had fallen. The wind, hitherto concealed, leaps from its ambush and lashes the earth with scourges of rain. The broken cisterns of the clouds can hold no water, and rivers run in the atmosphere. Dry ravines become turbid torrents, bearing cargoes of drift and rubbish on their swift descent. Confusion and chaos hold undisputed sway. In a moment the turmoil ceases. A gray veil of rain stands like a wall of granite in the eastern sky. The trailing banners of the storm hang from the frail bastions. The routed squadrons of mist, gray on violet, terrified fugitives, precipitately fly beneath the triumphal arch of a rainbow whose airy and unsubstantial glory dies with the dying sun."

A few years ago the great men of the time were fond of prophesying wonderful things for the frontier of Kansas. The poet Whittier wrote:

"On the lintels of Kansas,
That blood shall not dry;
Henceforth the bad angel
Shall harmless go by."

William II. Seward said, "Kansas, sir, is the Cinderella of the American family. She will live to defend, protect and sustain you." Charles Sumner said, "Constituting the precise territorial centre of the whole vast continent, Kansas is calculated to nurture a powerful and generous people. * * * She is worthy to be a central pivot of American institutions." Horace Greeley said, "In 1880 Kansas will have a million people." All of these prophecies, and many others like them, either have come true or are fast being realized. The census of 1880 showed a population of only a few hundreds less than one million people, and before the year expired the population unquestionably exceeded the limit of Mr. Greeley's prophecy. The following table gives the population of the organized and unorganized counties June 1, 1880, as shown by the United States Census, and also the total vote cast in each county for state treasurer, Nov. 2, 1880:

ORGANIZED COUNTIES.

COUNTIES.	Population.	Vote.	COUNTIES.	Population.	Vote.
Allen	11,463	2,411	Lyon	17,379	3,676
Anderson	8,991	1,996	Marion	12,471	2,036
Atchison	26,488	5,035	Marshall	16,147	3,676
Barbour	2,661	501	McPherson	17,145	3,328
Barton	10,326	1,961	Miami	17,806	3,794
Bourbon	20,518	3,853	Mitchell	14,917	2,758
Brown	12,830	2,882	Montgomery	18,127	3,764
Butler	18,591	3,954	Morris	9,228	2,012
Chase	6,089	1,448	Nemaha	12,468	2,707
Chautauqua	11,078	2,310	Neosho	15,136	3,079
Cherokee	22,075	4,911	Ness	3,322	537
Clay	12,320	2,669	Norton	7,004	1,301
Cloud	15,348	3,116	Osage	19,654	4,397
Coffey	11,456	2,466	Osborne	12,472	2,083
Cowley	21,561	4,376	Ottawa	10,325	2,301
Crawford	16,642	3,718	Pawnee	5,349	949
Davis	6,996	1,439	Phillips	12,012	2,029
Decatur	4,180	500	Pottawatomie	16,317	3,538
Dickinson	15,261	3,138	Pratt	1,890	328
Doniphan	14,264	3,264	Reno	12,776	2,174
Douglas	21,773	4,766	Republic	14,945	2,688
Edwards	2,419	416	Rice	9,297	1,923
Elk	10,665	2,222	Riley	10,428	2,205
Ellis	6,183	1,149	Rooks	8,062	1,466
Ellsworth	8,529	1,597	Rush	5,498	807
Ford	3,123	676	Russell	7,357	1,429
Franklin	16,852	3,738	Saline	13,861	2,890
Graham	4,262	815	Sedgwick	18,928	4,011
Greenwood	10,560	2,324	Shawnee	29,120	6,087
Harper	4,139	1,050	Sheridan	1,574	208
Harvey	11,478	2,274	Smith	13,904	2,446
Hodgeman	1,708	267	Stafford	4,768	784
Jackson	10,722	2,375	Sumner	20,944	4,032
Jefferson	15,574	3,458	Trego	2,535	468
Jewell	17,524	3,467	Wabaunsee	8,761	1,826
Johnson	16,958	3,672	Washington	15,145	3,020
Kingman	3,730	720	Wilson	12,764	2,878
Labette	22,753	4,598	Woodson	6,539	1,403
Leavenworth	32,345	5,845	Wyandotte	19,152	4,376
Lincoln	8,586	1,518			
Linn	15,326	3,315	Totals	989,934	201,623

UNORGANIZED COUNTIES.

COUNTIES.	Population.	COUNTIES.	Population.
Arrapahoe	3	Scott	43
Buffalo	191	Sequoyah	568
Cheyene	37	Seward	5
Clark	163	Sherman	9
Comanche	372	Stanton	5
Foote	411	Stevens	12
Gove	1,197	Thomas	161
Grant	10	Wallace	686
Geeley	3	Wichita	14
Hamilton	68		
Kansas	9	Total of unorganized counties	6,682
Kearney	159		
Lane	634	Total of organized counties	989,934
Meade	296		
Rawlins	1,626	Total population of the State	996,616

The population of the principal cities and towns of the State, according to the census of 1880, is shown in the following table. The information in the succeeding chapter, however, is more accurate as to the present time:

City	Pop.	City	Pop.	City	Pop.
Leavenworth	16,651	Beloit	1,882	Larned	949
Topeka	15,528	Concordia	1,623	Marion Center	942
Atchison	15,381	Hutchinson	1,599	Kirwin	923
Lawrence	8,395	Hiawatha	1,439	Russell	923
Wichita	5,482	Humboldt	1,401	La Cygne	922
Wyandotte	5,402	Girard	1,353	Clyde	870
Fort Scott	5,373	Garnett	1,337	Blue Rapids	806
Emporia	4,500	McPherson	1,335	Fredonia	801
Parsons	4,106	Osage Mission	1,283	Hays City	792
Ottawa	3,858	Wamego	1,240	Washington	792
Salina	2,963	Marysville	1,235	Oskaloosa	767
Independence	2,910	Holton	1,175	Osborne	751
Wellington	2,832	Seneca	1,135	Howard	738
Winfield	2,766	Eureka	1,082	Sabetha	728
Abilene	2,667	Council Grove	1,070	Pleasanton	720
Newton	2,600	Great Bend	1,050	St. Marys	710
Olathe	2,362	Burlingame	1,048	Louisburg	700
Junction City	2,332	Peabody	1,042	Stockton	700
Paola	2,163	Valley Falls	1,030	Ellis	668
Oswego	2,145	Minneapolis	1,017	Waterville	638
Manhattan	2,104	Florence	1,001	Osawattomie	600
Osage City	2,025	Iola	1,001	Nickerson	573
Burlington	2,008	Dodge City	996	Caldwell	548
Clay Center	1,986	Chetopa	958	Sedan	525

FOLIATION OF GRANITE.

CITIES AND TOWNS OF KANSAS.

KANSAS CITY — WYANDOTTE — LEAVENWORTH — ATCHISON — LAWRENCE —
TOPEKA — BURLINGAME — OSAGE CITY — MANHATTAN — EMPORIA —
NEWTON — WICHITA — MISCELLANEOUS.

HE foregoing tabulated statement of the population of towns is subtantially correct, though Topeka has grown so rapidly of late as to have overtaken Leavenworth; and Atchison has a suburban population of at least 2,000 souls, on the Missouri side of the Missouri river, which, by rights, should be counted as part of the city. It may also be stated in a general way that all the cities and towns named, especially those located in the central and southern part of the State, are growing with a steady, healthful growth. In this connection something special should be said of those Kansas cities through which the tourist is likely to pass.

Atchison, the most northerly of the three eastern termini of the Atchison, Topeka & Santa Fe Railroad, is a rugged young city of about 16,000 people. Its growth has not, as a rule, been as rapid as that of many Western cities, but it has never known a collapse, and, steadily, from year to year, it has held the even tenor of its way, until now its trade is of the sure, substantial sort, its society refined and cultured, and its population, as explained above, second to none of its sister cities. Atchison has extensive grain-shipping and pork-packing interests, and her manufactures are important.

Leavenworth, the metropolis of Kansas, (there is more or less strife now concerning this title,) is the next city south of Atchison on the Missouri river. It enjoyed a rapid growth in early days, being one of the most important outfitting points for the far western trade. It has, therefore, a more mature, Eastern look than any other place in Kansas. It is the location of Fort Leavenworth, the State penitentiary, and a large number of wood-

2

working factories, iron foundries and smaller manufactories of great importance to the State. Leavenworth has ample railroad communication, a charming situation, and all the characteristics of a modern city whose institutions are of a high order and whose people are in earnest.

Kansas City (unfortunately in Missouri, as Kansans say,) is emphatically a Kansas town. Kansas trade has called it into being, and furnished it the nourishment necessary to its wonderful development. Perhaps no better brief description of Kansas City and the country beyond, as far as Lawrence, has been written than that by Bishop Hunt in the New York *Independent*. The Bishop writes:

LIGNITIC SANDSTONE.

"In a half hour I was standing in that wonder of depots—the Union— in Kansas City. This same city is a key to our whole territory. Think of its growth. A citizen told me that when his Eastern eyes first saw the place, fourteen years ago, there was only one railway track there, which soon lost itself as it trailed its solitary length up along the Kansas or Kaw river. Now twelve great railroads centre there. There are given times when most of the trains leave, and unless you wish to take one of them, you will do well to stand and look on. It seems as if the whole world has its carpet-bag in hand and is going to the next place. The tracks are not shut in by a great building, covered over with a glass roof; but are in the open air, the raised platforms along them being protected by light and delicate iron roofing, supported by graceful pillars. You thus have all the advantage of protection from the weather and perfect light and ventilation.

"The new census puts Kansas City up to some 60,000. It is a marvel of growth. The most of the residences are on the bluffs, where are also the best hotels and the finest retail stores, and where, until recently, the heaviest business was conducted. But the broad flat delta, formed by the junction

SCENE ON THE ARKANSAS RIVER.

of the Kansas river with the Missouri, is destined to be the business part of the whole city. The bluff will be a place of churches, residences and stores, while the great manufactories will be down in 'The Bottom.' The largest beef and pork packing houses in the West, I have been told in the world, are already in this level part of Kansas City. The Fowler Brothers are just completing their's. Across the Kansas river lies Wyandotte, spread out over the flats, and building up so rapidly that, like Kansas City, you have to give your orders for bricks nine months ahead before you can begin to build your house. There is no break in either population or business during the whole hour and a half walk from the outer rim of Wyandotte, across the Kansas river, along the Kansas City bottom, over the innumerable railway tracks, and up the steep bluff, where the neat homes of Kansas City, the majestic, stand and throw their evening shadows across the broad and islanded Missouri.

"My destination in Kansas was Lawrence, about forty miles beyond Kansas City and up the southern bank of the Kansas river. One grows a little meditative as he takes his seat in the cars. The past begins to come in upon him, and he goes back to the days when the first battle of the republic since 1812 was fought on Kansas soil. When the treaty was signed in Paris, on the 30th of April, 1803, which gave us the Louisiana purchase, of which Kansas was a part, no eye could foresee the relation which this unknown State should occupy toward our national life. 'John Brown's soul' had just begun to march, for he was only wearing cotton pinafores, and lacked a month of being three years old. Some thirty miles away there once stood the old house of Osawatomie, which his own hands built, after he had snuffed, in the East, the morning air of the coming crisis, and had come to the heart of the hastening cyclone. Whether Kansas was to be a free or a slave State did not depend on the pro-slavery party in Missouri or its champions in Congress; but on the conscience of the whole country. Brown and his four brave sons knew all this part of Kansas—its trails, its strategic points, its river depths—as well as any Indian that had made it his home centuries before Columbus saw the light in Genoa the Proud. Brown turned all his wisdom to good account. His was the free lance of New England love of liberty. Lawrence, now a thriving city—with its beautiful university looking down over it, full of the hum and stir of honest and pushing thrift; catching now its nerves of power from the current of the river, now carrying its wheels by steam; educating its boys and girls with early and utmost care; driving its trade westward and southward with a steady eye on the march and consolidation of population; rearing its beautiful churches with sublime faith in the Power which gave freedom to all the broad acres of the State; and treasuring the traditions of its heroic history with honest pride—is a miracle of love of liberty, tenderness toward the slave, and of far vision into the future. It is the only American Troy we have. Every one of its plains and copses sings an Iliad. The marks of the first balls in the struggle for the slave's rights can still be seen in some walls and trees. A strange admiration of the vanished hands came over me as I walked the streets of this growing and historical place. It will hand down the name of Amos Lawrence and the Massachusetts and New England aid societies with a precision and power of high moral significance which Alexander could not give to the city of his name and fame. The streets you walk over are full of meaning. The first one I struck was Massachusetts street; and so it was to the end—New England names, New England faces, New England life. There is no place on the continent where Puritan ideas have projected themselves into the future with more definiteness than just here in Kansas. The air is that of Virginia; but the flow in the veins is that

HOTEL ON THE MOUNTAINS.

of the men who landed on Plymouth rock. There can be but one focus of thought in a nation at a time, and Kansas was that very thing all the way along from 1854 to 1858. It was the smelting-furnace of sentiment for four other years, 1861 to 1865. But all is now peaceful and plentiful in Kansas."

Eleven miles beyond Lawrence, on the south bank of the Kansas river, is the village of Lecompton, once the capital of Kansas, now a "cheerful mourner" over her own departed greatness. Fourteen miles further on is Topeka, the present capital, not mourning in the least, but rejoicing in the prosperity which Dame Fortune grants her at every turn of the wheel. Topeka is the pivotal point of Kansas politics, and the State offices there located are a constant attraction to strangers from abroad as well as to residents of the State. Biennial sessions of the legislature are held in the

SCENE IN HUTCHINSON, KANSAS.

(26)

splendid new capital building, which is now approaching completion. A visit to the State House, especially if some time can be devoted to the State library, the collections of the Kansas State Historical Society, and the museums of the State Board of Agriculture, is well worth while. Topeka also has one of the State Insane Asylums, the State Reform School, and two institutions for higher education—Washburn College (Congregational) and Bethany College (Episcopalian). And, lastly, Topeka is the home of the Atchison, Topeka & Santa Fé Railroad, whose Kansas City and Atchison

MOUNTAIN SCENE.

lines here unite, and where machine shops and general offices give employment to some 2,000 men, at an expense of many thousands of dollars. Topeka is a handsomely situated city, amply laid out with broad streets and plenty of room generally. Its residences are growing every year more attractive, and its business accommodations are improving rapidly with the increased demand. New churches, new schools, new hotels, a new Federal building, a new depot and a new opera house are some of the works under way or recently finished. The society of Topeka will bear the most critical inspection—not in the sense that it will "bear watching," but in the sense that it is up to the standard of Eastern cities of the same size. No one should consider that he has seen Kansas until he has seen its capital.

Leaving Topeka, the Atchison, Topeka & Santa Fé line to Colorado and New Mexico passes through the immense coal fields of Osage county, in which are located the flourishing towns of Carbondale, Burlingame and Osage City. From Burlingame the Manhattan, Alma & Burlingame line reaches Manhattan, where is located the Kansas State Agricultural College, one of the most successful institutions of the kind in the country. At Emporia the line crosses the Kansas and Texas division of the Missouri Pacific Railway and sends a branch south to Howard. Emporia has the State Normal School, the beautiful buildings of which may be seen at the head of the main street of the city, to the right of the west-bound train. Emporia has a growing trade, and is considered one of the best towns in the State.

A brief mention of several of the points of interest along the line, or its branches, will be in order. Cottonwood has 450 people, a hotel, newspaper, school house, church, elevator, five stone quarries, and a stone-sawing establishment. Cottonwood Falls, county seat of Chase county, is a thriving place. Halstead has 600 people, two hotels, one school house, two churches, two newspapers and a grist mill. Burrton has 600 people, two hotels, a school house, two churches, a newspaper, two elevators and a grist mill. Florence has 1,200 people, two hotels, three churches, a bank, a newspaper, a school house, a grist mill, an elevator, a lime kiln, and three stone quarries. From Florence branch lines lead to El Dorado, McPherson, Lyons, and other prosperous places. Marion Center, county seat of Marion county, has 1,100 people, a school house, four churches, two banks, one newspaper, two hotels, an elevator, three stone quarries, a court house, and syrup factory. McPherson Center, county seat of McPherson county, has 1,500 people, three hotels, four churches, three newspapers, one school house, three elevators, and one grist mill. Lyons, county seat of Rice county, has 1,200 people, three hotels, one school house, one church, one newspaper, a grist mill, and an elevator. Peabody has 1,200 people, two hotels, two banks, two newspapers, a school house, four churches, a public library, two grist mills, and four elevators. Newton has 3,100 people, five hotels, three banks, three newspapers, two school houses, six churches, three elevators, two flouring mills, and a nursery. From this place a branch line runs to Wichita, Wellington, Caldwell, Winfield, Arkansas City, and other points of importance. Hutchinson, county seat of Reno county, has 2,150 people, two banks, four hotels, four churches, a school house, two flouring mills, three elevators, a creamery, three newspapers, and a court house. Nickerson is a lively little city of 700 inhabitants, and is the terminus of the eastern division of the road. Sterling is twice as large, and has the usual quota of banks, newspapers, school houses and churches. Ellinwood and Great Bend, both in Barton county, are live, go-ahead places, the former containing 700 and the latter 1,500 people, with a full complement of civilizing influences. Larned, the county seat of Pawnee county, has 1,250 people, three hotels, a grist mill, an elevator, a bank, two newspapers, two churches, a school house, and a stone quarry. Kinsley, the county seat of Edwards county, has 500 people. Dodge City, the metropolis of Ford county, contains 1,000 people, and has a brick school house, a church, a bank, four hotels, two newspapers, a buffalo robe tannery, and a court house. Wichita, on the branch south from Newton, has nearly 5,500 people, and is a booming business point. Cimarron, Garden City, Syracuse and Sargent are small places in the western counties. Many of the places which have been mentioned are mere hamlets, but their age must be considered, and their future enlargement guessed from the history of like towns which have attained greatness further east.

AGRICULTURE IN KANSAS.

METHODS OF FARMING — CORN AND WHEAT — SUGAR CANE — RICE CORN —
LIVE STOCK STATISTICS — THE QUESTION OF RAINFALL,
AS TREATED BY AN EXPERT.

N a State where land is so uniformly good as it is in Kansas, it would be a somewhat difficult matter for the casual observer to say what locality had best right to claim supremacy. There is, in fact, but one way to determine this question, and that is by examination of the crop statistics. These undoubtedly place the valleys of the Kansas, the Cottonwood and the Arkansas in advance of all other sections, as will be shown elsewhere. Agriculture in Kansas is necessarily different from that of far Eastern States, owing to the marked difference in climatic influences. The method of farming that gathers wealth from almost barren hills and circumscribed areas of valley land, does not succeed in the rich and vast prairies of the West, where ten acres is hardly as one further east. Hence there arises the system of working large farms with the most improved machinery and a large force of men. It is no unusual sight in the valleys mentioned to see corn fields of 1,000 or 2,000 acres, stretching away from the railroad in one unbroken mass of green and yellow. Corn and wheat are kings. The value of the former product, in 1880, was $25,000,000, and of the latter $21,000,000, or over two-thirds of the total valuation of the crops of the State for that year. Regarding the agricultural progress of the State, Mr. Pliny L. Bartlett contributes the following interesting facts:

"The total number of acres cultivated in 1880 in excess of the acreage of 1879, was 1,098,958, or 14 per cent. greater. The valuation of all field products in 1880 was over $3,000,000 greater than in 1879. The production of wheat alone increased about 33¼ per cent. In live stock of all kinds in the State, the valuation increased, from 1879 to 1880, nearly 12 per cent., and this notwithstanding the fact that the value of animals slaughtered or sold for slaughter in 1880 was 50 per cent. greater than in the year preceding. Farmers got 45 per cent. more for their market-garden produce, and 33¼ per cent. more for poultry and eggs, in 1880. The wool clip improved 40 per cent., and so on through the whole category of farm products in Kansas. When the statistics for 1881 are compiled, the gains for the year will, in every department, show a marked improvement on those of 1880. Take, for instance, corn and sheep. The acreage of corn in 1880 was 3,554,396, and the product 101,421,718 bushels; in 1881 the number of acres planted was 4,182,653, an increase of 18 per cent., while the yield promises a corresponding ratio of increase. The number of sheep in the State has

FORT YUMA, FROM YUMA CITY.

PHOTO-HILL ENG. CO. N.Y.

increased in the past year from 426,492 to a round million, as nearly as can
be estimated from authentic reports. Here is an advance of *133 per cent.* in
a single year, which shows that sheep husbandry is the great 'boom' of
the period in Kansas."

Close on the heels of the corn and wheat interests of Kansas come two
new features of Kansas farming, sorgho-sugar cane and rice corn. In 1880
a field of 600 acres, near Larned, was devoted to the growing of sorgho-
sugar cane, and the result of the experiment proved the wisdom of the far-
seeing projector of the enterprise. All that is now needed in Kansas to
place it in the front rank of sugar-producing countries, is machinery for
crushing the cane and making the sugar. This want will soon enough be
supplied by the capitalists, who are already turning their attention in this
direction. The reasons for making these large prophecies about Kansas
sugar are based on the following facts:

"1. The cane can be successfully grown in any season, even in a year of
severe drouth. 2. It can be matured in ninety-five days from planting, the
earliest varieties ripening about August 10th ; and by regulating the time
in planting, the cane can be ripened just as fast as required, up to the
middle of November. 3. Sugar can be made from the cane from August
10th till November 1st, and in favorable seasons till November 10th or 15th.
Syrup can generally be made from the cane for a week or two after the frost
has spoiled the cane for granulating. This is the longest season yet found
in any part of the United States for working ripe cane. 4. Owing to the
higher altitude and drier atmosphere, the cane is richer in saccharine matter, and the juice of a better quality than that produced in the Mississippi
valley. 5. In consequence of the longer season, the richer cane, the fine
climate for drying the crushed cane to use it for fuel, and the certainty of
the crop, sugar can be manufactured more cheaply in southwestern Kansas
than anywhere east of the Missouri river. 6. It will yield to the farmer a
revenue of $2.50 per ton, or $25 per acre, based on the light average yield
of ten tons of cane per acre, and the cost of producing it is very light."

The rice corn, dhoura, or Egyptian corn, is coming to the front with
Kansas farmers as a food for man and cattle. It is much like sorghum in
appearance, and the grain resembles rice. Prof. Geo. E. Patrick, of the
State University of Kansas, has made an analysis which shows rice corn
to be superior to common corn in its nutritive qualities. The yield ranges
from fifteen to forty bushels per acre, regardless, almost, of rain or drouth.
Only the heads are harvested, and the grain is threshed like wheat. When
ground it is much like corn and wheat mixed. The advent of rice corn
will have a great effect on the cattle business, making assurance doubly sure
for an ample supply of nutritious feed.

Speaking of stock, Kansas is fast assuming a front rank in the value of
its cattle, sheep and swine. For the year 1880 the assessor's rolls show the

total value of Kansas cattle to be $17,968,128, swine $7,689,780, and sheep $1,492,722, which amount has been considerably increased since that date.

No article on Kansas would be complete without reference to the subject of moisture and its distribution for agricultural purposes. It is appropriate, therefore, that this sketch should embody an extract from Mr. H. R. Hilton's recent essay before the Kansas Academy of Science, Mr. Hilton having made the rain question a special study. Among other things Mr. Hilton said:

FARM SCENE IN KANSAS.

"In respect to its rainfall, Kansas is divided into three parts, or belts. The eastern belt has an average rainfall of thirty-three inches, the central belt an average of twenty-five inches, and the western belt an average of twenty inches. This average is based on the rainfall of eight years. The sufficiency of the rainfall depends largely on the nature of the soil. Eastern Kansas, with its black loam surface soil, resting on a clay formation, requires a greater amount of rainfall than central Kansas, with its deeper surface soil—a dark sandy loam, and its more porous subsoil of marl clay. The latter soil takes in more rapidly the rain that falls, stores it deeper below the surface, and retains it longer for the use of plant life; in other words, it wastes less and requires less. Every farmer in Illinois, Indiana, Ohio or New York, who has had any experience with drainage, can testify that where the soil is well drained a much less amount of rainfall is necessary to produce as good results as were obtained before the soil was drained, simply because the moisture-storing capacity of the soil had been increased, and, in consequence, crops could sustain themselves through a longer period of drouth without serious injury.   *   *   *   *   *

"To those who have not given this subject serious thought, it may at first seem that such changes as have been effected in this State by civilization are greatly exaggerated; but when you come to think of it, there would be a violation of some well-known law of nature if settlement of the country did not produce these results that I have attempted to relate. For instance, there can not be evaporation where there is no water in some form or other, and there can not be humidity in the air when there is no evaporation, and where there is no humidity there will be deficient rainfall, as the slower the evaporation and the more humid the air the greater will be the precipitation, for the moisture in the air has a greater affinity for the moist places on the earth than for the dry places.

"In what I have related here to-night we see another illustration of the order, economy and design that characterizes everything in nature.

"Nothing is wasted. The climate and vegetation of the plains prior to settlement were best adapted to the wants of life then existing on them. When man came, with his intelligence, industry and perseverance, conforming to nature's laws, the wilderness yielded up its barrenness and conformed itself to his wants. It was only by the united efforts of a great tide of industrious men and women that this great change could be wrought. To straggle off in detached bands, remote from each other, would do no good. They must go forward as a compact mass; and in this battle with the wilderness it is the vanguard that must do the hardest fighting, and clear the way for those who bring up the rear.

PRESCOTT, ARIZONA.

"As civilized man moves westward step by step, possessing the lands conquered from the elements, the red man recedes farther and farther into the wilderness, and as the red man and the buffalo recede before civilized man, so the grass of the buffalo and uncivilized life recedes before the vegetation of civilization. The march of human progress in Kansas seems to have taken equally as strong hold on its animal and vegetable life, and even the rain supply down to 1879 gave evidence of having caught the infection.

"The season of 1879, with its severe drouth, is a flat contradiction of the theories I have advanced; but I do not claim that this progression westward is annually continuous. Excessive dry seasons and wet seasons are a part of the history of every State and every country. For fair and satisfactory evidence we must take the average of a succession of years, and not the most favorable or unfavorable ones."

Before leaving the subject of Kansas agriculture, reference will again be made to stock raising. The following table shows the growth of stock interests during the years since 1865:

YEARS.	Cattle.	Swine.	Sheep.	Horses.	Mules.
1865	262,303	95,425	82,662	32,469	2,490
1870	373,967	206,557	109,688	117,786	11,786
1875	708,328	292,658	106,224	207,376	24,964
1878	872,243	1,195,044	286,241	274,450	40,564
1879	976,463	1,264,494	322,020	324,766	51,981
1880	1,115,312	1,281,630	426,492	367,589	58,303

Nothing could speak better than the above for Kansas as a great stock-raising State. The figures prove that in Kansas there is a food supply and a water supply such as to enable stock of all kinds to live and prosper. These two facts, added to the general healthfulness of the climate and the mildness of the winters, are alone sufficient to warrant almost unqualified success in every branch of the stock business.

THE ARKANSAS VALLEY.

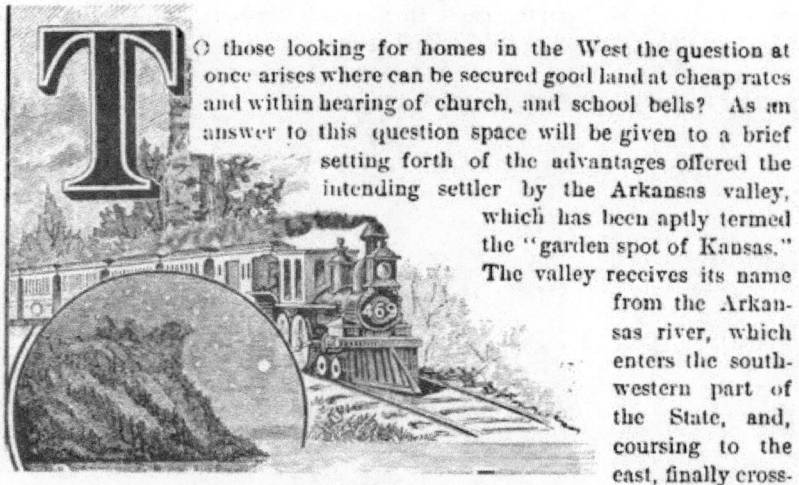

O those looking for homes in the West the question at once arises where can be secured good land at cheap rates and within hearing of church, and school bells? As an answer to this question space will be given to a brief setting forth of the advantages offered the intending settler by the Arkansas valley, which has been aptly termed the "garden spot of Kansas." The valley receives its name from the Arkansas river, which enters the southwestern part of the State, and, coursing to the east, finally crosses the southern boundary into the Indian Territory. The valley proper extends only a few miles on each side of the stream, but the country designated by that name is many miles in extent, and comprises nearly the whole of south-central and southwestern Kansas. In its borders is located the extensive land grant of the Atchison, Topeka & Santa Fé Railroad Company, which has been partially settled by a class of people who have made it blossom with bustling cities and towns, school houses and fine farms. Concerning the capacity of this land for bringing forth seed for the sower, these facts may be *apropos:* for instance, the average yield of corn in south-central Kansas, from 1875 to 1879, was forty-five bushels per acre. In southwestern Kansas the average had been fully thirty. These two portions of the State, in 1878, exceeded all other sections in the production of winter wheat, and in the value of all crops produced. This position it still maintains. The winter wheat acreage of the State for 1880 was 2,215,937. The following ten counties, viz.: McPherson, Sumner, Sedgwick, Barton, Cowley, Reno, Butler, Harvey, Rice, and Marion, ranking in the order named, have an acreage of 699,149, or nearly one-third the entire acreage of the seventy-nine organized counties in the State. Of the ten leading winter wheat counties of the State having the largest acreage, seven are in south-central Kansas, and none of these seven had an existence prior to 1870.

The past two seasons have been generally unfavorable to the oats crop of Kansas, and we find the acreage reduced from 573,982 in 1879, to 477,827 in 1880. The acreage of ten Arkansas valley counties in 1880 is 128,855, or

MOUNTAIN SCENE.

$26\frac{2}{3}$ per cent. of the total acreage of the State. Of the ten counties having the largest acreage seven are in the Arkansas valley. The average yield of oats, from 1875 to 1878, was thirty-eight bushels; in 1879 and 1880, twenty bushels per acre. There were, in 1880, 25,507 acres of broom corn in the State, of which McPherson county had 6,039 acres. McPherson, Rice, Pawnee, Reno, Rush and Stafford counties report 11,100 acres, or 43 per cent. of the entire State acreage. This is one of the most profitable crops of the State, is raised successfully in the driest season, and, owing to the superior soil, and fine climate for curing, it commands the highest market price. The yield is from one-third to one-half ton per acre. Millet hay is a successful crop everywhere in Kansas. Ten counties in the Arkansas valley report 25 per cent. of the acreage of the State in 1880. It yields two to three tons per acre. It is used largely as winter feed for sheep in southwest Kansas. Irish potatoes, of large size and fine quality, are raised in large quantities by mulching, and find a ready market, at good prices, in the mining regions. Sweet potatoes are also a very successful and profitable crop. Castor beans, peanuts, flax and tobacco are also raised to a limited extent.

It will be inquired what are the prices and location of lands for sale in the counties named. The subjoined table refers almost entirely to railroad lands, as the government lands have been so nearly exhausted:

COUNTIES.	Acres Sold.	Acres for Sale.	Maximum and Minimum Price per Acre.	Av'ge Price Good Farming Land per Acre.
Osage	520.28	3,374.06	$3 50 to $6 00	$5 00
Lyon	279.99	155.87		
Wabaunsee	4,603.58	8,525.36	3 00 to 6 50	5 50
Morris	8,246.41	24,701.10	2 50 " 7 00	4 50
Butler	29,365.47	28,673.94	5 00 " 9 00	6 00
Greenwood		640.00	4 00 " 4 00	4 00
Chase	20,117.61	113,728.52	2 00 " 9 00	6 00
Marion	162,675.11	48,787.09	2 25 " 9 00	6 00
McPherson	94,545.90	8,473.35	2 50 " 8 50	6 50
Harvey	149,319.30	20,651.59	3 00 " 10 00	7 00
Sedgwick	58,914.98	25,786.04	4 00 " 13 00	7 00
Reno	150,535.37	164,196.86	1 25 " 8 00	6 50
Rice	108,264.61	61,194.74	1 50 " 8 00	6 50
Barton	149,277.82	31,732.57	3 00 " 9 50	6 00
Stafford	3,281.70	151,791.11	1 50 " 5 00	4 00
Pawnee	106,562.83	113,558.19	1 50 " 8 50	5 50
Edwards	62,375.30	81,743.70	1 50 " 8 50	5 00
Rush	8,739.79	53,378.16	3 00 " 6 50	5 00
Ford	22,173.31	92,968.92	3 00 " 8 00	5 50
Hodgeman	7,347.80	73,111.99	3 00 " 7 00	5 00
Totals	1,116,538.19	1,104,200.51		

For information about Kansas, of too minute or specific a nature to come properly within the space of this book, application may be made, by letter or in person, as follows: (1) To W. F. WHITE, General Passenger and Ticket Agent, A., T. & S. F. R. R., Topeka, Kansas, in regard to rates, distances, accommodations, and all other matters pertaining to travel through the State; and (2) To A. S. JOHNSON, Land Commissioner, A., T. & S. F. R. R., Topeka, Kansas, in regard to lands, crops, stock raising, and all matters pertaining to the agricultural interests of the State.

COLORADO IN GENERAL.

GEOGRAPHY AND TOPOGRAPHY — ALTITUDES OF TWO HUNDRED AND FIFTY
POINTS — THE CENSUS REPORT OF THE POPULATION OF
COUNTIES — TREES, PLANTS AND MINERALS.

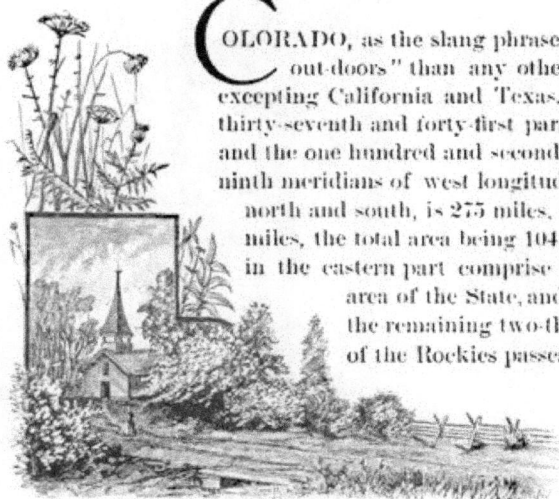

COLORADO, as the slang phrase has it, "covers more out-doors" than any other State in the Union, excepting California and Texas. It lies between the thirty-seventh and forty-first parallels of north latitude and the one hundred and second and one hundred and ninth meridians of west longitude. Its average extent, north and south, is 275 miles, and east and west, 380 miles, the total area being 104,500 miles. The plains in the eastern part comprise about one-third of the area of the State, and the mountains occupy the remaining two-thirds. The main range of the Rockies passes through the centre of the State from the north to the south. The plains in the eastern part are drained on the north by the South Platte and on the south by the Arkansas. The continental divide follows the summit of the main range from north to south. In the central part of Colorado the mountains form four vast basins, called parks—North Park, South Park, Middle Park, and San Luis Park. North Park, with its area of 2,500 square miles, at an elevation of about 9,000 feet, has a north-central location. Just south of North Park is Middle Park, with its area of 3,000 square miles, at an elevation of 8,500 feet. Still south of Middle Park is South Park, with its area of 2,200 square miles, at an elevation of 9,500 feet. The fourth park, San Luis, is near the south line of the State, has an area of 8,000 square miles and an elevation of 7,000 feet. The mountains are drained chiefly by the Arkansas, the Rio Colo-

LARNED IN '74.

RES. RICHARD BONTE.

(33)

rado, the Rio Grande and the Platte. The altitudes of Colorado range from 3,000 feet, the lowest, to about 14,400 feet, the highest, making an average of about 7,000 feet. In the most famous mountain regions of Europe and Eastern America, vegetation stops at an elevation of 5,000 feet; and in the Alps, the line of eternal snow is not higher than 7,500 feet. But in Colorado vegetation ceases only at an altitude of 11,000 feet, and perpetual snow does not begin short of 13,500 feet. Fruits and flowers grow at an elevation of 11,000 feet, and heavy timber is found at 12,000 feet. The altitudes of the most important points in Colorado may be learned from the following table:

	FEET		FEET		FEET
Alma	10,453	Evans	4,745	Longmont	4,957
Arapahoe Peak	13,520	Freeman's Peak	11,700	Lost Fork Peak	12,300
Arkansas Divide	7,500	Fort Collins	4,966	Lillie's Mount	11,483
Agency Peak	12,120	Fairplay	9,964	Littleton	5,362
Alamosa	7,000	Fall River	7,719	Lone Cone	12,500
Animas City	6,850	First View	4,479	Lake City	8,550
Animas Forks	11,200	Fisher's Peak	9,400	La Plata Mount	14,311
Antelope Park	9,000	Fort Garland	7,945	Long's Peak	14,271
Argentine Pass	13,100	Fort Lyon	3,784	Los Pinos	9,290
Baldy Peak	24,176	Galena Mountain	13,200	Malta	9,700
Bakersville	9,753	Georgia Pass	11,487	Maroon Mountain	14,003
Bald Mountain	11,493	Glacier Peak	12,654	McNassers	8,153
Bergen's Peak	9,773	Golden Peak	9,650	Monument	7,020
Bent's Fork	3,923	Grand Lake	8,153	Manitou	6,357
Bergen's Ranche	7,752	Granite	8,883	Massive Mount	11,368
Berthoud's Pass	11,462	Grizzly Peak	13,956	Montezuma	10,113
Black Hawk	7,975	Golden	5,729	Middle Boulder	8,067
Boulder	5,536	Golden Gate	6,225	Middle Park (av.)	8,500
Boulder Pass	11,613	Gold Hill	8,463	Mineral City	11,500
Breckenridge	9,490	Granada	3,485	Morrison	5,922
Buffalo Springs	8,719	Gray's Peak	14,251	Mt. Hamilton	13,800
Blanca Peak	14,413	Green Lake	10,000	Mt. Æolus	14,054
Beaver Brook	6,175	Greeley	4,779	Mt. Arkansas	13,647
Bison Peak	12,400	Georgetown	8,580	Mt. Byers	12,778
Bradford Junction	8,069	Helmet Peak	12,042	Mt. Kendall	13,380
Buckskin Mountain	14,022	Hesperis Peak	13,135	Mt. Morrison	7,908
Buffalo Peaks	13,541	Hartsels	8,700	Mt. Holy Cross	14,176
Capitol Mountain	13,997	Handie's Peak	13,997	Mt. Powell	13,398
Conejos Peak	13,183	Hague's Peak	13,832	Mt. Ouray	14,043
Costilla Peak	12,634	Hunt's Peak	12,446	Mt. Rito Alto	12,989
Crestone Peak	14,233	Hamilton	9,743	Mt. Princeton	14,196
Cuchara	5,980	Hamilton Pass	12,370	Mt. Wilson	14,280
Culebra Peak	14,097	Hillerton	7,000	Mt. Audubon	13,462
Carbonateville	9,800	Hoosier Pass	11,314	Mt. Cameron	14,000
Castle Peak	14,115	Horseshoe Mount	13,806	Mt. Elbert	14,351
Chicago Lakes	11,500	Hot Springs	7,725	Mt. Evans	14,330
Centreville	7,800	Howardsville	9,700	Mt. Flora	12,878
Cleora	6,570	Hughes	5,070	Mt. Guyot	13,565
Conejos	7,880	Hugo	4,952	Mt. Harvard	14,375
Cañon City	5,260	Italian Peak	13,350	Mt. Lincoln	14,295
Caribou	9,905	Idaho Springs	7,585	Mt. Rosalie	14,340
Central	8,300	Irwin's Peak	14,192	Mt. Vernon	6,421
Colorado City	6,342	Jamestown	7,123	Mt. Wright	11,800
Colorado Springs	5,990	Jones' Pass	12,513	Mt. Yale	14,187
Cunningham Pass	12,090	James' Peak	13,240	Mt. Sneffels	14,158
Dayton	9,441	Julesburg	3,590	Nederland	8,263
Deer Trail	5,087	Kenosha Pass	10,226	Northern Palisade	8,250
Del Norte	7,750	Kenosha Cone	12,469	Nevada	8,800
Denver	5,240	Kenosha Summit	10,139	North Park (av.)	9,000
Divide	7,500	Kelso Cabin	10,888	Oro City	10,704
Egeria Park	7,500	Kokomo	9,700	Osborn's Lake	8,821
El Moro	5,950	Kit Carson's Peak	14,100	Ouray	7,640
Empire	8,583	Leadville	10,247	Pagosa Springs	6,800
Estes Park	7,500	La Veta	6,968	Pagosa Peak	12,674

	FEET		FEET		FEET
Pidgeon's Peak......	14,054	San Luis Peak........	14,100	Teocalli Mountain ...	13,113
Park View Peak....	12,433	Silver Cliff	8,500	Trinchera Peak	13,540
Prospect Hill	8,893	Snow Mass Mountain..	13,961	Torry's Peak	14,336
Parrott City	8,611	Stewart's Peak	14,032	Tarryall	9,913
Purgatory Peak	13,719	Squaw Mountain	11,733	The Chief	11,000
Parry's Peak	13,133	Summit Peak	13,303	Trinidad	6,100
Pike's Peak	14,147	Shavano Peak	14,239	Twin Lakes	9,182
Platteville..........	4,900	Simpson Peak.....	14,055	Uncompahgre Agency	6,403
Pueblo	4,703	Saguache..........	7,745	Uncompahgre Park...	14,235
Puncha Pass	8,609	Salt Works..........	8,826	Uncompahgre P'k (av.)	7,200
Quandary Peak	14,260	Sangre de Cristo Pass.	9,451	Ute Pass	11,200
Queen's Park	7,554	San Luis Valley.....	6,400	Ute Peak	9,664
Rosita..........	8,500	Silverheel Mountain..	13,650	Venno Peak	12,800
Ralston Buttes	10,590	Silverton	9,400	Veta Pass	9,340
Rollinsville..........	8,323	Snowy Range	11,700	Yeulie's Peak	13,450
Rio Grande Pyramid .	13,773	Sopris' Pass	12,972	Vasquez Pass	11,500
Red Cloud Peak......	14,092	South Park (av.)	9,500	White River Agency .	6,490
Raton Pass	7,770	St. John....	10,625	Webster..........	9,156
South Boulder Park ..	8,533	St. Vrain's............	5,250	Weston's Pass........	11,676
Sugar Loaf	8,933	Sultan Mount.........	13,336	Whale Peak	13,104

The following table gives the population of Colorado as shown by the United States census of 1870, and that of 1880:

COUNTIES.	Population 1870.	Population 1880.	COUNTIES.	Population 1870.	Population 1880.
Arapahoe..............	6,829	38,607	Jefferson..............	2,390	6,811
Bent	592	1,654	La Plata..............	New	1,110
Boulder	1,939	10,055	Las Animas	4,276	8,909
Chaffee..............	New	6,503	Larimer	838	4,862
Conejos..............	2,504	5,616	Lake	522	23,787
Costilla..............	1,779	2,885	Ouray	New	2,677
Custer	New	7,968	Pueblo	2,265	7,617
Clear Creek	1,596	7,857	Park	447	3,956
Douglas	1,388	2,485	Rio Grande	New	1,946
Elbert	510	1,710	Routt	New	140
El Paso..............	987	7,903	Saguache	304	1,972
Fremont	1,064	4,730	San Juan	New	1,087
Grant	New	417	Summit	258	5,449
Gilpin	5,490	6,493	Weld	1,636	5,603
Gunnison	New	8,764			
Hinsdale	New	1,508			
Huerfano..............	2,250	4,149	Total	39,864	195,224

The increase here shown, for the past ten years is 155,370, a wonderful showing indeed, but one which will be surpassed by the decade ending 1890. At that time Colorado will have three-fourths of a million people.

The principal trees and plants of Colorado are as follows: vine maple, box elder, common yarrow or milfoil, monk's hood, red baneberry, red grass, onion, lick, speckled alder, juneberry, wild hog peanut, many-cleft anemone, wind flower, blue columbine, rock cress, trailing arbutus, sandwort, Mexican poppy arnica, wormwood, white sage, New England aster, milk vetch, mahonia, blue barberry, Rocky mountain birch, New Jersey tea- or red-root, field chickweed, wall flower, prince's pine, leather flower,

common virgin's bower, bird weed, coral root, golden corydalis, white
lady's slipper, white larkspur, larkspur, American cowslip, whitlaw grass,
stick-seed, willow-herb, worm-seed mustard, flowering spurge, American
columbo, mountain shrub, wild yellow lily, twin flower, yellow flax, fog
fruit, wild lupine, musk mallow, horsemint, peppermint, spearmint, lung-
wort, monkey flower, marsh cress, yellow weed, beard tongue, moss pink,
valerian, bitter poplar, cottonwood, American aspen, primrose, buttercup,
fragrant sumach, staghorn sumach, Missouri currant, white flowering
raspberry, stone moss, moss catch-fly, red flowering sida, meadow violet,
meadow-sweet, ladies' tresses, yellow pea, spiderwort, verbena, violet, and
soap-weed. New forms of plant life are being added every year to the
Colorado catalogue, both by discovery and by importation.

SHIP OF THE DESERT AT ANCHOR.

The minerals found in Colorado are as follows: actinolite, moss agates,
banded agates, geode agates, alabaster, albite, alumina, amber amethyst,
amianthus, amygdaloid, anthracite, antimonial silver, antimolite, apaphyl-
lite, aragonite, arsenicate of iron, arsenicate of copper, auriferous pyrites,
auro-tellurite, aventurine quartz, azurite, transparent barytea, opaque
barytea, basalt, beryl, biotite, bismuth blende, black copper ore, black
jack, blue copperas, bog-manganese, brittle silver, bog iron, brown iron
ore, calcareous spar, calcareous tufa, chalcedony, carnelian, chabogite, red
chalk, chrysocalla, fire clay, semi-bituminous coal, fossil copal, copper
oxide, copper antimonial, copper pyrites, grey copper, nickel copper,
variegated copper, vitreous copper, native silveras, cuban, dolerite, dalo-

mite, epidota erubescite, fahlerg, brown feldspar, green feldspar, red feldspar, white feldspar, flos ferri, fluor spar, foliated tellurium, galena, green
garnet, gneiss, native gold, common granite, graphic granite, graphite,
green earth, greenochite, gypsum, heavy spar, hematite, horn blende,
hydraulic iron, horn silver, red Iceland spar, idocrase, iridium, iridosmine,

GARDEN OF THE GODS.

arsenicate of iron, carbonate of iron, hematitic iron, hydrous oxide iron,
magnetic iron, meteoric iron, silicate iron, specular iron, sulphuret iron,
sulphate iron, titanic iron, micaceous iron, spathic iron, iron pyrites, jasper,
kaolin, labrodanite, lounanite, lava, arsenicate lead, codmiate lead, sulphate
lead, telluride lead, carbonate lead, iridiate lead, argentiferous lead, cupre-
ous sulphate lead, lepidolite, leucite, lydian stone, malachite, manganese,
marl, native mercury, mica, malybdenum, naphtha, natrolite, nickel, nitrate

FALLS OF THE YOSEMITE.

of soda, iron ochre, plumbic ochre, uronic ochre, olivine, opal, orthoclose, pitch blende, rosy quartz, greasy quartz, smoky quartz, ripidolite, ruby silver, common salt, schist, schorl, syenite, silicified wood, sulphuret silver, antimonial silver, native silver, telluric silver, vitreous silver, glance silver, false topaz, trachyse, uranite, wolfram, and wood opal. These minerals are found in comparatively equal distribution all over the mountainous portions of Colorado. Further information about gold, silver, copper, coal, etc., will be found elsewhere in this book.

CITIES AND DISTRICTS OF COLORADO.

PUEBLO — DENVER — LEADVILLE — SILVER CLIFF AND ROSITA — DURANGO AND SILVERTON — DOLORES AND RICO — THE GREAT GUNNISON — ROBERT E. STRAHORN QUOTED.

NTERING Colorado by the Atchison, Topeka & Santa Fe Railroad, the first city of importance is Pueblo, terminus of the road named, and junction of the Denver line, the Leadville line, and the south and southwestern line of the Denver & Rio Grande Railway. The population of Pueblo is about 8,000, and its growth is steadily in the right direction. Its railway facilities, its steel works, its railway shops, its mining business, and its lesser manufacturing and commercial interests, combine to render it one of the most attractive and most important cities in the State. It is situated in what might be called the plains region, but is near enough to the mountains for all practical purposes of commerce.

Denver is located near the western border of the plains, distant but twelve miles from the Rocky mountains, and nearly in the centre of the State on a line drawn from north to south. It is the metropolis and capital city of Colorado, and has enjoyed a growth and prosperity in the past few years equaled by that of no other city of similar size and pretensions in the Union. Possessing all possible natural advantages, it has, in addition, a pushing, driving, restless, ambitious people, who stop at no difficulty and surrender to no enemy. The broad, smooth streets are lined with beautiful houses and wide-spreading shade trees. The business blocks are of truly metropolitan proportions, and the public buildings are of modern design and the most elegant finish. The present population of the city is about 35,000, and the increase is steady. In the issue of January 1st, 1881, the Denver *Tribune* gave the following list of what it called "Facts about Denver":

"That the city has gained 15,000 population in eighteen months. That over 1,000 new buildings have been erected during the past year. That these buildings aggregate in value nearly three millions of dollars. That we will have at least three new local roads before the first of next January. That we will have rail connection to all parts of the State in twelve months. That the population and business will increase forty per cent. in 1881. That there will be a sewer system completed for the city. That the suburbs will be built up to an extent which people do not dream of. That the manufacturing establishments will increase in number a hundred per cent. during the coming year. That the new court house will be completed. That ground will be broken for new government buildings. That the real estate boom will extend further out the coming spring, and be more marked there than in the centre of the city. That the union depot will be completed some time this year. That everything favorable which can happen to an enterprising city will happen."

Leadville, in the year 1880, made for herself a record which was scarcely foretold even in the prosperity of the previous year. Old mines have continued fruitful and new mines have constantly been discovered. The rude mining camp has become a well ordered city, and nothing is now lacking to make life there as pleasant as it is profitable. The city is, as is well known, situated almost directly west of Denver, in what is known as the upper Arkansas valley, right in the heart of the mountains, and in what is probably one of the richest mineral districts of the world. The marvelous mineral statistics of Leadville for the year 1880 are condensed in the following table:

Months.	Pounds of bullion	Ounces of silver.	Ounces of gold.	Tons of ore shipped.	Value of silver.	Value of gold.	Value of lead.	Val. of ore shipped.	Total for month.
Jan....	5,167,429	1,045,356	151	570	$1,994,509	$3,080	$269,546	$148,900	$1,616,035
Feb....	5,092,719	808,758	169	610	916,292	3,390	292,742	173,181	1,385,605
March	5,040,238	743,403	91	1,275	841,916	2,120	293,925	166,132	1,304,093
April	4,953,673	636,716	4	925	724,320	80	246,932	109,394	1,080,728
May	6,177,660	864,388	4	873	986,164	80	292,737	109,683	1,378,664
June	4,227,828	649,489	....	887	730,281	......	193,005	126,997	1,040,283
July	4,598,738	676,227	300	664	730,367	6,000	206,932	77,885	1,041,184
August	6,996,039	769,248	350	1,162	878,989	7,000	349,790	128,391	1,364,170
Sept....	7,524,747	848,715	251	2,947	959,027	5,060	375,365	217,147	1,556,599
October	6,413,950	757,366	196	1,690	858,365	3,824	298,721	127,453	1,288,463
Nov....	5,091,082	625,858	12	817	708,156	240	263,431	68,500	1,040,027
Dec....	5,866,851	583,880	157	60	656,783	3,110	262,372	7,000	929,295
Totals	67,721,856	8,979,399	1,688	12,410	$10,195,169	$34,014	$3,335,507	$1,460,363	$15,025,153

This showing is positively unequaled in the history of silver mining anywhere in the world; and the half has not yet been seen or guessed. The year 1881 will see an output of vastly greater value than that of 1880, though there will be much less fuss and outcry made about it. Lessons have been learned, methods have been determined, and the work will go quietly on.

CASTLE ROCK.

Silver Cliff has a population of over 5,000 people whose good fortune it is to have as many churches, schools, newspapers, hotels and other such public institutions as any town of its size in the East. Its location is a happy one, the view of the Sangre de Cristo range from that point being one of the grandest in Colorado. Silver Cliff's tributary mines are among the best in the State, and so its business interests are buoyant.

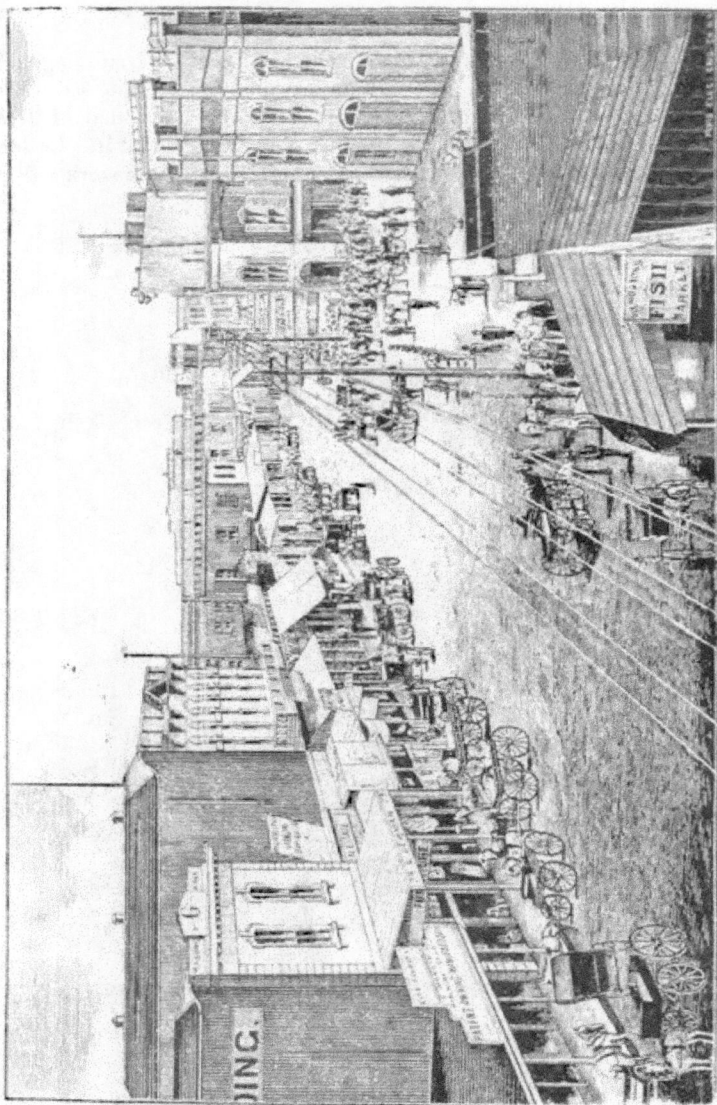

LOS ANGELES.

Rosita has about 2,000 people and a location of unusual beauty and advantage. Its growth has been and promises to be steadily ahead. Silver Cliff and Rosita are situated in the Hardscrabble mining district, which has been made famous by the history of such mines as Bull-Domingo and Bassick. Speaking of the Hardscrabble district, Mr. Z. L. White, in the New York *Tribune*, gives the following bit of interesting history:

"The discovery of true fissure veins in the neighborhood of Rosita antedates by five years any of the 'rich strikes' that have more recently made the Hardscrabble district so well known; and it is not at all surprising that this should be so. Eight years ago prospectors in Colorado only looked for two kinds of mines—placers and fissures. They never expected to find

CONCENTRATION WORKS

a broad belt of country everywhere impregnated with silver, nor did they search for great chimneys or blow-outs of ore. They never had heard of such mines, and, unless they found a gulch rich in placer gold, or a crevice in the rocks filled with quartz and containing a pay-streak of ore, they camped only for a night and then passed on to some more promising region. Some old miners from the 'Northern Diggings,' as the lodes and placers about Black Hawk, Central City and Georgetown were then called, followed the German colonists into the Wet Mountain valley in 1870, and in December of that year several mining claims were located, of which the G. W. and Senator were the most promising. But even these yielded a very low grade of ore, and none of them were opened to any depth until the fall of 1872, when one very cold, stormy night three prospectors returning from the Ute Reservation pitched their tents in the darkness at the Rosita Springs. In a few days they organized the Hardscrabble mining

4

district, adopting the name of a little creek in the mountains, and during the winter months examined some of the rounded hills in this vicinity very superficially. In the spring of 1873 many of the mines in true fissures that have since been productive were discovered, the town of Rosita was laid out, and the business of taking out ore began in earnest.

The progress of the Denver & Rio Grande Railway through the southern part of Colorado, toward Silverton, is making a number of very lively towns in that section. Durango, which is practically the terminus of that portion of the road, is booming. Real estate took an early jump, and is still in the air. Settlers of a permanent sort are rapidly going in. Durango has a good location, lying near the southwest corner of Colorado, not far from the New Mexico line, in the fertile Animas valley, and is, together with Silverton, a distributing point for the great San Juan country, one of the most important mining regions of the West. It is located favorably not only from a mining standpoint, but from considerations of agriculture and stock raising. Over 3,000 people were in Durango early in the year, and thrice that number will be there before the year closes.

Silverton, the county seat of San Juan county and the great distributing point for the San Juan mines, is 250 miles from Pueblo and about forty miles from Durango. Silverton is supplied with water by three streams, Cement creek, Mineral creek and the Animas river. Over 1,000 people call Silverton home, and there is every indication of a steady increase for years to come. The town is surrounded by good mines, and two large reduction establishments are already worked to their utmost capacity. One of these is owned by the New York and San Juan Reduction Company, and the other by the Melville Mining and Reduction Company. The most important mines in the vicinity are, first, those on Hazelton mountain, one and a half miles above town; the most prominent mines being the group owned by the New York and San Juan Reduction Company, Aspen, Susquehanna, etc.; second, those on Cement creek, owned by Governor Tabor, the Alaska, the Altea, and others; those on Sultan mountain, near the town, the Empire, Hercules, Great Republic, Great Central and Waterwitch, all owned by the Melville Mining and Reduction Company; third, the North Star, one of the great mines of this wonderful country, owned by Ambald & Williams; and fourth, those of Cunningham Gulch. the Pride of the West, owned by the mining company of that name; Highland Mary, owned by Edward Innes, of New York. There are other mines and groups of mines not yet famous but fast coming into notice.

No better description of Dolores and Rico and their mining prospects can be written than that given recently by the official correspondent of the New York *Mining Record.* The letter is as follows:

To the Editor of the N. Y. Mining Record:

"*Sir*—Dolores, the new and at present the most promising and inviting camp for the consideration and investigation of capitalists who may wish to invest in mining properties, is located in the southwestern corner of Ouray county, Colorado, about sixty miles north of the New Mexico line, and about the same distance east of the eastern line of Utah. The town of Rico is about forty-three miles distant in a northwesterly direction from Animas City, in the Animas valley.

"The most important source of success to a mining camp, especially to a carbonate mining camp, with ores mining from 25 to 1,000 ounces in silver to the ton, is accessibility, cheap transportation and cheap fuel. All these advantages are enjoyed by the Rico and the Dolores carbonate camp. Pioneer Mining district, of which Rico is the centre, was organized in 1879, shortly after the discovery of carbonate ores on Telescope mountain (Nigger Baby Hill). The district embraces all that portion of Ouray county lying on the waters of the east and west forks of the Rio Dolores and their tributaries, and includes within its boundaries all of the carbonate deposits of southwestern Colorado, so far as at present known. Rico is located in about the centre of the district, on the east fork of the Dolores, about thirteen miles south of the divide between the lake fork of the San Miguel and the headwaters of the former stream. Three miles south of the divide on the east fork of the Dolores, and ten miles north of Rico, are found extensive coal banks, upon which there has already been made sufficient development to prove its superior quality and inexhaustible quantity; it will make a fine quality of coke, having been thoroughly tested as to its coking qualities by Prof. E. T. Sweet, analytic chemist, of Silverton. It is a splendid quality of blacksmithing coal, and has been used by the blacksmiths of Silverton for the past three years. This coal bank is ten miles from Rico, up the east fork of the Dolores. A wagon road can be constructed to it at a cost not to exceed $1,000; six miles of the road of this distance of ten miles having already been constructed to accommodate the two saw-mills located there, and six miles up the river from Rico. This road continued twelve miles further will connect at Hoffman, on the lake fork of San Miguel, with the toll road from Ouray, and give to the camp wagon communication from the north.

"Believing that cheap transportation and cheap fuel are first to be considered as the most important points to the success of any silver mining camp in any country, we have spoken of them as regards this camp, before alluding to the mineral wealth in carbonate ores which surrounds the town of Rico in every direction. We spent the greater portions of the months of August, September and October at Rico, during which time we availed ourselves of every opportunity to obtain accurate information of the extent and value of the mines in the camp, and as a result of this study of the resources of Pioneer Mining district, we do not hesitate to take the chances of sacrificing our reputation as a prophet by predicting that Rico will be a second Leadville, in all that expression implies, to wit, a town, the growth and prosperity of which is unsurpassed in the mining history of the world. To warrant us in this prediction we have the following facts: First, within a radius of two miles of Rico there are at present, open and paying, two carbonate mines for every one which Leadville could boast of eighteen months ago. Second, the formation is the exact counterpart of that of the Leadville district, the contact of limestone and porphyry being perfect; the limestone forming the foot wall, and the porphyry the hanging walls of veins or deposits of ore which are capped in many instances with iron. The veins or deposits vary in width from a few inches to over twenty feet. The exact similarity of the Rico ores to those of the Leadville district has been most satisfactorily and fully demonstrated; all of the various characters of carbonate ores having been found in abundance, including hard and soft sand and gray carbonates. There are at present in the camp at least fifty paying carbonate mines, as a result of the work of discovery and development, covering a period of a few months. When we say paying mines, we mean mines the ore from which will stand sixty-five dollars for transportation, twenty dollars for treatment, and leave a handsome margin of profit to the producers. With smelting works, cheap transportation, and cheap fuel, at least one hundred properties will be immediately added to the paying list. The mines which will thus be made paying properties are similar to those from which at Leadville, at the present time, the great bulk of her mineral production comes—mines which produce from five to two hundred tons of ore per day, which will run from twenty to one hundred ounces in silver per ton. All these properties, unproductive and unprofitable to-day, which are owned by poor men, and which can be bought for from $5,000 to $50,000, furnish a golden opportunity for the capitalists. Such an opportunity for safe investments, guaranteeing immense profits, is not presented by business enterprises of any kind in any part of the world. Here again, to illustrate, we must hazard our prophetical reputation, to wit: The $5,000 to $50,000 mining properties of to-day will be more readily sold in eighteen months' time at prices ranging from $50,000 to $5,000,000. The Dolores Carbonate camp has been examined by many of the most eminent geologists and mining experts in this country, and we have yet to hear of one who has not given the most flattering reports of its extensive wealth and resources in carbonate ores. The most prominent mines, as far as yet opened and at present worked, are the Grand View, Alma Mater, Little Jim, Cross, Hope, the Bertha with a twelve-foot pay streak running well in gold as well as high in silver, Pelican, Yellow Jacket, Glasgow with fifteen feet of pay ore, Ethlena, Gertie, Democrat, Edith, Melvina, Pigeon and Wabash, on Telescope mountain (Nigger Baby Hill), from half to one mile and a half from Rico; the Newman, Rico Muldoon, Black Demon, O. G. Marston and Little Annie, on Dolores mountain; the Puzzle, Lucky, Highland Mary, Lady Elgin, Little Susie, Elgin Boy, Little Carrie and St. Louis, on Expectation mountain; from all of the above mines, mill runs from 75 to 1,000 ounces in silver to the ton have been obtained, while from at least ten of these mill runs, in lots from three to twenty tons, have given from 250 to 1,000 ounces in silver to the ton. In this camp New York capital is already largely interested in some of the very best properties, and we feel confident that the result of these investments will be most satisfactory to those interested; giving larger profits upon the amount invested than has been realized on a like amount sent out of New York into any other business enterprise for years."

The facile pen of Mr. Robert E. Strahorn, the well-known American traveler, who has without doubt seen as much of the western part of the United States as any other living writer, thus illuminates the somewhat gloomy history of the greatest mining region now open to the public. He says:

"The Gunnison country may well be termed 'Our newest West.' This too, in face of the fact that its entire eastern boundary lies within twenty miles of districts which have been important producers of the precious metals for from twelve to twenty years. Next door to civilization, easy of access, fairly safe and open to development as it now is, and promising to be the El Dorado of 1881, it deserves such fragments of history as we can at this period gather. In the early days of Rocky mountain exploration this whole region was vaguely defined as 'the Grand River country,' its fine stream, now called Gunnison, being then known as the South Fork of the Grand. Our earliest tangible knowledge of its geography and probable utility comes from Governor Wm. Gilpin, who, in 1845, a mere stripling, returned from Oregon to St. Louis, crossing its entire length from west to east. Crossing southern Utah by one of the old Spanish trails, his course then lay through the valleys of the South Fork of the Grand and Uncompahgre rivers, thence over Cochetopa Pass, at the southeastern rim of the Gunnison country, and thence to Bent's old fort on the Arkansas. He was enthusiastic in his description of the valleys and the country generally, and although pursued at intervals for 100 miles by savages, embodied his knowledge in a map which is now on exhibition at the Executive office, Denver.

"The interval between 1845 and 1853 only records vague stories from trappers and Mormons—the former boasting of the region as an ideal game field and of the riches in certain almost inaccessible gulches, and the latter taking care to let the world know only what dangers were threatened by savages. This last claim was well supported, or the Mormon crime speciously covered, when in 1853 Captain Gunnison's name was given the region at the expense of his life. While exploring in this vicinity that year for a Pacific railroad route he was killed—history says by Indians, but subsequent developments point to the Mormons as the murderers. In 1854 the indomitable old 'Pathfinder,' General Fremont, passed over the same country from east to west, but even his glowing tributes to the beauty and richness of the region did not serve to bridge the seven-year gap which ensued with tales of genuine pioneering.

"Not until 1861, when some prospectors who approached from California Gulch (where Leadville now stands) and named Washington Gulch, Taylor

Park, Rentz's Gulch, and Union Park, near the head of Slate river, was there any positive development. Such discoveries as they made created considerable excitement, and under ordinary circumstances would have led to a general stampede and permanent occupation of the country, but one morning of the summer named twelve men who were riding along the Washington Gulch trail were killed by Indians. This wholesale massacre,

BALANCED ROCK.

which gave a gloomy side defile the name of Dead Man's Gulch, sent a thrill of terror through every incoming prospector. The outrage was magnified each time its story was repeated, and the result was an almost entire abandonment of the country by the whites. Not even the stories of 'pound diggings,' of golden bullets that the Indians used, and of the famous 'Snow-Blind Gulch' along the Cochetopa, where, it was currently believed, two miners whip-sawed boards for flumes and washed out a pound of gold each per day, and finally, when the snows of 1862 fell, becoming snow-blind, they perished, an easy prey to savages or storm—not even these lured the most daring in the then populous gulches of Central Colorado to exploration. I have had 'Snow-Blind Gulch' pointed out to me near the headwaters of the Tomichi, with its traces of mining in the long ago—the old whip-saw pit, the rotten sluices and overgrown prospect holes. There are no 'pound diggings' or golden bullets there, but gold in the quartz of neighboring hills in paying quantities.

"A few faithful ones, however, remained, fortified themselves in Washington Gulch, living almost wholly for months at a time on game and fish, and harassed, as probably intruders deserved to be, by renegade Utes. In 1863

MANITOU HOUSE, MANITOU, COL.

three men, whose names, I am sorry to say, have passed from history, still 'held the fort,' and, with such rude sluice-boxes as they could fashion by hand, made from $5 to $20 per day. These placers have been worked almost constantly, under all sorts of discouragements, with fair results, ever since. The rifle went hand in hand with the shovel, and the skeletons often exhumed in these days of peace indicate many a thrilling chapter of unwritten history.

"Developments in quartz mining date back to the summer of 1872, when George and Lewis Waite, two old California gulch miners, crossed the mountains to see what could be found on the western slope. They passed over sixty miles of mineral country, failing to detect what have since developed into some of the finest gold and silver quartz districts of Gunnison, and hardly called a halt until they reached Rock creek, an important tributary of Roaring Fork of Grand river. They were encouraged by long-since abandoned surface-diggings, and soon discovered an enormous vein of

ON THE DENVER & RIO GRANDE.

gold and silver bearing quartz, which was fitly named the 'Whopper.' The lode was afterward traced across the gulch and over an adjoining mountain. A hundred miles of difficult defiles and steep heights lay between the Waites and an ore market, but they have been tunneling Whopper mountain almost steadily ever since, quitting work only temporarily at long intervals, when compelled to go back to civilization for powder and a 'grub stake.' Occasionally they would drive a pack-mule laden

with ore from the Whopper or other discoveries they made nearly to Denver or Cañon City, and return with the necessary flour, coffee and bacon. Thus they continued year after year, slowly pushing to the heart of the great mountain, and patiently piling up tons upon tons of the rich ore, laying up treasures for the inevitable day of reward. Although anticipating a little I can not resist adding here that the Waites made their well-earned 'home stake' in 1879 when mine hunters with capital poured into the country from Leadville.

"A small band of prospectors from Denver and Golden, headed by Jim Brennon, also entered the Rock Creek district in 1872, and their reports

resulted in the first organized attempt at occupying the land in 1873, when
Dr. John Parsous, Prof. Sylvester Richardson and thirty picked moun-
taineers, including any assayer, smelter, geologist and botanist, entered from
Denver. Machinery for testing and reducing ores on a small scale was
taken along. This necessitated wagon transportation, and the only practicable route was via Sagauche and Los Pinos Agency, at the southeastern
boundary of the Gunnison country. The Utes had, some ten years before,
exchanged San Luis valley for about all of Colorado lying west of the 107th
meridian, and had the whites been protected in their rights no trouble would

ATCHISON, KANSAS.

have ensued from their going as far west as the present site of Gunnison
City. The agency itself was located twenty miles east of Indian soil, but
Gen. Charles Adams, then in charge, said the expedition could only go by
permission of the Utes. A heated controversy and a tie vote were finally
settled by Ouray in favor of the whites. This was undoubtedly the turning
point in Gunnison's history—all praise to Ouray—for remnants of the
expedition made valuable discoveries of gold, silver, coal, iron, copper, lead,
etc., and, more than this, let the outside world know of their success.

    "In March, 1874, a colony was formed in Denver to settle upon agricul-
tural lands in Gunnison valley, and, in the winter following, twenty persons,

all told, were scattered for thirty miles along Gunnison and Tomichi valleys, while the mining districts contained a still smaller showing on account of the San Juan stampede of the previous fall. The county and town of Gunnison were organized in 1876, but not until late in 1878, when prospectors fresh from Leadville and San Juan found rich gold and silver ores, and what they called carbonates, at the head of Quartz creek, near the present site of Pitkin, at the head of Tomichi river and in other localities, did the region attract the attention it deserved. In the spring of 1879 the grand influx began. Probably 20,000 men participated in the wonderful discoveries at Ruby Corner, Gothic, Crested Butte, Tin Cup,

GRACE GREENWOOD'S COTTAGE,

Killerton, Roaring Forks, and other camps. At the height of these developments last fall came the Ute outbreak, and the Thornburgh and Meeker massacres; and for weeks, during the last working season at these great altitudes, scarcely a day passed that did not witness some act of Indian deviltry in sight of the various mining camps, such as setting fire to the valuable forests, stealing horses, or even killing a straggling prospector. Scarcely a man was to be found at many of the best camps when winter set in, and there were no adequate supplies for even the few who had the courage to remain.

SAN DIEGO.

PHOTO ELIC. ENG. CO.

(64)

"In spite of these discouragements 5,000 mines have been recorded in Gunnison county, the new discoveries at present averaging 300 per week. Several smelters and a dozen saw-mills and planers are at work. The permanent population of 500 last fall has grown to 12,000—and if I may judge from appearances, most of these people are here to stay. An assessed valuation of about $1,000,000 has been created here on the borders of Indian land in one year. Highways, upon which daily stages run, traverse all parts of the country, and I believe the first Concord coach made its appearance in Gunnison less than sixty days ago. Seven or eight newspapers appear weekly in a field totally unoccupied three months ago. How appreciative residents are of good home literature may be judged from the fact that the first copies of three or four leading journals sold at from $50 to $100 each on the day they were issued, and I hear $50 freely offered for a complete file of eight to twelve numbers. Substantial churches, school houses and county buildings are being erected. A dozen streams are strung for miles with houses of prosperous ranchmen, thousands of cattle, sheep and horses dot the hills, trains of rich ores are to be seen going to the railroad sixty miles away, and other trains are unloading vast quantities of mining machinery and a winter's supply of groceries."

The Gunnison country has an area of not less than 10,000 square miles, being 110 miles long by eighty miles wide. The most important part of this territory is the Elk mountain range, with its many spurs and foot hills. This range is one of the rockiest of all the Rockies. Great granite shafts, shot from some mighty bow in the earth's centre, have broken and re-broken the original surface, until now there are seven peaks in the range rising to a height of 14,000 feet, and many times that number reaching an altitude of 12,000 feet. Fissure veins are here the characteristic deposit, and these are reinforced by vast beds of coal and iron. The principal streams are the Gunnison, Uncompahgre, Cochetopa, Tumichi, Taylor, East, Ohio, Eagle, Rock, Roaring Fork and Slate, with their hundreds of smaller tributaries, all emptying into the Rio Colorado. The Gunnison is not an agricultural country, but with irrigation much can be done in this direction. For stock-raising purposes there are large areas of perennial pasturage, where bunch grass, blue grass and other varieties furnish the richest of grazing.

Some idea of the distribution of mineral in the Gunnison country may be obtained from the following verbal chart: Ruby Camp, ruby silver, brittle silver and sulphurets; Washington Gulch, ruby silver, carbonates and argentiferous galena; Slate River, galena; East River, galena and gray copper; Copper Creek, native silver, ruby, sulphurets and gray copper; Maroon Creek, copper; Spring Creek, carbonates; Cement Creek, carbonates; Tin Cup Gulch, carbonates; Roaring Forks, galena and gray copper; Tumichi, galena; Union Park, gold; German Flats, gold; Anthracite Creek, anthracite coal; Coal Creek, iron and coal. This is but a general outline of the lay of Gunnison's mineral. The particulars must be gathered from the study of individual mines.

The most important towns and mining centres of the Gunnison country are Gunnison City, Ruby Camp, Pitkin, Gothic, Washington Gulch, Irwin, Crested Butte, Hillerton, Virginia City, Red Cliff, Tin Cup, Willard, Cochetopa and Aspen. Gunnison City now has some thousands of people, a court house worth $15,000, a hotel worth $20,000, a school house worth $7,000, a bank representing a capital of $10,000,000, and other public or semi-public enterprises on a like generous scale. Irwin has about 1,500 people, 300 houses, and a brisk upward tendency in its real estate. Gothic, at the mouth of Copper creek, on East river, has about 2,000 people, and some of the best mines of Colorado in its vicinity. Ruby Camp has its famous Forest Queen mine, and many others of scarcely less importance. Pitkin, on Quartz creek, is one of the most important silver camps in the State. Washington Gulch has a magnificent outlook. Its mines are rapidly developing a richness which the most enthusiastic prophets of 1879–80 did not foresee. Among the best of these mines are the Gypsy, the Highland, the Gavitt, the Miner's Delight and the Baxter. At Crested Butte are limitless fields of coking coal, nearly equal to the best quality of that article from Pennsylvania. The vast deposits of anthracite coal at Ruby Camp are among the wonders of the wonderful Gunnison. The coal is of unsurpassed quality and the quantity is practically boundless.

COLORADO RESORTS.

CLIMATE — DENVER — COLORADO SPRINGS AND MANITOU — LEADVILLE —
THE EARL OF DUNRAVEN.

HE climate of Colorado is like that of Kansas, only more so. Having a greater elevation, it is drier, and its snow-covered mountain peaks temper the hottest rays of the summer sun. The atmosphere is pre-eminently dry, pure and electrical. It is itself a tonic, and its purifying and invigorating effect on the human system is wonderful. These facts are becoming known the world over, and the favorite summer resorts in the State are more and more liberally patronized every year. And what are the "summer resorts" of Colorado? A timely question. The entire State is a summer resort, and a good one; but what is meant by this expression is simply that class of cities and towns that are located near either medicinal springs or specially attractive scenic sections, and have ample hotel accommodations for summer visitors. Among the best of such places may be named Denver, Georgetown, Idaho Springs, Colorado Springs, Manitou, Cañon City, Alamosa, Wagon Wheel Gap, Pagosa Springs, Twin Lakes, Soda Springs, Aspen, the various parks and many of the smaller places on the line of the Denver & Rio Grande Railway. Denver is a good point for a summer location by reason of its ample railway communication, which renders all parts of the State comparatively easy of access. Colorado Springs and Manitou are beautiful places, surrounded by magnificent scenery and provided with good hotels. They are justly in great favor. Twin Lakes, Soda Springs, and the vicinity of Leadville generally, were thus described recently by a writer in one of our magazines:

"Leadville has many of the attributes of a metropolitan city, its theatres, its water-works, its letter-carriers, and its suburban resorts—Soda Springs and Twin Lakes. The drive to the foot of Mount Massive, where a large spring, strongly impregnated with soda, bubbles up from the earth, is

GARDEN OF THE GODS.

delightful. The sun shines brightly upon the mountain flowers, growing so hardily in the seemingly uncongenial soil, upon the pines and willows, giving something of greenness and cultivation to the barren, rocky ravines, and upon the gaily equipped horses and riders. The road to Twin Lakes leads through a desolate region, over sandy hills, through dusty dales, past no dwelling; nothing but barren ground and lonely, cheerless rocks. Four hours bring one to the summit of a high hill, and everything is changed: below are the lakes, lying in a natural basin, dark and blue in the afternoon sunshine; above are the mountains, stretching away in long serrated ranges to the west, and on the shores of the lakes are the hotels and cottages. The lakes are only a thousand feet below Leadville, but the air has not that constant suggestion of snow; grass grows here; and the former owner, Long, of the famous Long & Derry mine, grew his own vegetables—something quite impossible in the 'Carbonate Camp.' The lakes lie at the foot of a mountain, on whose side the bright yellow leaves of the aspens, colored by the early frost, seem like great bunches of golden-rod in happy

UNLOADING SHIP OF THE DESERT.

contrast to the dark green of the pines. Further up the mountain all trees disappear, the snowy crest of Mount Elbert· seeming to guard with an ever vigilant eye the clear waters at its base."

Taking up the more prominent of the lesser resorts in alphabetical order, the claims of Alamosa first appear for consideration. This city of a thousand people is located in the San Juan country on the Rio Grande river, and in the beautiful San Luis Park. South of the town are valuable meadows, and twenty-five miles distant rises the peak of Sierra Blanca. Animas Forks is situated fourteen miles north of Silverton, at the forks of Rio de las Animas, in a wild country 11,584 feet above sea level, and is the centre of a large mining district as well as a favorite resort for those who enjoy rare air. Antelope Springs is a wayside inn, half a mile north of the Rio Grande and fifty-six miles west of Del Norte. It is surrounded by a

MENNONITE SCENE.

country in which game is abundant, and the pine-clad mountains as rough and rugged as they make them.

Antonito is a lively town seventy-nine miles west of Alamosa in a level park, surrounded by agricultural and meadow lands. A mile from Antonito is the old Mexican plaza of Conejos, containing a Catholic church, convent, chapel and academy. It is a typical Mexican town. The Roaring Park district, in which Aspen, the county seat of Pitkin county, is located, is a favorite resort for sportsmen. Immense herds of elk and black-tailed deer, and not a few bears abound in the woods, while ducks and geese are found near the streams. Aspen is thirty miles due west from Leadville, "as the crow flies." Brown's cañon is a gorge cut through the foot-hills by that prince of engineers, the Arkansas river. It is second only in grandeur to

ADOBE FIRE PLACE.

the Royal Gorge. The tourist will see it just after leaving South Arkansas station on the Denver & Rio Grande Railroad. Its height is so great that the observer becomes lost in amazement while viewing the overhanging cliffs and forbidding gorges, and instinctively seeks a safe retreat from a possible down-dashing boulder. Buena Vista is a city of 2,000 people, thirty-seven miles from Leadville, in Cottonwood Park, and is one of the gateways to the Gunnison. A back ground of mountains and in front the lovely Cottonwood river, make Buena Vista a charming summer resort. Cañon city, county seat of Fremont county, is located on the Arkansas river, at an elevation of 5,400 feet, and has a population of 2,000. It is

situated in the midst of remarkably fine scenery, but its chief attractions are
its hot and soda springs, which are known far and wide.

Del Norte is in the northwest part of San Luis Park, on the Rio Grande
river, at a point where the valley is only one-fourth of a mile in width. The
site is exceedingly picturesque, a view from Del Norte comprising a glimpse
of cottonwood groves, high cliffs, San Luis Park, and the peaks of the Sangre

ANVIL ROCK, MONUMENT PARK.

de Cristo—"blood of Christ"—range. Durango, in La Plata county, is a
lively place, and is fast becoming a commercial centre. It lies on the east
bank of Animas river, on a high plateau, 6,410 feet above the sea, and is
reached by the Denver & Rio Grande Railroad. Among Colorado cañons,
Grape cañon ranks with the first. It receives its name from the profusion
of wild grapes growing on its lower slopes. The tourist can reach it by
rail or by stage from Cañon City. Perhaps Red Cliff and the Mount of the
Holy Cross are as interesting to the average traveler as any other places in
Colorado. To get to the former place, one starts at Leadville, crosses

Tennessee Park, and climbing Mother range, crosses it and descends to the romantic village of Red Cliff, which is located at the foot of Horn-Silver mountain, near Battle mountain. The easiest trail to the Mount of the Holy Cross is from this place. This mountain derives its name from the fact that two deep depressions, one horizontal and one vertical, cross each other at right angles on its eastern slope.

Pagosa Springs lie four miles south of the San Juan range, on the river of the same name. The chief attraction is a cluster of hot springs, the largest of which is forty feet in diameter, the water being exceedingly hot and charged with saline material. The celebrated Poncho Springs are located a short distance from South Arkansas, and are fifty in number. The locality offers numerous attractions as a pleasure resort ; the scenery is grand and inspiring, views being had of Mounts Ouray, Shawano, Antero, Harvard and Princeton. In the Wet Mountain valley, which is an old lake basin, lying between the Sangre de Cristo range and the Greenhorn mountains, are three prosperous towns, Silver Cliff, West Cliff and Rosita, all of them pleasantly situated and exceedingly prosperous. Prof. Hayden regards the view of the Sangre de Cristo range, from the Wet Mountain valley, as the grandest in Colorado. In this portion of the range rise four peaks, all of which are higher than Pike's Peak. Saguache, thirty-three miles from Del Norte, is located near San Luis Lakes, a large body of marshy land and shallow ponds, in which ducks are found in plenty. The town is surrounded by a rich farming region, and at least one-fifth of its inhabitants are Mexicans.

In this brief *résumé* of Colorado resorts mention has not been made of two objects of peculiar beauty and grandeur. These are, respectively, Toltec Gorge and Veta Pass. The first of these is located on the Denver & Rio Grande Railroad, nearly thirty-four miles from Antonito. The road climbs to the crest of the range, and, following along the steep mountain sides, just below the summit makes a bend of four miles and dives into a tunnel in the cliffs—all this distance at a height of 1,200 feet above the valley. The tunnel is passed, and shortly after emerging from it the gorge is reached. At the brink of the chasm the track is 1,100 feet above Los Pinos creek, and the view is one of wild, weird beauty, hardly surpassed on the continent. Veta Pass, on the road from Pueblo to Antonito, seventy-one miles distant from Pueblo, is one of the most interesting of its kind. From the station of La Veta to the top of the range the track ascends at the rate of 211 feet to the mile, until an altitude of 9,339 feet is reached. The view from the cars is certainly unique and never to be forgotten. Indeed, few travelers can make the trip without a nervous tremor and apprehension.

Hunting and fishing, as the chief industries of a camp life, are always in order, and none who have so spent a season will ever be content with anything else. The free, bright life of him whose cares are far away and whose sleep is sweet, is not to be improved upon. It is absolutely one of the finest experiences of a lifetime. The Earl of Dunraven, in his fascinating account of a hunting season in Colorado, has the following paragraph:

"In spring and summer the scenery and climate are very different. Ice and snow and withered grass have passed away, and everything is basking and glowing under a blazing sun, hot, but always tempered with a cool breeze. Cattle wander about the plain—or try to wander, for they are so fat they can scarcely move. Water-fowl frequent the lakes. The whole earth is green, and the margins of the streams are luxuriant with a profuse growth of wild flowers and rich herbage. The air is scented with the sweet-smelling sap of the pines, whose branches welcome many feathered visitors from Southern climes; an occasional humming-bird whirs among the shrubs, trout leap in the creeks, insects buzz in the air; all nature is active and exuberant with life."

NEW MEXICO IN GENERAL.

GEOGRAPHY AND TOPOGRAPHY—PAST AND PRESENT—RESOURCES—
CLIMATE AND HEALTH—REV. MR. FORRESTER
QUOTED—ARMY STATISTICS.

HE Territory of New Mexico lies between 31° 20′ and 37° north latitude, and 103° and 109° west longitude. The eastern boundary line is 345 miles long, and the western 390 miles. The average breadth of the Territory north of the thirty-second parallel is 335 miles. The area of the Territory is 121,201 square miles, or 77,568,640 acres. The surface of the Territory is composed of valleys, plains and lofty mountains. Entering from Colorado the Rocky mountains are found in two distinct ranges. The eastern range, highest and most rugged of the two, extends only to the vicinity of Santa Fé. The western range, known as the Sierra Madre, extends to the southern limit, forming a connection with the Sierra Madre of Mexico. Many of the peaks of the eastern range are above 11,000 feet in altitude, and are crowned with perpetual snow. The great inter-mountain plateaus have an elevation of from 5,000 to 8,000 feet. The valley portions—the Rio Grande being most important—are from 3,000 to 5,000 feet above the sea. Nearly two-thirds of the Territory lies east of the Sierre Madre range, the southeastern portion, or "staked plains," being high, level, and comparatively unproductive. South of the eastern range, between the Pecos river and the Rio Grande, is a series of valleys, intervening plains and low mountains. The country west of the Sierra Madre is of an irregular sort, there being a larger number of low mountains and narrow valleys. The most important river of the Territory is the Rio Grande del Norte, which rises in Colorado and flows south between the two ranges of mountains, crossing the southern boundary of the Territory at about the

NEAR SANTA BARBARA.

middle point. The second river in size is the Pecos, which rises in the
eastern slope of the eastern range, and, flowing south, joins the Rio Grande
in Texas. The Canadian river, a branch of the Arkansas, drains the northeastern portion of the Territory, and the San Juan, a tributary of the
Colorado, drains the northwestern section. The Gila and the Mimbres rise
in the southwest. Other important streams are the Chaco, Vaca, Puerco,

Zuni, Pinasco, Palomas, Torrejon, Gallinas, Cimarron, Mora, Utah creek,
Whitestone, Sapillo, Concha, Galisteo, Antonio, Bear creek, Gobezan,
Alacaso, Yeso, Toro, Azul, Ruidoso, Bonito, Tegique, Negrito, Berdio,
and Blanco. The altitudes of several of the principal points of the Terri-
tory are as follows: Trinidad, 6,034; Raton, 6,688; Las Vegas, 6,452;
Lamy, 6,531; Santa Fé, 7,013; and Albuquerque, 5,006.

Before New England New Mexico was. New Mexico saw the first implanting of European civilization in America, and Santa Fé, the capital, is beyond question the oldest city in the United States. In 1677 Mr. Peter Heylin, of London, wrote:

"Nova Mexicana is bounded on the south with New Biscay; on the west with Quivara; the countreyes on the north and east, not discovered hitherto, though some extend eastward as far as Florida. Extended

MEXICAN MOCKING BIRDS.

250 leagues from the town and mines of S. Barbara, and how much beyond that none can tell; the relations of this countrey being so uncertain and incredulous that I dare say nothing positively of the soil or people, but much less of the towns and cities which are said to be in it. So named by Antonio de Espeio, a citizen of Mexico in New Spain, by whom discovered and subdued.

"For first, they tell us of the people, that they are of great stature, and that like enough; but not so possible that they have the art of dressing chamois and other leather, as well as the best leather-dressers in all Flanders; or that they have shoes and boots so well sowed and soaled that no shoemaker in all S. Martins could do it better. Then for their towns, that they are very fair and goodly, the houses well built of lime and stone, some of them four stories, and in most of them stores for the winter season. The streets even, and ordered in an excellent manner. Particularly, they tell of a town called 1. Chia, one of the first chief towns of the province of Cuames, which is said to contain eight market-places, and all the houses to be plastered and painted in most curious manner. 2. Of Acoma, that it is situated on the top of a rock, a great town, yet no way unto it but by ladders; and in one place a pair of stairs, but exceedingly narrow, hewn out of the rock; exceedingly well fortified by nature, (they say true in that, if any things are true which they tell us of it), and all their water kept in cisterns (but nobody can tell from whence they have it). 3. Of Conibas, on a lake so called, the city seven leagues long, two broad; (a second Ninive) but the houses scatteringly built among hills and gardens, which take up a great deal of the room; inhabited by a people of such strength and courage, that the Spaniards only faced it, and so went away. Much of this stuff I could afford you, but by the taste we may conjecture the rest of the feast.

"The people more ingenious than the rest of the savages; exquisite at some mechan arts, especially in the making of their feather pictures, and so industrious withal, so patient both of thirst and hunger, that they will set at it a whole day without meat or drink, turning every feather to the light, upwards and downwards, every way, to see in which position it will best fit the place intended for it. No better goldsmiths in the world, nor men more expert anywhere in refining metals, curious in painting upon cotton whatsoever was presented to the eye. But yet so barbarous withal that they thought the gods were pleased with the blood of men, which sometimes they sacrificed unto them. They were so ignorant that when they first saw the Spaniards on horseback they thought the horse and man to have been one creature, and would ask what the horse said when they heard him neigh. So careless of the wealth of gold were they that they would part with great quantities of it for knives, glass beads, little bells, and such petty trifles. But whatsoever they once were is not now material, the Spaniards having made such havock of this wretched people that in seventeen years they destroyed above six millions of them, roasting some, plucking out the eyes of others, consuming them in the mines and mercilessly casting them among wild beasts where they were devoured. As for those who do remain, besides their own natural ingeniosities they have since learned the civilities and arts of Europe. What else concernes this soil and people we shall show more particularly, if we find it necessary, in their proper places.

"The countrey was first discovered by Augustino Royaz, a Franciscan frier, Anno 1580, who, out of zeal to plant the Gospel in the North, accompanied by two other friers of that order and eight soldiers, undertook the adventure. But one of the monks being killed by the savages, the soldiers plaid the poltroons and gave over the action. On their return, Beltram, a frier of the same order (from whose mouth we must have the former fictions), desirous to preserve the lives of his fellows which staid behind, encouraged one Antonio de Espeio, a native of Corduba, but a citizen of Mexico, to engage in such an holy cause; who, raising a band of 150 horse, accompanied with many slaves and beasts of carriage, undertook the busi-

PIKE'S PEAK.

ness. I omit the many nations of the Conchi, Pasaugates, Tobosi, Tarrahumares, Tepoanes, and many others as hard names, which he passed through in his way. But coming at the last to a great river which he called Del Noordt, there he made a stand; caused the countrey on both sides of it to be called Nova Mexicana, and a city to be built which he called New Mexico, situated in the 37° of northern latitude, and distant from Old Mexico 500 leagues; the name since changed to S. Foy, but still the metropolis of that province, the residence of the governour, and a pretty garrison consisting of 250 Spaniards. Some other towns he found at his coming hither, viz.. 2. Socorro, so called by the Spaniards because of that succour and relief they found there for their half-starved bodies. 3. Senecu. 4. Pilabo, and 5, Scriletfa; old towns but new christened by the Spaniards, when the inhabitants thereof did embrace the Gospel, each of them beautified by a church. 6. S. Johns, built afterward in the year 1599, by John de Onnate, who with an army of 5,000 followed the same way which Espeio went, and, having got a great deal of treasure, laid it up in this place that it might be no incumberance to him in his advance. This is the most I dare rely on for this countrey. And this hath no such wonders in it but what an easie faith may give credit to. Though I had rather believe the friers' whole relations than to go thither to disprove any part thereof."

IN NEW MEXICO AND COLORADO.

The modern commercial history of New Mexico, which covers the time since commercial relations were first established between New Mexico and the East, may be epitomized as follows:

1. Long, Nicollet and Fremont were practically the first discoverers of New Mexico interested in commerce.

2. The idea of establishing trade between the western cities and the northern States of Old Mexico was the first stimulus to travel in the direction of New Mexico.

3. La Londe, a Frenchman, was sent to Santa Fé by Mr. Morrison, of Kaskaskia, Ill., as commercial agent, in 1804.

4. James Pursley visited Santa Fé in a commercial way in 1805.

5. Pike went to New Mexico with his exploring and commercial party in 1807.

6. Knight, Beard, Chambers and eight others went with a train of goods, in 1812, to Santa Fé, and were held prisoners there for nine years, at the end of which time they were liberated and returned to the States.

7. Glenn, of Ohio, and Capt. Bicknell, of Missouri, merchants, went to Santa Fé in 1822.

OLD CHURCH—CAPISTRANA.

8 Eight merchants, with a party from Missouri, crossed to Old Mexico in 1824.

9. Caravans were furnished with Gove nm nt escorts in 1829. 1834 and 1843.

10. The treaty of Guadalupe Hidalgo, by which the United States came into possession of New Mexico, Arizona, California, Utah and Nevada, was made in 1848.

11. By act of Congress, approved September 9, 1850, New Mexico was defined and made a Territory, "*Provided*, it may be divided into two or more Territories; and, *Provided*, that when admitted as a State it shall be

TOLTEC GORGE.

with or without slavery, as the constitution may provide." By this act was secured the first definite settlement of the boundary between New Mexico and Texas.

12. After twenty-nine years of constantly increasing trade between New Mexico and the States, the Atchison, Topeka & Santa Fé Railroad entered the Territory in 1879.

The Territory contains about 100,000 Mexicans, 25,000 Indians, and 25,000 Americans. The American population has been increasing with marvelous rapidity, especially since the Atchison, Topeka & Santa Fé Rail-

road and its western connection with the Southern Pacific have made the
Territory the highway for a mighty trans-continental traffic.   The same
resistless energy which drove the Atchison, Topeka & Santa Fé Railroad
across the great plains of Kansas and Colorado, over the Raton range, 8,000
feet high, and the Santa Fé range, 7,500 feet high, through the Territory
to a connection with its western outlet, is now hard at work opening mines,
building towns, establishing schools and churches, encouraging manufactures, developing agriculture and stock raising, and otherwise urging the
Territory to its magnificent destiny as one of the richest and most powerful States of the Union.

The greater part of the certain prosperity of New Mexico will be due to
her advantage as a country for mining, stock raising and manufacturing.
The minerals of New Mexico are chiefly gold, silver, iron, copper, lead,
turquoise, coal and mica.   These are found in exhaustless quantities, the
only lacking requisite to their conversion into actual value having hitherto
been the means of ready transportation for men, material and the mineral
product.   With the advent of the railway this lack has been obviated, and
now the work of mining has been fairly begun.   More about the mines will
be said in the mention of particular towns and mining camps.   The valleys
and adjacent ranges of hills are a paradise for grazing.   Cattle and sheep
find food the year round from the rich growths of native grasses—principally the gramma or buffalo grass.   The native grasses do not decay as in
the regions of greater dampness, but cure in fine condition, retaining all
their natural juices.   Sheep raising is already conducted in New Mexico on
a magnificent scale, though the native breeds have been allowed to greatly
deteriorate.   With good blood and good methods New Mexico will give the
country more sheep product than any other southwestern district.   The
manufacturing interests of the Territory have already begun to grow.   Coal
inferior to none other found in the world, and numberless streams of a sort
to furnish fine water power, together with all necessary timber, mineral and
other raw material, are the factors which must combine to produce a manufacturing interest of colossal proportions.   The fruit and grain products of
the Rio Grande valley are by no means insignificant.   The grapes raised are
of extraordinary excellence, possessing a superior flavor and producing wine
equal to that made anywhere else in the world.   In regard to fruit it may
be stated in a general way, that wherever water may be had, either by
wells, springs, or the ordinary methods of irrigation, fruit may be grown in
every variety and of the best quality.   In this connection, as an example of
what is meant, may be quoted an article, first published in the Santa Fé
Trail, on "The Bishop's Garden," as follows:

"One of the most charming places in the Territory of New Mexico is the
garden belonging to the residence of good Bishop Lamy, of Santa Fé.
The venerable bishop has been a resident of Santa Fé for thirty years, and

during all that long period he has been carefully working out many of the
material as well as the spiritual problems presented to him in his peculiarly
exalted position. Among the former is the possibilities of horticulture in
the Territory. The result of the bishop's experiment is truly remarkable.
The garden in question is located in the heart of the city of Santa Fé. Its
long, wide avenues reach out from the bishop's home toward the north and

NEAR ECHO CANON.

east. On every side are rows and clumps of flourishing fruit trees of every
sort. Peaches as fine as ever were seen; large, richly-flavored apples, with
"keeping" qualities rarely equaled ; pears, perfectly formed, without spot
or blemish of any sort ; plums of all colors, satin-skinned, full of juice ;
cherries nearly as large as the plums ; apricots as fine as those of any
climate ; dates as good as those from across the water ; prunes and quinces
fit for show at a world's fair ; oranges as good as the best from Florida,
though not in large quantities; almonds and other nuts; grapes, such as

6

described elsewhere in this paper ; strawberries, raspberries, blackberries, currants, gooseberries, and other small fruit in great abundance,—all these, together with the finer sorts of agricultural products, and a profusion of the most beautiful flowers, may be found in the bishop's garden, the result of his wise forethought and patient waiting.   At one side of the garden, extending some little way into it, is another feature which should not be forgotten : a splendid perennial spring supplies water for a large pond, or series of ponds, in which are thousands of flashing trout, so tame that the

LAKE NEAR GEORGETOWN.

gardeners frequently catch them by hand as they come to the surface for food.   Flocks of water-fowl frequently settle upon these ponds for a rest on their way from river to river, so that a dish of trout may almost always be supplemented by some sort of delicate wild fowl.   Bishop Lamy believes that wherever water may be obtained in New Mexico the same results may be accomplished ; and he thinks that where streams or springs are not found naturally, they may be had, *almost invariably*, by boring.   At the

MORMON TEMPLE, SALT LAKE CITY

risk of trespassing on the bishop's good nature, the *Trail* advises all visitors to Santa Fé to try for a glimpse of the garden herein described."

A fine description of the climate and sanitary characteristics of New Mexico has been written by the Rev. Henry Forrester, of Las Vegas, whose fifteen years' residence in the Territory well qualifies him to testify. Mr. Forrester says:

MOUNTAIN GROUSE.

"It is doubtful if the climate of New Mexico is excelled by that of any other part of the world. It varies, of course, according to locality and altitude, but the atmosphere is everywhere dry. This moderates the effect of the heat in the southern valleys, and that of the cold at the higher altitudes and latitudes. When the thermometer is at 110° at Mesilla there is no such unpleasantness as there is in the city of New York with the thermometer at 90°. At Santa Fé, which is about 7,000 feet above the level of the sea, the summers are very pleasant, though the thermometer sometimes registers as high as 95°. In the winter it seldom gets to zero, and when it does get 4° or 5° below that, the cold is not felt unpleasantly, unless one happens to be traveling, or is exposed to the wind. There are generally three or four deep snows, from six to twelve inches, during the winter, and many lighter ones. There is a regular rainy season, but it is not what is generally understood by that term. There is no continuous rain; indeed, there is seldom a day without sunshine. The rain comes generally in showers, occasionally in storms, but seldom lasts more than a few hours at the longest. The season begins about the first of July and lasts two months. There are occasional heavy rains, and many light showers at other times; and when there are snows in and near the mountains, the southern valleys and the lower table-lands get rains. Snow seldom falls in the Mesilla valley. When it does, it melts at once. The winters there are very mild. It is hot in the summer, but one can always keep reasonably comfortable in the house, and the nights are scarcely ever unpleasantly warm. Then, as the mountains are only about twenty miles distant, it does not take long to get a cool atmosphere, even when the temperature in the valley is highest. One can find almost any temperature desired by changing altitude. North of Santa Fé, where the elevation is greater, the winters are colder in proportion. In the summer the dwellers in the large valleys are troubled, as are localities in the East, by mosquitos, gnats, and other like pests, but in the mountains there are none of these things. A peculiarity of this climate is its electric condition. The atmosphere seems to be highly charged with electricity. Sometimes there are electric disturbances that prevent for hours the working of the telegraph. The air is beautifully clear, and the sky can scarcely be excelled by that of Italy. It is almost impossible for one to correctly estimate distances, everything appears so much nearer than it really is."

The meteorological characteristics of the Territory may be seen from the following official figures: The mean temperature at Santa Fé (latitude 35° 41′, elevation 6,842 feet) for six years has been as follows: spring, 49.7°; summer, 70.4°; autumn, 50.6°; winter, 31.6°; year, 50.6°. For the year ending September 30, 1873, the mean temperature at the same place was 49°; of the warmest month (July), 71°; of the coldest month (January), 29°; total rainfall, 8.59 inches; greatest monthly rainfall, (in August), 2.79 inches; highest temperature observed during the year, 88°; lowest, 5°. Speaking further of the health of the people of the Territory, as affected by the climate, Mr. Forrester remarks:

"It may well be supposed that with such a climate as that above described New Mexico has few diseases. In the mountains there is some tendency to catarrh, rheumatism and neuralgia. The first is very prevalent; the others are less so. Some persons who come here with these diseases are relieved. Some get them here for the first time. Most persons, exercising ordinary care, would not contract them. In some of the southern valleys ague prevails at times. The people of the lower Rio Grande valley were troubled with that disease for three summers prior to 1880. It had not existed before for some twenty years, when it had prevailed for two summers. There are now no visible causes that have not existed all the time, so it is impossible to say what caused it at the last time of its occurrence. Smallpox went through the Territory from south to north in 1876 and 1877, and was very fatal among the Mexicans. It was said that several thousand persons died of it. Few Americans had it, and scarcely any of them died. That the Mexicans suffered so much may be attributed to the fact that few of them were vaccinated, and to their carelessness and want of management. Corpses were carried in open coffins through the streets to the churches, where the people were necessarily exposed to infection. Diseases that are cured here —when curable—are malarial and bilious troubles, lung affections, asthma,

A NEW MEXICAN BURRO TRAIN.

and general debility. When not curable they are generally relieved. Persons with heart-disease, nervous difficulties, or consumption in its later stages, should not come to the mountain regions. The Mesilla valley is the great sanitarium for phthisical patients. It combines three advantages not found together elsewhere: moderate altitude, mild temperature, and dry air. Persons suffering with rheumatism or neuralgia are often cured by bathing in the water of some of the hot springs. There are several groups of these in the Territory. Most of them are medicinal, and those that are most accessible are visited now by many persons. The group near Las Vegas, now accessible by rail, has long been known and used. It is supplied with hotels having all modern conveniences, and newer and larger hotels, bath houses, etc., are in course of construction. Other groups of springs now used are the Ojo Caliente (O'-ho Cäl-ee-en-tä), about seventy miles north of Santa Fé, and Hudson's Hot Springs on the stage road between Mesilla and Silver City. All these springs are said to be good for skin diseases, as well as for rheumatism and neuralgia."

The statistics of the United States Army Reports demonstrate the important fact that New Mexico has the lowest ratio of respiratory diseases to be

found in the country, the cases being 1.3 per thousand; while in various
other localities the proportion ranges from 2.3 to 6.9. A very striking
evidence of the curative character of its wonderful climate is found in the
army records of the time of the rebellion. Among the troops originally
sent there in 1861 there were some 350 cases of catarrh. At the expiration
of a year no cases were reported, and all who had the disease and remained
in the country were cured. Dr. Symington says: "In a residence of eight
years in New Mexico, I have never seen but two cases of phthisis among
natives." In addition to its dryness and purity, the atmosphere is electric
in an extraordinary degree. It belongs, perhaps, rather to the sphere of
scientific speculation than that of absolute demonstration, as to how much
this electricity and its correlated developments of ozone has to do with the
extraordinary healthfulness of the Mexican climate; but there is little
doubt of its being an important element. It is thought, also, by the best
scientific observers that these "electric" properties of the Hot Springs of
Arkansas and Las Vegas have much to do with their beneficial efficacy;
and of such properties it is fair to assume the latter have the larger proportion. It is the invariable experience of those who go to New Mexico from
the heavy and moist atmospheres of the Mississippi valley and the Atlantic
coast, that they find a fascination and inspiration in its unequaled climate.
To those who are well it is an exhilaration, and to the invalid a marvelous
tonic.

CITIES AND DISTRICTS OF NEW MEXICO.

TRINIDAD—RATON—LAS VEGAS—AN ANALYSIS OF THE WATERS OF LAS
VEGAS HOT SPRINGS—SANTA FÉ THE OLDEST AMERICAN CITY.

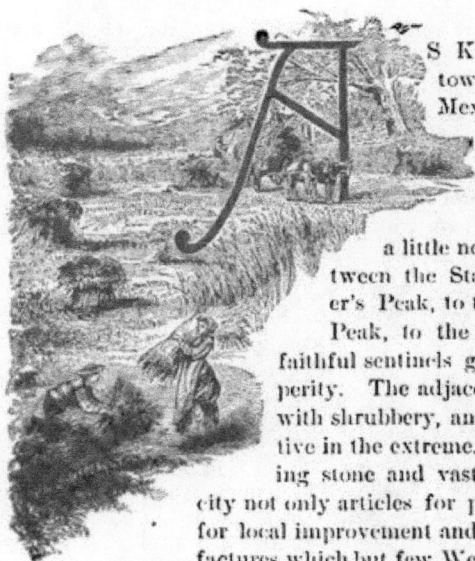

AS Kansas City, Mo., is a Kansas town, so is Trinidad, Col., a New Mexican town—in the sense that the New Mexican trade is chiefly what has built it up and is now sustaining it. It has an advantageous location, a little north of the boundary line between the State and the Territory. Fisher's Peak, to the south of it, and Simpson's Peak, to the north of it, stand like two faithful sentinels guarding its growth and prosperity. The adjacent foot-hills are well covered with shrubbery, and the entire vicinage is attractive in the extreme. Deposits of the finest building stone and vast areas of good coal give the city not only articles for profitable export, but facilities for local improvement and the encouragement of manufactures which but few Western cities enjoy. Testimony to the truth of this statement is found in the substantial style peculiar to the buildings of Trinidad, and in the extensive coking-ovens and other outgrowths of the coal supply. The city has a population of about 3,000 people, and its business importance is steadily increasing, in spite of the development of the towns further south. Well supplied with churches and school houses, the social atmosphere of the place is unusually pure. The people, though differing greatly in nationality, are one in their efforts to build up a solid, flourishing town. Their success is certain.

Just across the Raton range, in New Mexico, is the growing town of Raton. A year ago it was a mere village; now its inhabitants number nearly 1,000, and bright hopes are entertained by them of the future prosperity of the place. It is located at the end of the Colorado division and the beginning of the Las Vegas division of the Atchison, Topeka & Santa Fé Railroad, and is therefore in many respects a creation of the railroad. Here are situated machine and repair shops, and the development of the coal seams in the neighboring hills gives promise of adding largely to the business of this thriving community.

SANGRE DE CHRISTO PASS.

Las Vegas, the first large city south of the Colorado line, is located on the Gallinas river, the old town and the hot springs being on the right bank, and the new town and the railway station on the left. The old town lies upon a broad slope to the south and east. It is built, in true Mexican style, around an open square, or *plaza*, which constitutes the principal market place. The houses are of the adobe style, built of unburned brick, and, with but few exceptions, one story high. The streets are narrow, irregular, and rather uninviting; but inside the houses—or within the *placitas* or little *plazas*—the

NEAR POINT FERMIN.

thick, dry walls of the adobe guarantee a dry, cool atmosphere, which, under the midsummer sun, is a *sine qua non* of comfort. Las Vegas boasts of two schools of a high grade, the oldest and largest being the school conducted (one branch for males and the other for females) by Jesuit Fathers; and the other, an academy, conducted by the citizens generally, without respect to denominational bias. The Jesuit Fathers publish a very interesting Spanish paper, devoted to the interests of their religious and educational work.

ON THE BORDERS OF NEW MEXICO.

The paper is ably edited by Father J. Mars, who is thoroughly posted on the Territory and its temporal as well as spiritual needs. The various Protestant churches are here well represented, and two or three first class newspapers lend invaluable aid to the conservative influence of the town. In fact, none need object to making Las Vegas a place of permanent residence on account of the lack of school or educational advantages. The new town of Las Vegas was recently reduced to ashes, or, at least, the greater portion of it; but new buildings have been erected in lieu of the ones destroyed, and now the place shows no signs of the accident which so lately befell it. Some of the largest mercantile establishments of the Territory are located at Las Vegas, and their trade extends as far as White Oaks to the southeast, and all along the line of the railway to the south. A large number of promising mines and prospects are located within a few miles of

Las Vegas, and the business incident to mineral development will soon be added to the present business of the place. An excellent eating house and other railway improvements add greatly to the advantages of the city. Las Vegas can hardly help prospering.

The Hot Springs of Las Vegas, to which reference has previously been made, are located about five miles northwest of Las Vegas, 130 miles south of the Colorado line and 250 miles south of Colorado Springs. These springs are found at the mouth of a beautiful cañon, which opens upon the plains four miles above the city of Las Vegas, and from that point winds romantically into the Spanish range of the Rocky mountains, the latter extending 150 miles southward from the Colorado line into New Mexico. The springs have an altitude of 6,400 feet — the elevation which has made Colorado such a favorite resort for those affected with pulmonary complaints — with a decided advantage over some of the northern resorts as to latitude and health-giving climate. The character of the waters is similar to that of the famous Hot Springs of Arkansas, as indicated by the following chemical analysis, made by Prof. F. V. Hayden, United States Geologist:

CONSTITUENTS.	Spring No. 1.	Spring No. 2.	Spring No. 3.
Sodium carbonate	1.72	1.17	5.00
Calcium carbonate (Magnesium " (	1.08	10.63	11.43
Sodium sulphate	14.12	15.43	16.21
Sodium chloride	27.26	24.37	27.34
Potassium	Trace	Trace	Trace
Lithium	Strong trace	Strong trace	Strong trace
Silicic acid	1.01	Trace	2.51
Iodine	Trace	Trace	Trace
Bromine	Trace	Trace	Trace
Temperature	30° F.	123° F.	123° F.

This showing speaks volumes to all who are familiar with the constituents of thermal springs in other parts of the country. The Las Vegas Springs will always possess important advantages over similar resorts elsewhere, in the greatly superior medicinal character of their waters, and a climate less bleak and harsh in winter and equally pleasant and bracing in summer. They are the most southerly resort attainable on that central elevated plateau, which may be considered the great sanitarium in this country for lung diseases, and which extends through Colorado and the upper half of New Mexico, along the eastern base of the Rocky mountains. The springs number twenty-two, and vary in temperature from 110° to 140° Fahrenheit. Their character and the efficacy of their waters is thoroughly established by the experience of the native population, and they will prove to be the only resort in the country combining a climate pre-eminently healthful and curative, with waters possessing the extraordinary specific virtues of the Arkansas Springs—the latter having an altitude of about 600 feet, with a hot and sultry climate, low lands, and a malarial surrounding country; while at Las Vegas Springs the altitude and clear bracing atmosphere is of itself exhilarating and invigorating to a debilitated person, being of course a wonderful auxiliary to the health-giving properties of the thermal waters. Herein this locality will always have an important advantage.

A VIEW OF MIDDLE PARK.

The accommodations at the springs are ample. To the comfortable hotels at first built has been added an elegant establishment, valued at about $100,000, where the most fastidious may be suited. A bath house, 200 feet by 42 feet in size, two stories high, affords every desirable facility for pleasant and beneficial bathing. The ladies' department has a large shampooing room, electro and vapor rooms, douche, rising, spray and tub baths, cooling and dressing rooms, parlor and reception rooms, all of which have been fitted up with all modern improvements. For parties desiring to camp out near the springs every advantage is offered. A line of horse cars will soon

connect the springs with the Las Vegas depot of the Atchison, Topeka &
Santa Fé Railroad, and horses or carriages may be had at rates as satisfactory
as those of any other summer resort. A visit to the springs in winter will
prove to some even more advantageous than a visit in summer, as the
climate has nothing of the harshness of an Eastern winter and the mineral
waters are perennially the same.

There are many other localities in the Territory where mineral waters and
attractive natural surroundings may be found by the summer tourist. At
present, however, no other special points will be recommended, because
none have as yet been provided with those artificial environments deemed
so essential by the greater number.

In May, 1880, the pioneer locomotive of the Atchison, Topeka and
Santa Fé Railroad turned away from the main line at Lamy and climbed
the hills by a crooked and circuitous trail into the ancient city of Santa
Fé. As it halted on the outskirts of the town, a great throng of Mexican

men, women, children and burros gathered about to inspect its mysterious
manifestations. They gazed, and wondered, and surmised, and were sur-
prised — superlatively so — when, whoop-a-la! went the engine's whistle
and a deafening shriek rent the long somnolent air. Away went the people
and the burros in mad haste to escape, precisely as went the natives in that
wonderful narrative for boys, the "Gorilla Hunters," when the genius of
the party played upon barbarian credulity with "phosphorus and ungodly
noises." Away they went, but they came again, and when they came again
they stayed and welcomed the locomotive and crowned it chief of all, so
that to-day Santa Fé and the locomotive are fast friends, and trouble will
fall upon the man who intermeddles with their friendship.

Santa Fé was old enough in 1880 to have seen any number of locomotives.
It was old enough, in fact, to have been the thrice great grandparent of the
first locomotive that ever shrieked. Santa Fé was then, as of course it is

now, the oldest town in America. It looks as though it might be the oldest
town in Europe as well. It looks as though it had been founded by Fates'
fugitives, of which Virgil sings, in the far away days before emigration
had become a science and colonization a business. The stones in its narrow
streets are worn smooth by the tramp of processional generations. The

SCENE IN NEW MEXICO.

houses, built of sun-dried bricks, look as if made by the children of Israel
in ancient days before cruel Pharoah cut off their rations of straw. The
bulky-headed burros, oldest, and some say wisest, of all the inhabitants
of the ancient country, wave their long ears and nod knowingly to the
tourist, as much as to say, we could a tale unfold as long as our ears, and as
thrilling as our voices. The Navajo Indians, leaning languidly against the
mud walls of the houses, from which they seem to have derived their own com-
plexions, display their wonderfully woven blankets and drive hard bargains

with those who wish to buy. The industrious Pueblo Indians display their curious pottery made into all unhappy shapes of gods, men and devils. The native artisans illustrate the process of making their wonderful filagree jewelry which so attracts the lover of things quaint and beautiful. The chiming bells of the schools and churches, over which Bishop Lamy—a counterpart of the immortal bishop of Les Miserables — has held a guiding hand for more than thirty years, call the stranger to scenes of worship, study and religious instruction generally. These bells would have been worthy of Father Prout's love for the bells of Shandon. They are bells that for years have kept the ears of an isolated people keenly alive to the matchless truths of the Christian religion. Santa Fé has a heart, and that heart is the great *plaza* or central square where the musical representatives of those of our nation's guardians commanded by General Edward Hatch assemble nightly to make sweet music for those who choose to listen. There is music in the heart of Santa Fé. On three sides of the *plaza* are business houses, and on the fourth side stands the palace of the Governor. This palace architecturally is as unpalatial as possible. It is only a long, low adobe building with whited walls and few windows. Mrs. Gov. Wallace, writing of the old palace, says:

"Santa Fé was a primeval stronghold before the Spanish conquest, and a town of some importance to the white race when Pennsylvania was a wilderness, and the first Dutch governor was slowing drilling the Knickerbocker ancestry in the difficult evolution of marching round the town pump. Once the capital and centre of the Pueblo kingdom, it is rich in historic interest, and the archives of the Territory, kept, or rather neglected, in the queer old Palacio del Gobernador where I write, hold treasure well worth the seeking of student and antiquary. The building itself has a history as full of pathos and stirring incident as the ancient fort of St. Augustine, and is older than that venerable pile. It had been the palace of the Pueblos immemorially before the holy name of Santa Fé was given in baptism of blood by the Spanish conquerors; palace of the Mexicans after they broke away from the crown, and palace ever since its occupation by El Gringo. In the stormy scenes of the seventeenth century it withstood several sieges; was repeatedly lost and won, as the white man or the red held the victory. Who shall say how many and how dark the crimes hidden within these dreary earthen walls?"

Looking down upon Santa Fé from the hill northeast of the *plaza* where are the ruins of old Fort Marcy, built in 1846, one may see, nearest, the old cemetery where the murdered Gov. Perez now sleeps; further on, the present military barracks and other buildings of new Fort Marcy; then the Governor's palace, and the *plaza*, out of which is lifted the tall shaft of the monument erected by the Territorial legislature in honor of the citizens of New Mexico who had fallen in Indian wars of the country, and also to

BIG TREES.

7

the Union soldiers who had perished in the battles of New Mexico; the Christian Brothers' college, where boys receive a good high school education, with particular attention paid to business qualifications; San Miguel church, which was partly destroyed in 1680 and was rebuilt by Vargas; across the street from this church the oldest house in Santa Fé, known to have been ancient in 1540; the convent of the Sisters of Loretta, north of the Brothers' college; the Bishop's cathedral, a cruciform building at the

HANGING ROCK CANON.

head of San Francisco street—the old mud building now being surrounded by a modern stone structure, which will, in time, extinguish its predecessor; the Bishop's beautiful garden, mentioned elsewhere; the chapel of Our Lady of the Rosary, built about 1700; the Guadalupe chapel near the church last mentioned; away in the distance the Cerillos and other mountains; and all about, and between the long, straggling, narrow streets and the little areas of field and garden marking the homes of 8,000 people, who, if they are not up with modern ideas, yet may boast of losing no time fretting about it; who, if not rulers themselves, yet have the satisfaction of not being much ruled by anybody else. The commerce of Santa Fé is holding its own in spite of great changes in the Territory, changes which at one time were prophecies of the city's speedy decadence. It is safe to say that Santa Fé will for many years be the largest and always the handsomest and most attractive city in the Territory of New Mexico.

Below Santa Fé, in the Rio Grande valley, the towns and villages of importance are more infrequent. Albuquerque is a thriving town of about 4,000 people. From this point the Atlantic & Pacific Railroad runs westward across Arizona toward California. Socorro is the headquarters of an important mining business, and is a place of great promise. San Marcial h s considerable importance as a railway point. Rincon is the point of junction for the main line and the El Paso branch. El Paso is an important town of five or six thousand people. The Southern Pacific and the Atchison, Topeka & Santa Fé system here cross, and from this point the Mexican Central extension is being constructed. Deming is a town of importance as the junction point of the Santa Fé and the Southern Pacific roads. Silver City is the county seat of Grant county, the favorite county for American settlers in New Mexico. Silver City is the centre of a great mining region, and its present 6,000 people will before long be very greatly reinforced. Grant county is a good one for stock raising, and Silver City reaps a benefit from this as well as from the mining business. Silver City is reached by stage from Lordsburg, fifty miles beyond Deming.

ARIZONA IN GENERAL.

GEOGRAPHY — TOPOGRAPHY — CLIMATE — VALLEYS — HOT SPRINGS —
PEOPLE — TOWNS — RAILROADS — SAN FRANCISCO MOUNTAIN.

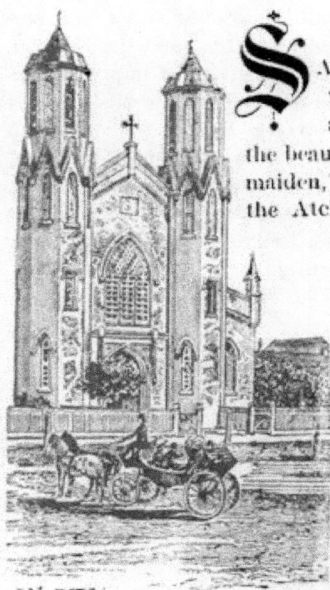

SAID Baron Alexander von Humboldt, "The wealth of the world will be found in Arizona and New Mexico." Arizona, "the land of the beautiful zone," or "the land of the beautiful maiden," has hitherto been almost inaccessible. But the Atchison, Topeka & Santa Fé Railroad has now opened the door of this wonderful territory to the civilization and capital of the East. The Territory of Arizona is bounded on the south by the Republic of Mexico, on the east by New Mexico, on the north by Utah, and on the west by California. Colorado touches it at the extreme northeastern corner, and Nevada impinges upon its northwestern boundary. Speaking with exactitude, Arizona extends from 109° to 114° 25′ west longitude, and from 31° 37′ to 37° north latitude, which corresponds to a width and breadth of nearly 325 miles each, and an area of 113,916 square miles, or of 72,906,240 acres. New York, Pennsylvania, New Jersey, Maryland and Delaware could be set down inside this square without crowding each other. Until 1863 this vast area was a part of New Mexico, but in February of that year was made a separate political division. Arizona is essentially mountainous, and a list of the ranges chopping it up like the ocean waves under a cross wind would be a very long one. The general "dip" of the land is to the southwest. In the northern and eastern parts the plateaux are nearly 6,000 feet high, while to the south and west they are but a few feet above the level of the sea. This grand slope is one vast network of mountains. Starting at the southeast corner and going west south of the Gila river the principal ranges are as follows: Peria, Pedrogosa, San Jose, Huachuca, Dragoon, Chircahua, Peloncillo, Pinaleno, Galiuro, Santa Catarina, Tortilita, Tucson, Santa Rita, Atasooso, Cababi, Quigotoa, Santa Estrella, Sierra de la Naril, Sierra del Ojo, and Mohawk range. Between the Gila river, which crosses the Territory from east to west across its southern third, and the Atlantic & Pacific Railroad, which bears westward midway between the Gila and the northern boundary line, are to be found the Big Horn, Eagle Trail, Plomas, Mt. Hope, Juniper, Black Hills, Verde,

A VIEW NEAR ANIMAS FORKS.

Mazatzal, Magallon, White, Apache, Gila, Salt River and Bradshaw mountains. The northern third contains the Virgin Range, Hurricane Ledge, Sheavwitz Mountains, Buckskin Mountains, Calabasa Mountains, Rabbit Hills, and the Vermillion Cliffs. The drainage of this network of mountains is almost perfect. The course of the Gila has been alluded to. Besides this river, which is over 500 miles long, there is the famous Colorado which as the San Juan flows westward from Colorado, unites with the Little Colorado at White Bluffs, and thence as the Colorado flows southwest and then south, forming the Nevada and California boundary lines, and receiving in its course the Pah-ria, Virgin, Williams' Fork and Gila rivers. The San Pedro, San Carlos and Verde are the principal tributaries of the Gila.

That Arizona is well wooded the following names would seem to signify: Navajoe Forest, Black Forest, Colorado Forest, Coconino Forest, and so on to the end of the chapter. Open plains are found in the southwestern and southeastern sections.

Though the climate of Arizona is essentially a warm one, yet the air is dry, pure and remarkably salubrious throughout the greater portion of the year. It is what might be called semi-tropical in the southern portion, where for two or three months of the year the heat is somewhat excessive, though cases of sunstroke are unknown. The winters are delightful beyond imagination by northern people.

LA VETA PASS.

"In winter," says J. Ross Browne, "the climate near Yuma is finer than that of Italy. It would scarcely be possible to suggest an improvement." In the mountains of western Arizona, for the greater part of the season the higher peaks are white with snow, rendering the pure, dry air deliciously cool and enjoyable, especially at night, when a good supply of covering is always in demand for the sleeper. Within a distance of 200 miles from north to south a greater variety of climate can be enjoyed than between Maine and Florida on the Atlantic coast. The climate of southern Arizona is superior to that of Florida, in that it is warm and at the same time dry.

YOSEMITE—BRIDAL VEIL FALLS.

As soon as this great sanitarium is fully known it will become for winter what Colorado now is in summer—a great resort for invalids. From the middle of June to October, however, the heat is intense, but travelers say that, even with the thermometer at 120 degrees, sunstrokes are of rare occurrence. This is due to the rarity of the atmosphere. The average rainfall at Fort Mojave is but little over five inches, distributed through August, December, February and June. At Camp Grant, which is said to be in all respects a medium climate, the diurnal variations of temperature are from fifteen to thirty degrees; the monthly range being about twenty-seven degrees, and the yearly extremes of heat and cold thirty-four and ninety-six degrees, respectively. There are, annually, about sixty-five days of rain and hail, and three of snow. At Camp Verde the temperature ranges from five degrees to 113 degrees, and the average rainfall is eight inches. At Camp Lowell, seven miles east of Tucson, the diurnal range is sometimes seventy degrees. Persons afflicted with pulmonary complaints experience speedy relief in this warm atmosphere, and many wonderful and well-authenticated cures of this nature are reported. The scenery is truly charming. It is not so rugged, perhaps, as Colorado, but it is, if possible, more pleasing. Instead of having a continuous mountain chain running in a given direction, it has isolated peaks and detached sections coming up out of the plain apparently at random. Yet, while her landscapes are thus beautiful to a degree that admits of no rivalry, Arizona has her towering peaks and deep cañons surpassing those of any other locality. The cañons on the Colorado river are some of them 6,000 feet, or more than a mile, in depth. Mention should here be made of the valleys of Arizona. They are numerous and fertile. In the valley of the Verde, settlements have been made to a considerable extent. Williamson's valley, near Prescott, contains not less than 500,000 acres, together with 300,000 acres of adjacent foot-hills, well furnished with bunch grass. Around Mount Hope, in Yavapai county, there are scores of beautiful valleys containing from 40 to 400 acres of land each; in fact, wherever a river runs, there, at some portion of its course, may be found as lovely depressions as exist anywhere in the United States. It is estimated that there are about 2,800,000 acres of land in the Territory, of the very best quality, with sufficient surface water near at hand to properly irrigate. At least 10,000,000 acres more, it is said, can be reclaimed by the use of artesian wells. As compared with Mojave county, in Arizona, the eastern portion of southern California and southern Nevada, in the same latitude, have the following relative standing: Agricultural, irrigable and arable, California and Nevada, 2 per cent.; Arizona, 25 per cent. Timber, California and Nevada, 6 per cent.; Arizona, 10 per cent. Grazing, California and Nevada, 88 per cent.; Arizona, 30 per cent. Barren, California and Nevada, 4 per cent.; Arizona, 35 per cent.

The following agricultural divisions of Arizona are of interest: 1. The Colorado river country. 2. The valleys of the Gila and tributaries. 3. The Santa Cruz valley, and certain parts of Pinal and Pima counties. 4. The Colorado-Chiquito. 5. The country around Prescott. 6. Mojave county.

As far as known Arizona is abundantly supplied with hot springs. They have been noticed in the Grand Cañon of the Colorado, also on the Gila and Prieto rivers, on the Mesa near Camp Lowell and near Tubac. The Monroe Hot Springs, on Castle creek, sixty miles south of Prescott, are

TABLE ROCK.

most widely known. The temperature of the water at the springs is 160 degrees, but two yards below it cools to 130 degrees.

In population and wealth Arizona is rapidly advancing. According to the census of 1876 the population consisted of 30,191 whites, besides 25,000 Indians. Since that time the increase has been rapid, and the census, if taken to-day, would probably foot up nearly 50,000. What were considered the wild dreams of Cremony, in his "Life Among the Apaches," published a dozen or so years ago, are now being realized; and the almost miraculous opening of the country, and the continuous discoveries of rich mineral deposits, lead to the belief that the next ten years will see an inflow of immigrants as yet unparalleled in its wonderful history.

The principal Arizonan towns are Yuma, Ehrenberg, Prescott, Florence, Tombstone, Benson, Tucson, Wickenburg, Phœnix and Globe. Yuma is located near the junction of the Gila and Colorado rivers, and is 466 miles from Deming, N. M., on the Southern Pacific Railroad. It was founded as a mission in 1700 by Father Kino. The population is now probably over 2,500. Ehrenberg is 130 miles above Yuma, on the Colorado river, and is a

LUCIFER FALLS.

town of nearly 1,000 inhabitants. Prescott, established in 1864, and county seat of Yavapai county, is a handsome, homelike city, situated in a small valley, surrounded by mountains, and boasting of a population exceeding 4,000. The capital of the Territory, first located at Prescott, was taken in 1867 to Tucson, but in 1877 was taken back to its first love. Phœnix, the county seat of Maricopa county, is situated two miles north of the Salt river, and is the business centre of a highly productive valley. It was founded in 1868, and contains nearly 800 inhabitants, half of whom are Mexicans. Wickenburg, a village of 300 people, is a mining town, situated at the forks of the stage road to Prescott from Ehrenberg. Florence, the county seat of Pinal county, lies on the Gila river, 225 miles from its mouth. It is the centre of the rich agricultural valley of the Gila, and contains about 1,800 people, evenly distributed between Americans, Mexicans and Spaniards. Globe is a recent vigorous outgrowth of mineral discoveries in the mineral district of that name, ninety miles northeast of Florence, on Pinal creek. The early origin of Tucson can not easily be traced, but it is

A VIEW NEAR LEADVILLE.

thought to have been founded but a few years after Santa Fé, in 1560. Up to 1800 it was a mere presidio, or garrison, with a population of a thousand souls. In 1856 it is described as containing only 400 inhabitants, while to-day it supports nearly 5,000 people. The future importance of Tucson is easily predicated. Tombstone is a recent "output." It was founded and named by a miner who made a wonderful strike contrary to the gloomy predictions of friends, who asserted that he would find his tombstone in the district to which he was going. It is the county seat of Cochise county, and is situated twenty-seven miles southeast of Benson, on the joint line of the A., T. & S. F. and Southern Pacific Railroads, being easily reached from Benson by a daily line of Concord stages. The buildings of the town are of a superior order, and church and school privileges exist in abundance. The present population is estimated at 4,000. Benson is an important station on the roads mentioned, and will increase in commercial importance with the opening of the road from that point south to Guaymas.

Two great continental lines of railroad occupy Arizona. The Southern Pacific and Atchison, Topeka & Santa Fé jointly operate a line entering the Territory near San Simon, not far from its southeastern corner, thence passing west to Benson, from which point, as the property of the Southern Pacific Railroad Company it bears away northwest to Maricopa, thence southwest to Yuma, and from there northwest to San Francisco. The Arizona mileage of these two corporations exceeds 350 miles. The other road starts from Albuquerque in New Mexico and passes along the thirty-fifth parallel of latitude, through a portion of Arizona which has a much more equable temperature than that traversed by the southern line. By the last of August, 1881, this important line had reached Winslow, 285 miles from its starting point, and nearly one-third of the way across the "silver zone" Territory. It is rapidly being pushed westward in the direction of Los Angeles, and when completed will offer a new route to intending tourists.

Before closing this chapter of "River to Sea," the reader may read, if he so choose, the following description of San Francisco mountain, a type of Arizonan scenery. The extract is from an article in the Santa Fé *Trail* by the writer of this book:

"One of the most attractive localities in Arizona is that of San Francisco mountain. The location is on the line of the proposed Atlantic & Pacific Railroad (the Albuquerque branch of the Atchison, Topeka & Santa Fé), and is about half way between the eastern and western boundaries of the Territory. The mountain is about 1,400 feet above the sea level. It is of volcanic formation, being itself an extinct volcano, and being surrounded by smaller mountains of the same character. The view from the summit of the mountain is magnificent in the extreme. To the northward, 150 miles distant, may be seen the lofty peaks of the Wahsatch mountains, in Utah, with the great plateau intervening, through which passes the Grand Cañon of the Colorado, with its chasms 6,000 feet deep, and its broken, winding way through the Buckskin range. To the northwest can be seen the mountains of San Juan, and to the east those of Fort Defiance, with all the immense intervening table-lands, where are located the curious villages of Moquies. These table-lands have, among their other curious inhabitants, thousands of Novijo sheep. To the southeast are seen the beautiful White mountains of eastern Arizona and New Mexico. To the south are vast

ranges of the Mogollon mountains, and at their right, southwest, great
forests of pine and juniper as far as the eye can reach. To conclude this
glorious panorama, they are in sight on the west and northwest the Bill
Williams mountain, 150 miles of the Atlantic & Pacific road, the Colorado
plateau, the Aubrey cliffs, and the mountains of southeastern Nevada. No
view in Switzerland equals this in the variety of its scenery or in the
magnificence of its distances. San Francisco mountain is covered to a point
far up its sides by a heavy growth of timber, while in the valley, at its
southern base, are 8,000 or 10,000 acres of perfect grass-land, without
stick or stone to break its smooth surface. This valley is surrounded by
small mountains, fringed with a rich growth of pines. At the northern
edge of the valley is a large spring, which furnishes an abundance of
water the year round. The valley has a southern exposure, and is much
warmer in winter than the unsheltered localities east and west. The
forests in the vicinity of the mountain are full of deer, antelope, bear, wild
turkeys and other fit game for the sportsman's weapon. There will some
day be a full-fledged summer hotel near the spring, within a mile of the
railway, and a settlement will probably be found soon at the base of the
mountain. The railroad is pushing steadily westward from Albuquerque,
and in a comparatively short time San Francisco mountain will wake up
and put on a new life."

THREE BROTHERS — YOSEMITE.

THE RUINS OF THE PECOS.

THE CITY OF CICUYE — THE PECOS VALLEY—THE MANNER OF CONSTRUC-
TION — MONTEZUMA'S BIRTHPLACE — HOW THE CULTURE
GOD CAME AGAIN TO HIS PEOPLE.

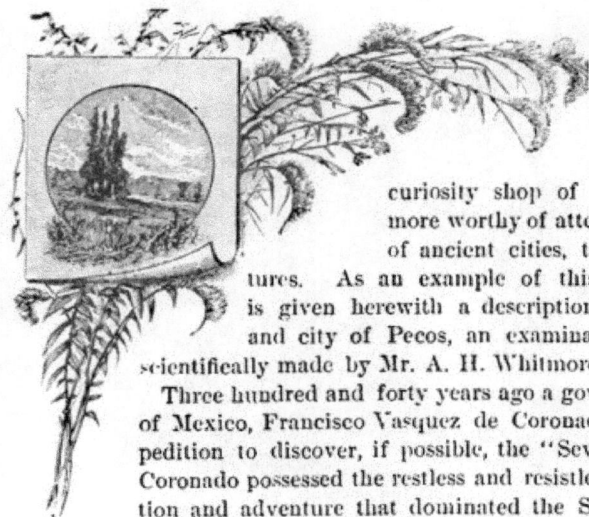

OF the multitude of quaint, queer and curious things to be seen by the tourist in New Mexico — the old curiosity shop of America — few are more worthy of attention than the relics of ancient cities, towns and manufactures. As an example of this sort of attraction is given herewith a description of the old church and city of Pecos, an examination of which was scientifically made by Mr. A. H. Whitmore, of Las Vegas:

Three hundred and forty years ago a governor of a province of Mexico, Francisco Vasquez de Coronado, organized an expedition to discover, if possible, the "Seven cities of Cibola." Coronado possessed the restless and resistless spirit of exploration and adventure that dominated the Spanish character in the fifteenth and sixteenth centuries. Like Cortez and Pizarro, he had courage, perseverance and determination, and, like them, extreme credulity. Nuno de Guzman was at this time president of all the territory on this continent acquired by Cortez. Among the slaves of Guzman was one who told his master strange tales of famous cities, of large population and fabulous wealth, situated far to the north. This slave described seven cities of great extent and wealth, whose mechanics wrought exclusively in gold and silver. These cities were only to be reached after long, weary days of toilsome travel over plains of oceanic dimensions far to the north. To these tales Coronado lent a willing and eager ear, and so thoroughly believed them as to organize and command in person the expedition before referred to. We will not follow him through the windings of his journey—a journey that took him as far north as the junction of the Arkansas and Little Arkansas rivers—a journey of toil, hardship and of bitter disappointment. It is sufficient for the present purpose to say, that in this journey Coronado and his little band of followers reached a town or city called Cicuye—a strongly fortified city, having houses four stories high. Of its position the historian says : "Cicuye is built in a narrow valley, in the midst of mountains covered with pines."   *   *   *   *

TEOCALLI MOUNTAIN.

"It is traversed by a stream in which we caught some excellent trout." Unquestionably the city of Cicuye is the same as is to-day known as the Ruins of the Pecos, and the stream mentioned no other than the Rio Pecos. The unanimity of opinion upon this proposition is not absolute, yet the weight of opinion and of evidence amply sustains the theory that the Ruins of the Pecos and the city of Cicuye, mentioned by the historian, are identical. The brief description of the historian closely agrees with the surroundings of the Pecos ruins. The ruins indicate that at one time they were "strongly fortified." The Rio Pecos at this point, until very recently, contained quantities of "excellent trout." A few writers have claimed for Santa Fé the honor of having been the Cicuye of the past ; yet as the Rio Santa Fé was never known to produce a trout, we must either conclude that Coronado's piscatorial achievements on the Rio Santa Fé amounted to an absolute annihilation of the trout, or that Cicuye was located elsewhere. To visit these ruins the traveler by rail over the Atchison, Topeka & Santa Fé Railroad should leave the road at Baughl's Station, 2,100 miles from Boston, 800 miles from Guaymas, and southwest from Las Vegas nearly fifty miles. Baughl's Station is situated at an altitude above the sea of 7,026 feet. It is nestled close under the eastern slope of the mountains that skirt the western edge of the Pecos valley. Distant from the station about one and a quarter miles and a little south of east, stands the grim old ruin of the Pecos church, looking quietly down upon the ruined Pueblos of the once populous and busy city of Cicuye. This impressive ruin is slowly but surely resolving itself into the clayey dust out of which, ages ago, its proportions were chiefly wrought. When it was erected is not known to-day. The Jesuit prelates say that the first priest of the Romish Church was settled here in 1529, and very likely the erection of the church soon followed. It was built in the form of a Roman cross and had an extreme length of 133 feet, and a width through the wings or arms of fifty-seven feet, and through the base or body of forty feet. Its walls were five and a half feet thick, built of adobe bricks, mostly eighteen inches long, nine wide, and four inches thick. It is difficult to determine the character and height of the roof at the present time, as nothing is left but the walls of the structure, and even they are far from perfect; in fact, the front wall and parts of the side walls are pretty much down. The few timbers that time and man have left in place are massive, and are rudely carved upon all pendent and exposed surfaces. For all purposes of description the church may be said to face the west, and in point of fact it varies from that direction but a few points. It stands upon an elevated ridge that runs north and south, or nearly parallel with the general trend of the valley. This ridge, from the church north, is not more than an average of 300 feet in width for at least a quarter of a mile. South from the church the ridge begins to widen and gently slope toward the south until finally it is lost in the common level of the valley.

Along the front of the church and ruined city runs the Rio Pecos, which is often but a thread of a stream which runs along its sandy bed for a few yards, then disappears, to appear again yards below. From the Pecos west the valley gradually ascends to the base of the mountains one mile or more away. On the east the valley is more broken and ridged, and it is, possibly, four miles to the mountains. Both the head and foot of the valley present the appearance of being closed by huge mountains. Certain it is that the Ruins of the Pecos are "in a narrow valley in the midst of mountains." Except upon the ridge first mentioned, no well-defined evidences of ancient habitation are to be found, although the ruins of walled enclosures are to be traced on the west and on both sides of the Pecos, in the

8

immediate front of the city. That two or more of these enclosures were constructed for water reservoirs, is evident. The others may have been for the stock-yards, or possibly enclosures of defense against a common enemy.

Contiguous to the church, and on the south, are the ruins of both stone and earth enclosures, the latter of which are nearest to and of about the same surface area as the church itself. Their location and formation suggest the possibility of buildings once connected with the church. From the church north for something like 1,200 feet the ridge is enclosed by ruins of a stone wall. This wall is built just at the edge, or more properly, just where the gentle sloping of the top leaves off and the abrupt declivity

PUBLIC SCHOOL LARNED

begins. This wall, which enclosed the entire city proper, as at present disclosed, was a parapet upon a natural rampart. Just within the wall on the west, and near the most abrupt declivity, in the one case, and overlooking the main passway through the wall in the other, are the ruins of mason work that suggest the probability of their having been redoubts and watch towers ages ago. About 200 feet north of the church, and against the walls on both sides the ridge, are the ruins of the ancient homes of the Aztecs— the first dwellings met thus far. These dwellings are grouped in two lines along the wall for 350 to 400 feet. The two groups or lines are separated by an open space some 200 feet wide. At an average of three stories, these two groups must have contained at least 225 to 250 dwellings.

Before describing the manner of construction, it should be stated that there appears to be a strong resemblance in the methods of construction

between the Cliff Dwellers, or Aztecs, and the Pueblos, although unlike in
so far as relates to situation. The houses at the Pecos ruins were all built
after one model, with some slight changes of detail. When Coronado was
here the houses were four stories high; they were built of stone cemented
together with mud. The roof is flat; made of poles and then earthed over.
The first house, or story, has an opening only at the top—through the roof.
The second house, or story, is erected in the rear of this opening and above
the first, and has an opening on to the roof of the first story. Each succeeding story is built back from the one underneath, like unto the steps of a
stairway. The first stories are, as a rule, connected by small openings and
passages, hardly large enough to permit an average person to crawl through.

Passing north along the ridge 250 or more feet, the ridge rising rapidly,
we come to the next group of dwellings. We are now on nearly the highest
part of the ridge. The buildings are built in this group about a circle, the
buildings making about three-fourths of the circle. The segment of the
circle not built upon is opened to the north. Within this opening is built
the south end of a larger group of buildings, built about an oval, and upon
the highest point of the ridge. The diameter of the circle is about sixty
feet. In the oval or ellipse the longitudinal diameter is about 200 feet
—possibly more—and the transverse diameter sixty-five or seventy feet. A
passage way leads from the ellipse into the circle, and from the circle two
passage ways lead—one to the southeast and one to the southwest. Another
passage leads from the ellipse on the east. To the right and left of this
passage, outside the building, are two water reservoirs fifteen to eighteen
feet in diameter—how deep they may have been could not be determined.
They are now nearly filled with earth and debris. The one on the right, as
the visitor passes into the enclosure, had an aqueduct leading somewhere
(just where could not be determined) possibly into one of the two reservoirs inside the ellipse. The aqueduct as shown at the edge of the
reservoir, and immediately under the bluff, has an inside diameter of nearly
two feet, and walls about one foot and a half thick. The construction of
the walls of this aqueduct is peculiar. The walls are circular and are built
of balls of cement that vary in size and shape—some flat, some oval, and
some round—with diameters running from four to ten inches. These are
laid together like bricks in cement and over the whole is a layer of the same
cement. The reservoirs inside the ellipse are larger than those outside by
eight or ten feet in diameter, and are at least six feet deep, as was disclosed
by digging to that depth. These two groups of houses must have contained not less than 800 to 900 rooms, the average dimensions of which were
about eight by ten feet and seven feet in height.

Upon the north the ridge slopes again some feet to a bare, flat-topped
ledge, reaching from bluff to bluff upon either side, and about 1,000 feet
in length before ascending. At this point the ridge again ascends rather

THE DEAD GIANT—YOSEMITE.

(116)

abruptly, and at the same time bends around to the east. Upon this elevation is to be seen a circular stone wall enclosing a space some thirty to forty feet in diameter. Evidently this was at one time a fort or watch tower. From this point, with a few additional feet of elevation, such as would be obtained in a fortification or watch tower, a lookout would have the greater part of the valley under his eye.

The reader has now gone over the ground that embraces the main features of the ruins, and enough has been accomplished, if he has been able to fix in mind a sufficient outline of the character and situation of this the traditional birthplace of Montezuma—the Culture God of the Aztecs. It was here that the sacred and everlasting fire was kept burning until the abandonment of the city, some time in the second quarter of the present century. This fire was dedicated to Montezuma. Upon his removal south he told the people of Cicuye to keep this fire burning, and that when he returned to them it would be down through the smoke and flame of this sacred fire. Warriors watched this fire by turns. Montezuma came not. Still the faithful watchers remained true to their trust through the years. Warfare, old age and disease decimated their ranks; still they watched by day and night. At last, reduced in numbers to a body so small as to preclude the possibility of longer keeping up the watch, three warriors took the remains of the fire into the mountains, where Montezuma himself appeared and received it.

The foregoing relates to people and to homes that antedate history, and although this be so, the ruins so hastily described are but ruins upon previous ruins, for, incorporated into the mud bricks and cement which in part comprise these structures, are bits of pottery, arrow heads and charcoal, showing that the soil selected for bricks and cement had been dwelt upon long enough to accumulate the debris of a town in quantities great enough to permeate every square inch of soil used in the construction of the thousand or more dwellings described. The reader must not confound the Culture God Montezuma with the monarch Montezuma, who was ruler over Mexico at the time of the conquest of Cortez.

EL PASO AND VICINITY.

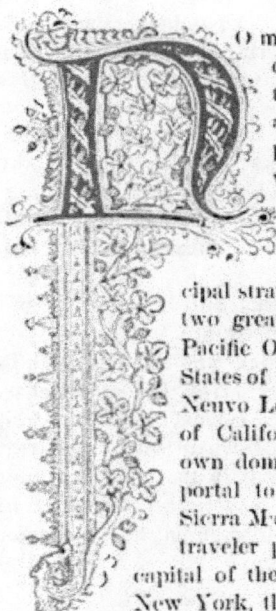

NO more delightful journey can be found than the descent of the middle valley of the Rio Grande: through the fragrant meadows, the bending orchards and luxuriant vineyards, where hangs the purpling grape; through the blooming lowlands walled on either side by the lofty peaks of rugged mountains, past some of the most enchanting scenery on the continent, to the border of Old Mexico, at El Paso, Texas. El Paso is the principal strategic point upon the long border line between the two great republics, stretching from San Diego on the Pacific Ocean along the northern limits of the Mexican States of Lower California, Sonora, Chihuahua, Cohahuila, Neuvo Leon and Tamaulipas, and the southern borders of California, Arizona, New Mexico and Texas, of our own domain. El Paso, the pass; and so it is—the grand portal to the marvelously rich mineral districts of the Sierra Madre—the gateway through which the wondering traveler passes to the still populous and still beautiful capital of the ancient Aztec kings. Here, 3,000 miles from New York, the Atchison, Topeka & Santa Fé, the Southern Pacific, the Texas & Pacific, the Galveston, Harrisburg & San Antonio and the Mexican Central railways—those gigantic transcontinental highways of commerce and travel—in their long stretches from ocean to ocean, and from the tropics to the frozen north, come together, as if in mutual greeting, upon the banks of the Rio Grande—the only instance in all history where so many great thoroughfares reaching to all the ends of the earth have concentrated at one point upon the boundary line between two great empires. This fact is most significant and suggestive of that prophetic period when all the dividing lines and barriers between peoples and races and nations shall be broken down and the "universal brotherhood of man" shall be proclaimed and established.

Situated at an altitude of over 3,000 feet above the sea level, far above the malarial line and yet below the line of frost; with a climate famous for its vigorous and invigorating influences upon the system; with a general, unvarying atmosphere of perfect purity and freedom from any depressing or enervating effects or conditions; surrounded far and near by a varied landscape of mountain, mesa, valley and river, unrivaled for picturesque

GOLD LAKE.

romantic beauty and impressive grandeur, El Paso has superior attractions as a health or pleasure resort at any season of the year, and as a place for present and constantly increasing opportunities and facilities for the successful prosecution of nearly every branch of inland trade. In every direction coal of a superior quality has been found, and active preparations are being made to open a large vein at Eagle Springs, about 130 miles below, on the line of the Texas & Pacific road. Rich deposits of iron, zinc, gypsum, lead, copper, argentiferous galena, metallic silver, silver carbonates and chlorides and gold characterize, in greater or less degree, every mountain, foothill and gulch in every direction on both sides of the international line.

There are the ancient shafts and drifts, some filled up by the mountain wash of two centuries, while others reveal great depths and traces of former active working, from which tradition declares more precious metal was once taken than has ever since been obtained north of Chihuahua City.

FISHING IN THE MOUNTAINS.

Old Virginia can not compare with the Rio Grande valley in the production of tobacco, and the great Mississippi cotton belt has here its rival when placed under an intelligent and careful system of cultivation. Every grade and species of cereal may be made to thrive and increase beyond any eastern idea of profitable and abundant yield. Emphatically one need only "tickle the earth with a hoe to make it laugh with a harvest." Beets of every variety attain enormous size, substance and weight; the onion outstrips its Bermudian rival, so much esteemed by epicures for its delicacy of flavor and size, specimens being frequently met with in the El Paso market weighing several pounds without attracting more than ordinary attention.

The apple, peach, pear, fig, apricot, nectarine, plum, pomegranate, and many other fruits, domestic and wild, and of the finest quality, abound in rich luxuriance. The grape-growing and wine-producing industry of the Rio Grande valley is of the highest importance. An eastern vine-dresser who visited the country about El Paso not long ago, and whose opinions of grape culture and the production of wine are entitled to more than ordinary weight, said: "The actualities and possibilities of this El Paso and middle Rio Grande valley for raising the grape in superabundance and of the most excellent quality, and for producing wines that will compare to advantage with the finer grades of the foreign product, can not be estimated." Another experienced grape-grower adds: "The time will come, and it is not remote, when some of the best wine known to the market will be produced in the valley of the Rio Grande, about El Paso. This product has already attracted marked attention and favorable mention among the best judges both in the Atlantic States and abroad."

The mesas, the foothills and the mountains abound in game. Here, four days and a half from New York, the hunter may mount a well trained animal and plunge at once into the primeval wilds. On the mesas he may find antelope, black tailed deer and rabbits, and in the mountains wilder game. The valley lands near the river and the lagoons swarm with duck of every species, wild geese, swans, plover, marsh fowl, snipe and other game birds, while the black and blue cat fish, silver buffalo, perch and soft turtle abound.

There is at present at El Paso a permanent population of over 3,000, and between 400 and 500 dwellings and business houses, as against about 450 people and about thirty five old adobe structures on the first of May last. This remarkable increase is mainly due to the apparent advantages of El Paso as a business, pleasure and health resort, and to the united influence of the two great railway lines, the Atchison, Topeka & Santa Fe and the Southern Pacific, both of which reached El Paso in May. The former connects with the Mexican Central—now in course of construction to the City of Mexico—by a substantial causeway and bridge, the first and only bridge across the Rio Grande border into Old Mexico. The Southern Pacific is rapidly completing connection with Galveston and the gulf steamship lines. Substantial depots, machine shops, freight houses, and, in short, all the usual accessories of a large railroad centre, are being constructed on the lands of the various railroads, while dwellings, business houses and shops are being

LAKE TAHOE.

(122)

driven forward to completion in every direction throughout the city. On every side there is observable that activity and enterprise so characteristic of our western towns. There are here several good hotels, two banks—with a prospect of another—many extensive mercantile establishments, some of them carrying immense stocks of general merchandise to meet a large and constantly increasing local and Mexican trade. The city has several hardware stores, one large plumbing establishment, several lumber yards, stock yards, a coal yard, two livery establishments, an omnibus line, two stage lines—one to San Antonio and the other into Mexico—several machine

SILURIAN SANDSTONE.

shops, harness dealers and makers, bottling works, brick yards, a real estate and mining exchange, three telegraph lines, two large market houses and two markets for domestic and foreign fruits, as well as various other establishments incident to a growing and prosperous city. Episcopalian, Methodist, Baptist, Presbyterian and Catholic church edifices have been contracted for by their respective societies, and work will be commenced soon on a large school house, the present accommodations in that respect being entirely inadequate—a fact which goes to show that this frontier city is not a colony of roving adventurers but a community of many families who make it home and home-like.

Details are given here so that the reader may have the more accurate and near view of El Paso as it is to-day. An ice manufactory, a planing mill, reduction works, tannery, iron works, and an extensive mining machinery

depot are projected, and are all likely to be in practical operation within four
or five months.   There is also a probability that the government will erect
here a large military post adequate for the accommodation of a garrison of
ten or twelve companies—in addition to Fort Bliss, located at "The Pass,"
about a mile above the city—and will create here a general military supply

A VIEW NEAR SILVERTON.

depot for the Mexican frontier.   Charters for three street railway companies,
a water works company and a gas company have been obtained, and charters
for several other corporations, including a hotel company and a banking
company, have been applied for.

Such is a true picture of El Paso and its environment to-day.   But it will
not do to hold up this picture to-morrow and say, "This is El Paso."   To-

morrow the whole scene will have changed; new enterprises will have been born; new plans will have been matured; new foundations will have been laid, and the Portal City will have taken another long stride forward toward that position which it promises to reach—the railroad centre and the most important commercial city in the great valley of the Rio Grande.

But no one who visits El Paso should fail to see the old Mexican town of Paso-del-Norte, on the opposite side of the Rio Grande, the northern terminus of the Mexican Central Railway. Once over the river the American visitor finds himself in what is to him a most peculiar, but at the same time a representative Mexican, town. Paso-del-Norte is composed entirely of adobe structures, so nearly all alike that seeing one is seeing all. The streets are irregular, crooked, unpaved, and have cobble stone side-walks. With the exception of the church, the military barracks, the aduana, or custom house, and the Mexican Central Railway offices, there are no public buildings. The church, of course, is the principal building; it is nearly 300 years old, and was built under the order of and internally decorated by the Franciscan Brotherhood, as a holy work. The vineyards and gardens are numerous, and extend down the river for miles, inclosed by fences sometimes twenty feet high and made of huge adobe blocks, moulded in a box on the spot where they are laid in the wall. These gardens are watered from the *acequia madre*, or mother ditch, which, having its source of supply from the Rio Grande by means of a dam at Fort Bliss, is extended for miles past the town, and is the only means by which the above mentioned vineyards and gardens are irrigated and made fruitful in a country where, save in the so-called rainy season, rains are more the exception than the rule.

From the battlemented and mud-plastered roof of the quaint old adobe walled cathedral of "Our Lady of Guadalupe"—which is reached by climbing up through the bell-tower, or campanile, by an admirably and curiously constructed winding stair of dressed Alamo logs—the enchanted vision lingers long upon the blue and purple-tinged summits and time and weather-scarred sides of the Organ, Guadalupe, Sacramento, Wind, Hueco, Blanco, Carrizo and Quitman mountains and ranges on the American side of the Rio Grande. On the Mexican side the eye rests with reverent awe upon the towering heights of the Amargosa and Boracho—flanked by their intervening retinue of foothills and mesas—the sierras of the Potrillos, San Blas and Candelarias with their sharp serrated peaks, among which, last year, the murderous Mescalero, old Victorio, met his deserved fate at the hands of the brave Terassas. Through the midst of this varied landscape flows the Rio Grande, gleaming in the ever bright and glorious sunlight as it pursues its tortuous way among the foothills or through the mesas, or plunges down some deep and rugged cañon of the sierras of San Carlos on its way to the gulf. The cathedral grounds are surrounded by a heavy wall, and were formerly used as a cemetery till the houses in this city of the dead were all occupied. Radiating in all directions from these grounds are the principal streets of the old town. One runs to the river and the old ferry over to the American side; another runs up the river and ends at the junction of various trails leading to Laguna de Guzman, Mexico, and to the upper valleys and the grand plateau of the Sierra Madre, New Mexico; another runs down the river to Guadalupe, San Ignacio, the Ojos Calientes, and on to Presidio-del-Norte; while still another street bears away to the wonderful "White Hills"—immense mounds and deposits of silica and iron sand—and thence on to Carrizal and the City of Chihuahua.

Nowhere can the eye turn without being arrested and held in interested gaze, whether upon the old triad of bells hung by cowhide thongs to the heavy cross pieces in the tower and rung by ropes attached to the clappers; or upon the plaza in front of the edifice with its old well in the centre, surrounded by ancient adobe seats whereon perchance the cavaliers and señoritas of Castile and Arragon were wont to spend the twilight hours in listening to the song and mandolin of some wandering troubadour; or upon the ancient tombs, with their Spanish inscriptions nearly obliterated by time and the elements.

There are quartered here in this old Mexican town various bodies of infantry and cavalry of the national and state (Chihuahua) forces. This garrison has no bearing upon international intercourse, but only as a protection against Indian outbreaks, which the advances of the railroads through their hunting grounds are making less frequent till soon they will be known only as episodes in the history of the valley.

THE MINES OF ARIZONA.

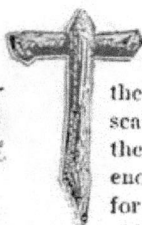

HE mines of Arizona are even now the wonder of the world, though the mineral wealth of the Territory has scarcely yet been touched. Some of the Arizona mines had already yielded enormous treasure before the facilities for railway transportation were available. There are mines of gold, silver and copper which have been worked 200 years by the Spaniards and Indians in their own rude style. Placer mines are quite numerous, and pay handsomely for the working, in spite of the cost of supplies.

The mineral wealth of the Territory consists of gold, silver, copper, iron, lead, platinum, tin, and almost every other mineral known to commerce. Some of her gold mines have already produced millions of dollars for their owners. Silver ledges, from two to two hundred feet in width, are seen in many localities. In some of these veins horn and ruby silver are found from one side to the other. The copper mines are absolutely without an equal in the world. The Clifton mine, in eastern Arizona, has become famous among miners everywhere. A half interest in it was recently sold for $800,000. The Black Hills, further to the west, are full of immense copper dykes, containing a very high grade of ore. Copper mountain, on the Agua Fria river, is an enormous deposit of ore, carrying from 30 to 40 per cent. copper, while the Antelope copper mines, near Prescott, carry from 40 to 75 per cent. Immense copper mines are also found in the Wallapai mountains, thirty-five miles west of Prescott, and on the Santa Maria, one of the tributaries of the Colorado river. The iron mines are no less important than the deposits of the more precious metals. Iron is found in abundance in many places. Within a

SAN XAVIER CHURCH, TUCSON, ARIZONA.

few miles of Prescott is an immense ledge of hematite iron, fifteen feet wide, which has been traced a distance of seventeen miles. All over the Territory, north, south, east and west, wherever mountains rise out of the plain, there are found vast quantities of all kinds of mineral. The whole Territory is seamed with it, making Arizona, as an intelligent Californian called it, "the treasure chest of the American continent." There can not be fewer than 25,000 mining claims now on record in the various counties of the Territory, and it is safe to say that more paying mines are found, in proportion to the number worked, than in any other region of the United States.

To enumerate the different mining districts of the Territory, and give an intelligent description of their location, so that, with the aid of a map, they could be satisfactorily studied, would be an impossibility in the necessarily limited space here devoted to the subject. A few of the more important districts only may be mentioned. These are located in a continuous range of gold-bearing rock, extending from near Wickenburg to within ten miles north of Prescott, and from the lower Hassayampa to the Agua Fria, an area of at least 1,000 square miles. Of the mining districts near Prescott the Weaver is the oldest. Several lodes are worked there

THE IRON SPRINGS—PIKE'S PEAK TRAIL.

which have yielded fortunes to their owners. The most southerly is the Humbug. Immediately north of this district is the Tiger or Bradshaw, where placers were worked prior to 1864, and quartz claims since that date. The Pine Grove, Peck, Walnut Grove, Hassayampa, Turkey Creek, Big Bug and Lynx Creek districts complete the list for Yavapai county, in which, up to 1876, out of 11,605 mines located and recorded in the Territory, 7,298 were in the districts named. Since then the proportion has decreased with the opening of newer and more remote sections.

In the Santa Cruz valley mining operations have been carried on since 1748, but not until recently to any considerable extent. Starting from Tucson and going south to the Mexican line, there are the Pima, Arivaca,

OAKLAND.

(130)

Oro Blanco, Patagonia, Arivaipa and Huachuca districts. In the immediate vicinity of Tucson but few lodes have been discovered as compared with those further south. The Arivaca is a rich district, in which many fine gold and silver mines are located, among others the Buena Vista and Mogul. The Oro Blanco district is best known because of the Ostrich mine (gold) located therein. It is eighty miles south of Tucson. The Pima lies thirty miles southwest. Arivaipa district, now known as the De Freese, is located 120 miles from Tucson, in a northeasterly direction. Both of these are justly celebrated for the richness of their ore bodies. Perhaps the most important district at present in the Territory is that of the Tombstone. Its sepulchral cognomen was put upon the place by a sturdy miner who said he should either find his fortune or his tombstone. He found a mine which did find him his fortune, and in his solemn hilarity he called it Tombstone. From this first mine the camp and district were named.

Tombstone is the county seat of Cochise county, and is situated twenty-seven miles southeast of Benson on the line of the A. T. & S. F. and S. P. railroads, and is reached easily by a daily line of Concord coaches running from Benson. The buildings of the town are of a superior order, and the heavy stocks of goods carried by the merchants are a sure indication of the prosperity of the town. There are three churches, a school house, and two daily and weekly newspapers; and these three are strong elements in civilization. The mines of the district have taken such rank in the markets of the nation that an extended mention of them in detail can not be out of order. First may be mentioned the Contention. This great mine has never been heralded, "boomed," or kept before the public, except by the excellence of its developments, the richness of its yield, and the regularity as well as the amount of the dividends it pays to its shareholders—which speak volumes both for the mine and for the great mineral district in which it is located. The property was stocked for $10,000,000, divided into 100,000 shares, and it shows in sight to-day probably one or two million dollars above this par valuation. The stupendous quantity of ore reserves, representing the $11,000,000 which competent judges estimate in sight, now stand in place in the mine. Eight hundred and ten feet was the greatest length opened at the time this estimate was made in February, and on a few of its six levels the linear extent did not exceed 500 feet, and in one or two instances below these figures. It took about $200,000 to place the property upon a paying basis, but if it had absorbed five times the amount the results so far obtained would have warranted the expenditure. The bullion yield of the mine to the last of January approximated $2,000,000. Of this aggregate, dividends to the tune of $675,000 had been disbursed to shareholders up to February, divided into eight consecutive dividends of $75,000 each, including the extra one paid last Christmas. In addition, the company in January last had $400,000 in coin and bullion in bank, besides $225,000 represented in tailings or slums at its mill, and besides 800 tons of first-class ore on dump at the mine, valued at $120,000, or $150 per ton, and besides, further, 2,000 tons, valued at $70,000 or $35 per ton.   Independent

CLIFF DWELLINGS, MANCOS CANON.

of these exhibits the company owns one of the finest twenty-five stamp mills in the district, costing not less than $125,000, and as complete new hoisting works as are to be found anywhere outside of the Comstock, and excelled not even there except in the matter of intrinsic cost and ponderosity.

The Tombstone M. & M. Co.'s property embraces eleven locations, covering 169 acres of surface. They include the celebrated Toughnut and the Lucky Cuss, the Goodenough, Survey, Defense, West Side, Tribune, East Side, Owl's Nest, East Side No. 2, and Owl's Last Hoot—the two latter

STAGE STATION, ARIZONA.

formed out of segregations from the East Side and Owl's Nest. The territory covered by these eleven claims is bounded on the northeast by the Wayup and the Toughnut, on the north by the Republic and Gilded Age, on the west by the Vizina and Survey, on the southwest by the Intervener and Blue Monday, and on the east by the Girard and Hawkeye. The first two of the above series were about the first locations made in the district, in August, 1877, the others following in the same month or next following one; and some two months subsequently followed the Western (Contention) and the Grand Central, the two having been staked out on the same day. The Arizona incorporators of the property were Mr. Gird, the present manager of the property at Tombstone, the Scheiffelin brothers, ex-Governor Safford, and the Corbin brothers of Connecticut. During the term of this organization the Gird ten-stamp mill was built, and in May, 1880, the Scheiffelin brothers disposed of their joint interests in the property to Philadelphia parties for $1,000,000; hence the present incorporation in the

EASTWARD FROM TOLTEC TUNNEL.

same month under the laws of Connecticut, where the present head office is, while the principal branch office is located at 432 Walnut street, Philadelphia. The property is now stocked for $12,500,000, divided into 500,000 shares, and up to the first of March had disbursed dividends to the total amount of $1,000,000, $450,000 in the ten months spanning the Arizona incorporation, and $550,000 for the eleven months' existence of the present incorporation. It has paid under the new order of things eleven consecutive dividends of $50,000 each, and had at the time these data were collected $200,000 coin on hand. It is shipping 70 tons of ore daily, and if it had sufficient mill capacity could ship three times the number of tons without making visible strain upon the resources of the mine, which are wonderful. The company has also a sum equal to $225,000 represented in the tailings at the mills; the Gird ten, and the Corbin fifteen stamps—in all twenty-five, and five more are now being added to the Corbin, which covers all the improvements to be made in milling matters until the water shall be introduced by the new company from the Huachuca range (Wa-chu-ca) which will be soon. With the introduction of this great desiderata, a new and brilliant future will open for the district, since it will promote at this

CATHEDRAL OF TAOS.

point the concentration of labor, capital and prosperity by rendering available thousand of tons of ore which will not now pay to ship to the San Pedro, but which will pay, and profitably, when mills of large capacity come to be erected in proximity to the apparently inexhaustible sources of their supply, scattered over the district in all but limitless abundance. In this property alone may be found, even now, many thousand tons of low-grade ore ($35 to $45 per ton) which will not pay to handle, and which, per consequence, is allowed to hang, to lie and to cling in place in the workings. And what is true of this, is true of every property in the camp. Even the Western Company (the Contention), with above 2,000 tons of such grade of ore on the dumps, is leaving behind in its driftings ore which could be worked with large profit were there water on the ground. Throw this to the flanks of the hills bordering the mines and there will be work for all, money for all, and prosperity unstinted for all in Tombstone. The ore is very high-grade, as proven by the assay records of the company, and as shown by the average of $144 per ton of the present daily shipments to the

reduction works at Charleston, on the San Pedro. Native silver, polyba-
site and horn silver are found adhering to the rocking in place at many
points in the mine. The chlorides and carbonates are also very rich; and
while it offers no great obstacle to profitable separation by pan process of
amalgamation, the ore is somewhat more leaded and permeated with other
bases than is the ore of any of the other large mines examined and mentioned in this sketch. Twelve per cent. will probably cover the lead, while
the ore ranges from $45, the lowest, to $125, $200, $300 and $600 per ton.

The property of the Grand Central Company bounds the Western on the
south, the Grand Central South on the north, and the Naumkeag on the east.
It is 1,500 feet long, the trend being north and south, and 600 feet wide.
It was located on the 27th day of February, 1878, on which date, or the day
previous, was located its northern neighbor, the Western. The work of
permanent development was commenced upon it one year ago. It is
opened by main and prospecting shafts; the former is now 370 feet deep,
but its lowest opened level is only 300 feet deep, yet above the level to the
surface and within the limits of 900 feet long are held in place not less than
80,000 tons of first-class ore, representing the gross amount of $8,000,000,
besides 6,000 tons stored on dump at the mine and 400 tons in the new
ore-bin, representing $640,000 more, or a total of $8,640,000 worth of ore
reserves to draw upon, and all out of the space given above. What will
outside skeptics think of this stupendous output from a mine upon which
the work of exploration was inaugurated one year ago?

The Head Center Company's ground was located in August, 1878. It is
1,300 feet long and 500 wide at its widest point, and the main inside vein seems
to run 1,000 feet through it, as demonstrated by surface outcrop and nearly
by underground driftings. It is bounded on the east by the Western and
the Contentment, on the north by the Tranquillity, and the Sulphuret on
the southwest; strike of surface outcrop, north ten east. Incorporated
under the laws of California on the 15th of January, 1880, on a basis of
$10,000,000, divided into 200,000 shares, the work of permanent develop-
ment was inaugurated upon the present 4½ by 3½ double-compartment shaft
on the 20th of December, 1879. Since this last mentioned date the work of
exploration has been continuous; and that no idleness existed around its
works is attested by the finely opened condition of the mine. This fine shaft
is 516 feet deep, is well built and substantially timbered from top to bottom,
and the north compartment receives the cage, while the other section
will be used for sinking purposes. The ore body is explored on the first
level 330 feet, polar course; on the second level 630 feet, same course;
on the third level 650 feet, like course; and on the fourth or 410-foot level
260 feet, same course. In the above is not included the large lateral drifting
or cross-cutting to be described below. To estimate correctly the vastness
of the ore reserves explored and given tangible existence in this property, by

means of the above longitudinal driftings, is about as impossible as would be
the task of numbering the sands of the ocean beach, for, like the Toughnut
series described above, its ore limits appear to be bounded only by the lateral
and the linear limits of the mine. We give therefore these limits, the character of the ore, and an estimate of at least $5,000,000 when the quality of the
ore is considered, and allow the interested reader to do the remainder. In the

BULLION AND SILVER ORE.

first and second levels of this mine are presented in many localities along
their explored sections ample evidences to support the belief that of the
noble metals, gold will largely predominate in the reduction returns.
The analytical tests made up to the present, though not entirely bearing out
yet largely support this theory, and the future mill returns will probably
exhibit more than 40 per cent. gold (present percentage). Visible to the
naked eye may be seen this precious metal in its free, pure state, permeating
the ore in place, impregnating here the porphyry and there the quartz constituents of the mineral, and glistening in the candlelight in a manner to
encourage hope, and to forcibly recall the lang syne days of the Golden State.

The Vizina property was incorporated under the laws of New York (April, 1880), with a capital of $5,000,000, divided into 50,000 shares, 12,500 of which were set aside for working purposes. Little of this amount has thus far been used, the mine having more than paid all expenses, purchase price included. The ore output has been about 1,600 tons, and the milling returns are about 80 per cent., which give an aggregate bullion yield of $125,000. The company is shipping daily to the Boston mill fifteen tons, equal to $1,200, or $36,000 per month. The hoisting works are northwest of the Tombstone

RUBY CAMP, ELK MOUNTAINS, COLORADO.

M. & M. Co., adjoining the Goodenough on the southeast and the Survey on the southwest. The Vizina vein courses through the northwest end of town. It is opened by three shafts, 36, 56 and 220 feet deep respectively, the last being the present new main working shaft, the others the old prospecting shafts. In the first the ledge was cut about twenty-five feet below surface. The new shaft has but one level 100 feet deep, and the shaft is now down 120 feet further in its course to the point where the 300-foot level is to be opened, which will leave a space of 200 feet between the two levels. The formation in the workings of this mine, as in the workings of all east of it, is highly metamorphic, and shows more talcose schist and vitreous looking but still mineralized quartzite than elsewhere seen in the district. The ground in the region of the present bottom of the shaft (220 feet deep) looks very favorable indeed, the structure more metamorphosed and compact, and

largely mineralized, showing that the dolomite and marbleized lime
higher up is fast disappearing as we descend. This property is an excellent one, and that there is a bright future before it none who carefully ex
amine it can doubt. As to the amount of reserves in sight, it is hard to say
with anything like certainty, but that they are large is evident enough, and

THE NEW CATHEDRAL, SANTA FE.

with small labor enough ore could be released from place to increase the
daily shipments to at least thirty tons, or double the quantity now shipped.
As in the case of other mines in the district yet but partially developed,
depth and drifting are alone necessary to place the Vizina among the most
valuable properties of the district. And when this depth comes to be
reached, the present metamorphic lime and quartzite will terminate and a
purely porphyritic under-structure take their place, the same as exists

southeast of the Girard in the region of the Sulphuret, the Head Center and Western.

The Grand Central South has a surface of 1,500 by 600 feet. It is opened by two shafts 600 feet apart. One of these is a single compartment prospecting shaft, well and substantially timbered with two and a half inch plank. It is situated on the slope of the hill, close to the north boundary, and is now 150 feet deep, all the distance in a highly mineralized vein formation, and the prospects at this depth are first class. Cross-cutting east from bottom (150-foot) is to be proceeded with without delay, and it is

CHICAGO LAKE.

safe to add, that the energy thus far displayed in the incipient development of this fine property will soon be rewarded in the cross-cutting. Everything looks favorable for an extensive mine ; in fact, it is only necessary to remark of its prospects and promises, that it is the immediate direct south, probably ten east, extension of the Grand Central, which shows above the 300-foot level, standing in place, and so developed that they can be readily released, not less than 90,000 tons of first-class reserves, and this estimate anticipates all the possible contingencies of the future.

The formation is a strong porphyritic, full of mineral for above 1,600 feet wide ; in fact, the whole vast belt is saturated with ore, which is liable to be struck anywhere and at any moment. Yet, despite this general diffusion of the precious metals, there are well-developed veins and ledges having regular strikes, pitches and walls, solid and well outlined. And these veins and ledges, or fissures, or whatever they may be designated, exhibit, where opened and followed, less faults or displacements and richer

GOAT ISLAND, SAN FRANCISCO.

ore, and more of it, than is to be found in any quarter of the coast outside of the Tombstone district. The bullion yield of Tombstone's mines for 1880 is given by local papers at $3,008,278. Probably four-fifths of this was in silver and the remainder in gold. The product came from the following sources: Contention, or Western mine and mill (nine months), $1,214,055; Tombstone Company, $913,443; Harshaw (four months), $365,455 ; Copper Queen (four months), $300,000; Corbin, $36,000; Boston and Arizona Reduction Works, $36,625; Sunset mill (short run), $22,500; Holland (trial runs), $18,000; other mills and arastras, $100,000. An item for $10,000 for placer gold that appeared in the published statements is omitted here because it was credited to another county—Pinal. The Contention product contained $909,607 in silver, and $224,448 in gold. The above is an excellent showing for a district but two or three years old, whose mines had been brought into fair producing condition at the beginning of last year. In fact, there are said to be several mines that gave little or nothing last year that have opened so as to show ore reserves insuring productions almost-equal to the best of those mentioned. The completion of mills is all that is needed to enable them to become regular producers and dividend-payers.

The road from Tombstone to Bisbee passes through Charleston, a thriving town on the San Pedro. The Tombstone Mill and Mining Co. have two mills at this point, one of twenty stamps, run by steam, and one of fifteen stamps, propelled by water power. The place has three or four stores, two hotels and several saloons. It has about 400 inhabitants. It does a large trade with Sonora, being situated on the main thoroughfare which leads up the San Pedro to the principal points in that State. And, speaking of the Sonora trade, the smuggling which is carried on across the border is deserving of some mention. At all points along the frontier this illegitimate traffic is extensively indulged in. The business is mostly in the hands of Mexicans, who are familiar with every trail and bridle path across the border, and who manage to elude very successfully the customs officers of both governments stationed along the line on either side. Mescal, tobacco and cigars are brought from Sonora, while dry goods are taken across from Arizona. Occasionally some dusky Dirk Hatteraick falls into the clutches of the myrmidons of the law, and his goods and chattels are confiscated by Uncle Sam. Owing to the length of the frontier, and the facilities for crossing, it is almost impossible to prevent this traffic. The Sonorans are free-traders of the most advanced type. Nothing galls them so much as paying dues of any kind to the government, knowing from sad experience that the one in power to-day may be sent to the " demnition bow-wows " to-morrow.

Between Charleston and Tombstone, and about two miles from the former place, is the old " Bronkow Mine," whose dark and bloody history has given it an unenviable notoriety all over southern Arizona. Discovered and first located by Emil Bronkow, a German engineer and metallurgist, in 1858, its history since then has been an uninterrupted series of violence and murder. Bronkow and three companions were the first victims—assassinated by Mexicans. Since then no less than seventeen men have been killed on this property. The graves lie thick around the old adobe house. Pros-

GUADALUPE CHAPEL.

pectors and miners avoid the spot as they would the plague; and many of them will tell you that the unquiet spirits of the departed are wont to revisit the place by the light of the moon and wander about the scenes which witnessed their untimely taking off. The gloomy old building is unoccupied, the present occupants of the mine, not caring to reside there, having put up a house some distance away. Although much blood has been spilt and many lives lost over this claim, it has not yet proven of much value. It is still in dispute, being guarded by men armed with Henry rifles.

After leaving Charleston, the road to Bisbee follows up the valley of the San Pedro to the new town of Hereford, nearly twenty miles. There is some fine farming land along the valley, and water in abundance near the surface. It is covered by a Mexican grant, however, which prevents its occupancy and cultivation. The Tombstone Mill and Mining Company have secured from the owners of the grant the water right from the boundary line down to their mills at Charleston, nearly twenty-five miles. No one can take out the water above them, and other companies operating in Tombstone are compelled to put up their reduction works lower down the river. The proposed town of Hereford contains at present four houses and a few tents, three of the former being in course of erection. The town site has been laid out by the Neptune Mining Company, who intend to erect reduction works at this point. It has a beautiful situation in the valley of

AMONG THE ISLES.

the San Pedro—here over half a mile wide—with the pine-covered ridges of the Huachucas on the west, the Mule mountains on the east, and the isolated Sierra de San Jose filling up the picture on the south. From Hereford it is five miles to the Sonora line, and a steady stream of travel is always going to and from that point.

Bisbee is eighteen miles from Hereford, following the road, but less than half the distance in a direct line. The town is situated in a deep cañon of the Mule mountains, and contains about fifty houses, built mostly of lumber. It has a population of nearly 200. The mines of this district were first discovered some five years ago by a man named Warren, who successfully worked them for silver, until compelled to leave on account of Indians. The first copper discoveries were made about two and a half years ago, and attracted little attention until they passed into the hands of the present company. As is generally the case, the original owners received

10

but little for their property; being in the chronic condition of treasure hunters, they had not the means to develop the claim, and parted with their interest for $18,000. A portion of the property lately changed hands on the basis of $1,200,000 for the whole! The Copper Queen, as far as opened, is an immense mountain of ore, averaging over 20 per cent. pure

HIEROGLYPHICS ON THE ROCKS, ARIZONA.

copper. The claim is opened by over 600 feet of tunnels, cross-cuts and winzes, exposing an ore body 160 feet in length, 120 feet in width, and over 150 feet in thickness. From careful calculations it is estimated that over $2,000,000 worth of ore is already in sight. A large excavation has been made in the side of the mountain, and the ore is quarried out and wheeled to a shute which delivers it at the smelter, a few feet below. It will thus be seen that the cost of extraction is merely nominal, and Superintendent Williams assured your correspondent that with his present facilities he could work ore carrying six per cent. copper. The smelter is a water jacket, with a capacity of thirty tons in twenty-four hours, and turns out daily six and one-half tons of copper, 95 per cent. fine. About forty men are employed at the smelter and in the mine. Another smelter of the same capacity is on the road, and will soon be running. Under the careful and efficient management of Superintendent Williams everything runs like clock-work. The Copper Queen is incorporated in New York, and is one of the best paying properties in the Territory. There are many other promising claims in the district, upon which but little work has yet been done. The Neptune Company, before alluded to, are the owners of eight or ten claims,

GARDEN OF THE GODS.

have spent a great deal of money in the camp, and are opening up some valuable copper properties. This company have surveyed a line for a railroad to the river, and intend to work their ores at the San Pedro. Bisbee is destined to become an important mining camp. Its ores are rich and easily reduced; it has an abundance of wood, a reasonable supply of water, and a fine climate. With all these advantages there is no reason why it should not become the copper camp of the Southern country.

He who bestowed upon Patagonia so uncouth an appellation must certainly have had a depraved conception of the eternal fitness of things, for surely nothing could be less suggestive of barren plains, ice and fogs and gigantic savages than this mountain paradise of southern Arizona. Elevated about 7,000 feet above the level of the sea, its gently sloping mountains covered with a luxuriant growth of grass and crowned with oak and cedar, with beautiful, lawn-like valleys lying between, it is the most delightful portion of the Territory that your correspondent has yet seen. Washington camp, the present centre of the mines of this region, is

SEAL ROCKS, NEAR SAN FRANCISCO.

situated about nine miles almost due south from Harshaw, and less than four miles from the Sonora line. About three miles from Harshaw is a lovely little flat among the hills, where are the ruins of the smelting works of the "Old Mowry Mine," owned and worked by Lieut. Mowry, of the U. S. army, before the civil war. A collection of adobe ruins is all that is left of what was once the liveliest mining camp in Arizona. The lofty brick

ON THE KANSAS RIVER.

chimney is still standing, a mournful monument to extinct enterprise and former active life. It is said that 400 Mexicans and their families were at one time employed at the mine and smelter, and the spot is yet pointed out—in the valley surrounded by beautiful oaks—where the festive Sonoran and his dusky mate whirled in the dizzy mazes of the fandango, and made the hills re-echo with their joyous hilarity. Every Saturday at twelve o'clock the force stopped work, and from then until morning there was a continuous round of dancing, drinking and gambling. Often, too, the treacherous Apache, concealed behind rock or bush, took a hand in the performance, and, with his piercing war-whoop, changed the scene of joyous pleasure into shrieks of agony and bloody strife. But not a sound disturbs the oppressive solitude of these ruins now, save, perhaps, the gentle *basso profundo* of some lonely prospector's burro, who has wandered hither with his master in search of some hidden bonanza. Apache warfare and civil war must answer for the destruction of this once prosperous mining enterprise. The "Old Mowry Mine" is now owned by parties in Tucson, and nothing is left to tell the stranger in these parts of the untiring labors and unceasing efforts of that true friend of Arizona, Sylvester Mowry, save the legend on the capping of stone near the top of the chimney, "Mowry Silver Mine, 1861." Six miles south of these ruins, and the mines of Washington Camp are reached. The hills are higher and steeper, and the growth of timber heavier than at Harshaw. The camp—a collection of tents, canvas-covered houses, with a few frame and adobe structures—is situated on an elevated bench, with the towering Patagonia mountains all round about. It is a delightful situation, and the climate is said to be perfection itself. From the town site a beautiful view of the Santa Cruz valley and the mountains of Sonora behind it, is obtained. The white tents of La Noria, at the southern point of the mountains, and just on the line, set off most charmingly this magnificent view. At La Noria are located the smelting works of the Holland Mining Co., and at the same point the W. C. Davis Co. are erecting works of a similar nature.

Matters in the Harshaw section are looking bright, and recent developments indicate that it will soon rival Tombstone as a silver-producing district. The Hermosa mine, owned by a New York company, is improving in quantity and quality as depth is attained. The twenty-stamp mill on this property has steadily produced from $75,000 to $100,000 per month since the mill started up in August last. The Hardshell mine, recently purchased by D. B. Gillette—formerly superintendent of the Hermosa—is proving superior to the former mine, at the same depth. A few days since a remarkably rich and extensive body of ore was struck in the same. The Trench mine, owned by Messrs. Haggin, Tevis and Gallagher, has within the past sixty days showed up a body of ore large in quantity and high grade in quality. This property has fine hoisting works, and is now prospected to a depth of 350 feet. The Alta mine, owned by Dr. Perrin and associates, at a depth of 175 feet displays a six-foot ledge of high grade ore, assaying from $150 to $2,500 per ton. The Chicago mine, owned by Messrs. L. Conley, Briden & Co., adjoins the Alta, and displays the same character of ore. When opened to the same depth as the former it will doubtless prove equally as valuable. There are many other claims located in the same mineral belt embracing the above-mentioned properties, but being undeveloped their value as yet is undetermined. Mining and milling in the Harshaw district is to-day done cheaper than in any other camp in the Territory. A notable instance is the Hermosa Company, which is running and milling (including transportation of ore) for less than $15 per ton. The town of Harshaw is situated among rolling hills, covered with grass and trees, and is amply supplied with pure mountain water. It has a population of about 1,000,

STREET SCENE, SAN FRANCISCO.

and is a year old. The climate is good, as the altitude is about 5,600 feet above sea level. Washington Camp, some eight miles distant from Harshaw,

OLD CHURCH AT MONTEREY.

is being rapidly developed, and is now showing up large bodies of fine ore, The W. C. Davis mine having been thoroughly prospected, its superintendent, Thomas Selby, has just shipped a large smelter, together with hoisting works adapted for sinking 1,000 feet. Other notable mines in this district are the Ohio, Emma, Grasshopper, Silver Bill and Belmont. Some of those mentioned have recently been sold to companies who are now preparing to erect hoisting works, mills and smelting furnaces. The work that has been

done during the past year has demonstrated the extent of the ore bodies, and the permanency of the camps seems no longer a matter of doubt.

What has been said of a general sort about Tombstone and other camps, may be applied to Phœnix, Shakespere, Globe, and the hundred other prosperous camps of the Territory. All are unfolding steadily the immensity of their resources. In conclusion, as summing up the mining business of the Territory may be quoted two Pacific coast authorities, the Los Angeles *Herald*, and the San Francisco *Alta*, both writing under the head of "The Mines of Arizona." The *Herald* says:

"Arizona to-day, with all intelligent men, eclipses Nevada. The glories of the old Silver State are those of memory and retrospection merely. Mines at a depth of from two thousand to three thousand feet are beyond the possibility of profit, especially with the extravagant management which has been bred in the bone of all Comstock mining magnates, or, more properly, stool pigeons. The sneer at Arizona has been principally because the mines of the Territory lacked depth. Just there is the strength of the Arizona mines. Tombstone is worth the played-out Comstock lode twenty times over, because the Tombstone mines are at trifling depths and yield dividends from the surface. The Nevada mines are a mammoth devil-fish, squirming and delving not only into the depths of the earth, but into the depths of the poor stockholders' pockets. Fortunately for the fair fame of Arizona, assessments are an almost unheard of thing. At the worst they are confined to the owners of the mineral properties, and that at a time anterior to their becoming stock propositions. None of the attractive properties which are now paying heavy dividends in Arizona have levied assessments. The Silver King, which has paid many dividends, and which bids fair to pay more, has never levied an assessment on stockholders. The same may be said of the leading Tombstone mines. Undoubtedly Arizona will, in the near future, play a leading part in stock speculation. Unless all signs fail, before the coming trans-continental railway systems below the snow belt shall have been completed, the attention of Eastern capitalists will be focused upon Arizona, a region which has practically developed itself in an extraordinary degree."

The *Alta*, quoting the above, adds the following:

"Arizona mines are now the popular mines, but hardly for speculation in the stock boards—we mean for investment by capitalists; and here we wish to say that a few of ours have got awakened at last to the fact that Arizona has very promising mines. Wherever the mines of Arizona have been developed to any considerable depth, they have, with but very few exceptions, proven richer in minerals with increasing depth, and foreshadow a permanency completely at variance with all theories of scientists and experts. Even small prospects on the surface generally develop into good ledges at less than 200 feet in depth. This is true not only in those districts where the mining excitement exists, but in all locations where minerals have been found. Tombstone has shown that her mines are practically inexhaustible; the Meyers district is showing astonishing richness; the Silver Bell and Silver Hill belt are adding to the wonders of the Territory; Patagonia is proving the truth of her predicted greatness; the California district is full of bonanzas; Dos Cabezas, Oro Blanco and Arivaca are fast growing in favor; and the rich leads of the Santa Ritas are beginning to show that they are not a whit behind the rest.

"There is one point that, it seems to us, is not sufficiently emphasized when the Globe district is discussed. We allude to the fact that the ores of the mines have continued to grow richer as depth is increased. There are but four mines in this entire mineral region that have reached any depth, and they are comparatively superficial. The Stonewall Jackson is down over 500 feet; the Mack Morris over 300 feet; the Centennial about 300 feet; and the Silver King over 500 feet. These Mines are all in the same mineral belt. The Stonewall Jackson is distant from the Mack Morris about eight and a half miles; the Mack Morris from the Centennial six miles; the Centennial from the Silver King thirty-five miles. Yet there is a similarity in the composition, the difference being in the proportions, some being richer than others. Then, if we take these facts as data, it is fair to assume that there is the greatest abundance of mineral deposits between these several points, and it only requires nerve and capital to substantiate this fact. The Arizona copper interests are going to be another of those trades which will grow to vast proportions. The consumption of the article is daily growing larger, and as it will be constantly put to more uses the greater will be the demand. To foster the copper interests of Arizona Territory is as necessary for the welfare of this community as to foster the interests of any other industry."

FALLS OF THE BOULDER.

(156)

CALIFORNIA IN GENERAL.

GEOGRAPHY — TOPOGRAPHY — PHYSICAL CHARACTERISTICS — CLIMATE —
POPULATION — COMMERCIAL AND AGRICULTURAL STATISTICS —
COMMERCIAL MATTERS.

REVIOUS to the year 1769 California was inhabited only by the Indians. The rule of the Spaniard began April 11th of that year, when a party of Franciscan friars, accompanied by some soldiers, arrived at San Diego, and settled in what was then Upper California. In time twenty-one missions were founded. All were near the coast. The first and most southern was founded in 1769 at San Diego, and the last and most northern at Sonoma in 1823. San Francisco was established in 1776. These missions in most cases have served as nuclei for what have since become thriving cities. The era of Mexican dominion began in 1822, when the independence of Mexico was first formally announced. The American and commercial era dates back to 1846, when the stars and stripes were hoisted at Monterey. The first discovery of gold occurred soon afterwards. This was followed by an invasion of fortune-hunters from the East. Of the famous days of '49, when the trail from the Missouri river two thousand miles to the Pacific coast was thronged with the chivalry of the land, little need be said. The battles with savages, the fight against poverty, the fruitless wanderings from place to place, the eternal hoping against hope on the part of the many and the realization of hope on the part of the few—all these things are familiar. But concerning other and more common matters less is known. California extends from latitude 32° 31' to 42°. It has a coast line of 1,097 miles, and in general shape is a parallelogram 800 miles long by 190 wide. It contains 155,000 square miles, or 99,000,000 acres.

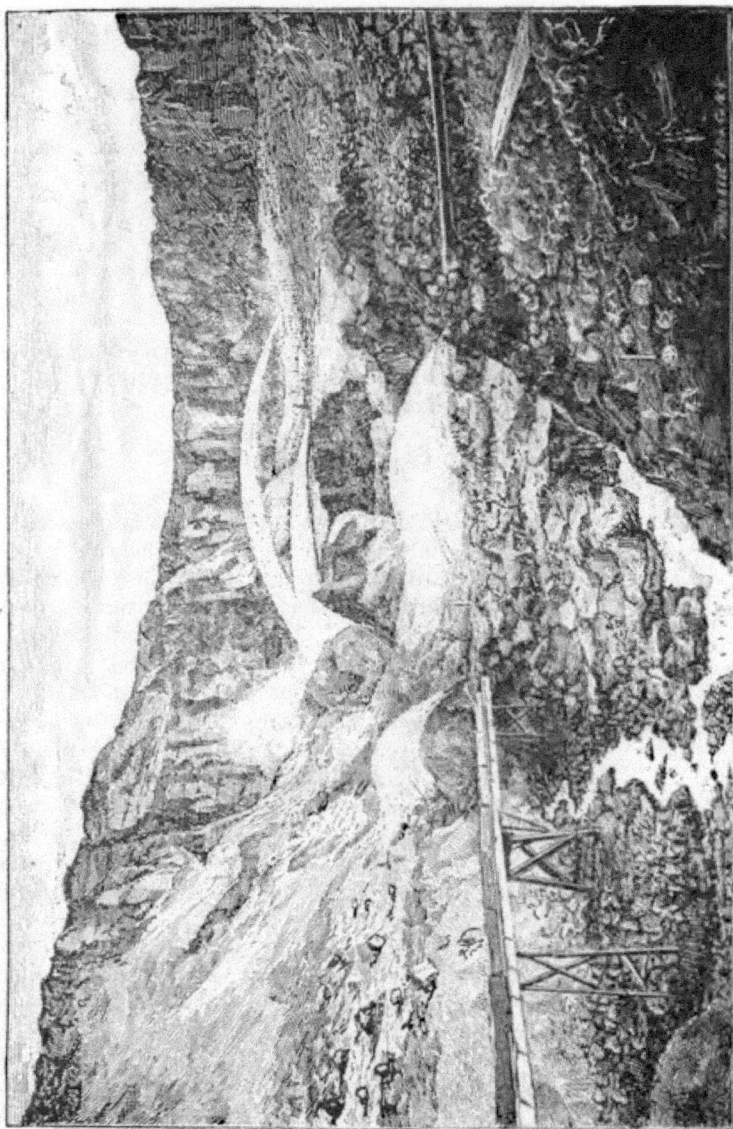

HYDRAULIC MINING.

The topography of this vast domain is peculiar. It is doubtful whether any other portion of the United States contains so many volcanic peaks, vast masses of granite, rough mountain ridges, lovely, fertile valleys, desert wastes, broad bays, beautiful lakes, fine rivers, extensive marshes and impenetrable forests. The division of the State into coast and interior districts, separated by the coast mountains fifty miles inland and extending the entire length of the State parallel to the ocean, is a striking feature. The interior district is again subdivided into the Sierra Madre range, the Sacramento and the Klamath basins and the Colorado desert. Of the total area of California it has been estimated that one-fourth is occupied by the mountains and valleys of the coast, another fourth by the Sierra Nevada mountains, 30,000 square miles by the Sacramento basin, 10,000 by the Klamath basin, 15,000 by the Colorado desert, and the remainder in what has been termed the "enclosed American prairie." The height of the Coast range varies from 2,000 to 6,000 feet, and in width it averages thirty miles, being composed of one main stem (the Diablo range) and many branches bearing to the west, known as the Santa Susanna, Santa Inez, Santa Barbara, Santa Lucia, Gabilan and Contra Costa ridges. The coast rivers are necessarily short. The more important ones, going south from San Francisco, are San Lorenz, Pajaro, Salinas, Cuyama, Santa Inez, Saticoy, Los Angeles, San Gabriel, Santa Ana, Santa Margarita, San Luis Rey, San Dieginto and San Diego. The majority of these streams are, during dry weather, swallowed up by the sands; in winter they run bank full. The only navigable coast stream is the Salinas. North of San Francisco the main streams are the Russian, Elk, Eel, Mad and Smith rivers, none of which are navigable. California has two important capes, Mendocino and Point Arguello, the former being perhaps the stormiest place on the coast. Forty miles from San Francisco in a westerly direction are the Farallanes islands, and southward lie the Santa Clara, Santa Catalina, San Clemente, Santa Rosa, San Nicholas, Anacapa and Santa Barbara groups, all rocky and barren excepting Santa Cruz, which has a few trees and is well watered. Four fine land-locked harbors are also found on the shore line—Humboldt, Tomales, San Francisco and San Diego—all well protected by narrow peninsulas. A peculiar feature of the borders of the bays mentioned, and of the Tulare and Kern lakes and the Sacramento and San Joaquin rivers, is the existence of large areas of swamp lands, both fresh water and salt, aggregating nearly 3,000,000 acres.

The Sierra Nevada range in California is 450 miles long, seventy miles wide, and has a height of from five to eight thousand feet above the level of the sea. The western slope is sixty-five miles long and the eastern but five miles, terminating in what is known as the Great Basin, which is 4,000 feet above the sea. The Sacramento basin, lying between the two great ranges, is 400 miles long, fifty miles wide, and is drained by the Sacramento from the north and the San Joaquin from the south, both uniting and breaking through the Coast range to the Pacific. The western slope of the Sierra Nevada is drained by the Pit, Feather, Yuba, American, Cosumnes, Mokelumne, Calaveras, Stanislaus, Tuolumne, Merced, San Joaquin, King's, White and Kern rivers, all over 100 miles long and carrying considerable water. The most noted lake of this range is lake Tahoe, which is twenty miles long, ten miles wide, and 6,000 feet above sea level.

The Klamath basin lies north of latitude 41°. It is watered by the Klamath river and its tributaries, the Trinity, Salmon, Scott and Shasta.

The enclosed American basin is a triangular district enclosed to the north by the basin of the Columbia, east by that of the Colorado, and south and west by the Sierra Nevada and Coast ranges. It is an elevated tract, barren and mountainous, containing the most sterile land in the entire West. The chief stream is the Mojave, which rises near Mt. San Bernardino, and, running northeast a hundred miles, sinks into the sand. The next most important stream is Owen's river. The Colorado desert lies in the south-eastern part of the State, and contains about 10,000 square miles.

The population of California, according to the Federal census of 1880, was 864,686. Of this number 572,006 were native born, and 292,680 foreign; 767,266 were white, and 97,420 were colored. The latter included 75,025 Chinese, 16,130 Indians and Half-breeds, ninety-four Japanese, two East Indians, and one Sandwich Islander. The population of California is divided as to industries pursued as follows: commercial, 268,684; agricultural, 92,002; mining, 30,700; mixed industries, 45,900; farm, town and hamlet, 427,400.

California is cosmopolitan. All nations have contributed to its population. Society is, therefore, as varied in its character as could possibly be imagined. The migratory nature of the people who flocked to the Pacific coast in the early days has exercised a powerful influence in the social life of California, and endowed it with liberal tendencies far removed from the exclusiveness of the East. The journey across the plains in the days of '49 was of itself an education; and the struggle for existence after arrival, the large fortunes made and lost, and the general uncertainty of life itself, have produced a race strong in the elements of aggressiveness and freedom. The Californian is hospitable. He lives to enjoy life, and spends money while he has it, trusting to his good fortune for replenishment of the depleted purse. His home is, as a rule, furnished elegantly, the table supplied with all the delicacies of the season, and dress is regarded as a matter of importance. To the new-comer, be he rich or poor, Crœsus or Bohemian, the hand is extended in hearty greeting, provided the stranger is polished and entertaining. Mere wealth, where wealth is found in all businesses, is not esteemed as high as the man, apart from his external possessions. In no other State is the individual so free from the trammels of custom and the restraints of an artificial social world, since a large proportion of the people live remote from home influences, accountable to themselves only, yet in no wise abusing their liberty, or becoming lost to all deference for law and order. As to his physical characteristics the coming Californian will be, says a certain writer, "plump, ruddy in complexion, full in the chest, and melodious in voice." "The beauty of the women," says W. F. Rae, "is without the pale of controversy. They have the soft and delicate beauty of Italy, combined with an intelligence wholly American, and a physique wholly English." So much for the individual.

California has an excellent system of public schools, free to all children between the ages of five and fifteen. The method of instruction approximates to that of New England, and the teachers are mostly natives of that highly intellectual region. A State university has been organized and liberally endowed, and sectarian colleges are scattered along the coast from Santa Rosa to Santa Barbara, the Catholic schools being probably the most largely patronized. Church organizations are numerous and well sustained, the principal sects being, in the order named, the Catholics, Methodists, Baptists, Congregationalists, Presbyterians and Episcopalians. Secret societies exist in every town of importance, and literary organizations are met with on every hand. In fact, in going to California you do not go out of, but into, the world.

California has a climate which is simply capital—capital, not perhaps in the strict sense of political economy, but still capital; a climate which is not only a source of wealth indirectly but directly, inasmuch as it can be appropriated by as many mortals as the railroads and steamships can ever bring together. Much has been written of the influence of external nature upon national character. It is considered as established that extreme cold dulls the intellect; that extreme heat debases morals and enervates the body; that the temperate zone only can produce a really high and pure civilization. It has further been noted that the people of mountainous countries are, other things being equal, superior to the people of level countries, and the dwellers on the sea coast to those of the interior. The Californian, like the Greek, has every advantage of natural surroundings. He is neither dulled by extreme cold nor demoralized by extreme heat; he aspires with the mountains; he drinks in the many-sounding sea— figuratively speaking; actually he has something better to drink. In other parts of the temperate zone men get more than an occasional taste of both the torrid and the frigid; in California it is not so. The Pacific slope enjoys warmer winters than the Eastern States, and cooler summers. The nights are always cool; the days never oppressively sultry. There are no violent storms of any kind; the air is dry and invigorating. California is 800 miles long, lying north and south. Moreover, a part of the State is quite elevated, and a part is on a sea level. Of course this makes a great variety

11

ON GRAND RIVER, MIDDLE PARK.

of climate; though, on account of oceanic influences, there is less than would be supposed. The most distinctly marked climatic regions are, the western slope of the Coast range, the Sacramento basin, the Klamath basin, the Colorado desert, and the coast region south of Point Conception. Of course the western slope everywhere has the most equable climate, and the nearer the sea the lower the mean temperature. This is due to the strong sea breeze prevailing throughout the summer.

From San Francisco, south, the mean temperature of the winter differs but little from that of the summer. The lowest record ever " made " by a San Francisco thermometer was 22°. Snow rarely covers the ground, and then only for a few hours. It very rarely freezes in the daytime, and the whole winter season is a rich hazy Indian summer. The mean temperature of the summer months in San Francisco is not above 57°. Very seldom does the mercury register more than 80°, and no matter how warm the day, one must sleep under blankets at night. Warm woolen clothing can never be dispensed with. Prof. Robert Von Schlagintweit has said: "The climate of California resembles in general character that of Italy, but has not its objectionable effect, the depriving the people of the disposition to energetic mental and physical effort." The following table, taken from Mr. Hittell's valuable book on California, will give the reader a very good idea of the thermal peculiarities of San Francisco. It shows the number of days in twenty years when the thermometer reached 80°.

YEARS.	March.	April.	May.	June.	July.	Aug.	Sept.	Oct.	Nov.	Total.
1852	2	2	....	1	....	....	8	....	1	14
1853	.	....	1	3	..	...	3	3	....	10
1854	...	1	....	...	4	2	2	3	....	12
1855	1	2	1	2	2	3	6	3	....	20
1856	3	....	....	....	....	3	3	2	....	11
1857	2	....	..	2	...	2	4	4	....	14
1858	....	....	1	....	2	....	3	1	....	7
1859	....	....	1	3	...	....	....	2	....	6
1860	....	....	1	....	....	....	2	....	....	3
1861	....	....	....	....	....	....	....	....	....	....
1862	....	....	....	....	....	....	....	....	....	....
1863	....	....	....	....	....	....	....	....	....	....
1864	....	....	....	....	....	...	....	2	....	2
1865	...	..	2	....	....	....	3	....	....	5
1866	..	2	....	1	....	....	....	....	....	3
1867	....	2	1	2	4	...	4	....	....	13
1868	....	....	..	....	....	....	....	3	..	3
1869	....	....	1	....	....	....	3	....	....	4
1870	..	....	2	....	2	1	....	2	....	7
1871	....	....	....	....	....	....	....	2	....	2
Total	8	10	19	14	14	11	41	27	1	136

In a series of twenty-three years the rainfall at San Francisco varied from seven to fifty inches per annum, and this great variability of precipitation is noticeable everywhere in the State. In the south the annual rain-fall is only about ten inches, and in the vicinity of Yuma it is even less than this. The lack of rain, where agriculture is an object, is compensated for by systems of irrigation, either from living springs or from streams which draw their waters from the perennial snows of distant mountains. Many of the streams are like the Nile in respect to regular inundation of adjacent low-lands.

A VIEW OF THE TOP OF THE SNOWY RANGE.

The peculiar position of California upon the direct line of exchange between the lands of the Pacific and the largest commercial centres of our own country, the limitation set by nature and by chance to the number of her own industries, and her 1,000 miles of coast line—all serve to make California commercially active. To San Francisco is fast centering the trade of western South America, of Central America, of the Pacific islands, of Australia, China and Japan. As the great West continues to develop, there must inevitably spring up all along that 1,000 miles of Pacific coast busy trading towns and cities, such as dot the Atlantic from Maine to Florida. A variety of reasons unite to make it probably and almost certain that the metropolis will always be as now, San Francisco. The railroads are there, the capital is there, the best or second best harbor is there, and the men who will shape the course of business in California for some time to come, are there. But other localities have advantages.

There are other available points with good harbors and surrounded by rich territory—Crescent City, Trinidad, Bodega Bay, Monterey, Santa Barbara, Humboldt Bay. But by far the finest harbor of the whole coast is that at San Diego. A correspondent says of it: "As we rounded Point Loma, upon which stands a large government lighthouse, I was very forcibly impressed with the safety of the entrance to this land-locked harbor. From the entrance to the head of the bay, thirteen miles, is a narrow peninsula, which forms an absolute breakwater, while the lofty hills on the opposite side serve as a complete windbreak. The shore side of the harbor is in the shape of a horse-shoe, the beach being uniformly level the entire thirteen miles, while immediately back of this is a low circle of semi-hills, forming not only an elegant location for a city, but affording excellent drainage, sightly spots for homes, as well as beautiful views of the surroundings. The harbor is probably a mile wide at the upper end, near National City, while the width of the channel over the bar is about 1,000 feet. There is a depth of thirty-two feet of water on the bar at the lowest of low waters. As the average tide is nearly four feet, this gives them thirty-six feet at high tide. Captain Duncan Johnston, of the British ship Trafalgar, of Glasgow, now lying in the harbor, informs me that he came in last week under sail, and without the assistance of a tug, with his vessel drawing twenty-two feet. The ship is of iron, with iron masts, is registered as first-class, and was loaded with 2,450 tons of steel rails from Antwerp,—long tons, being 2,250 pounds to the ton,—and is one of the largest vessels made."

The chief exports of California are the grains, and horticultural and mining products. The sum total of these exports, per annum, is something more than $75,000,000. The imports from foreign countries reach $20,000,000, and from the other States of the Union, $30,000,000. The annual product for exportation is about $85 per capita; in no other State is it much more than $20. At present the chief shipping points are San Francisco, Oakland and Vallejo. The annual export in wheat and flour is at least, twenty-five millions; wool, four or five millions; wines and grapes, two to three millions; ores, two to three millions; fish, lumber, hides, one to two millions, etc. By way of imports the State pays more than ten millions for provisions, sugar, coffee, tobacco, etc.; and then for coal, kerosene, iron, dry goods, hardware and manufactures of all kinds, forty millions. Like most undeveloped countries, California ships raw materials and receives in exchange, manufactured products. This is true of the South and West generally, but it will not be so long. Where there are ample facilities,

CALIFORNIA PEARS.

(166)

it is cheaper for the artizan to go to the raw material than to transport the material to the artizan. New England by force of organization and sharp competition will keep the supremacy in manufacturing as long as she can, but the result, the final result, is certain.

The commercial facilities of California, besides her great coast-line and many harbors, are her navigable rivers and her railroads. The Sacramento river, the Feather, the San Joaquin and the Colorado are all navigable; the Sacramento to Sacramento City, for vessels drawing three feet; the Feather, seventy-five miles, for vessels drawing fifteen inches; the San Joaquin 130 miles, to Stockton, for vessels drawing five feet of water; the Colorado 453 miles, to Hardyville, for steamers or tugs of two feet draught. Canals may be constructed at comparatively small expense as soon as the trade of the country shall demand it.

The chief arteries, however, for the life blood of internal commerce, must be the railroads. The Central and Southern Pacific systems, and the lesser occupants of the territory, penetrate every region which offers the prizes of commerce, and in California, as elsewhere, have worked changes, reforms and developments which never by other means could have been accomplished.

For many reasons, the Golden Gate State may be considered the finest country in the world for farmers and cattle raisers, with large capital or small. The climate is mild and healthful; no hyperborean winters or tropical summers interrupt work; no expensive buildings are necessary, and building material is abundant and cheap; soil and climate are peculiarly adapted to the raising of wheat and barley, as proven by the large yields and fine quality of both grains; where irrigation supplies plenty of water, no country in the world can produce such magnificent root crops—potatoes, beets, turnips, onions, sweet potatoes, carrots, pumpkins, melons and cabbages. There is record of pumpkins weighing 250 pounds, beets 120 pounds, potatoes seven pounds, etc. Cattle need little protection and no cultivated feed. The greatest variety of the finest fruit can be raised, tropical and otherwise, commanding the markets of the world. On this subject may be quoted the very accurate statements made in the new Rand, McNally & Co.'s Atlas of the World, viz. "The wonderful climate and fertile soil of the Sacramento and San Joaquin valleys and the rich lands of the coast render California one of the richest agricultural States in the Union, although scarcely one-thirtieth part of its area is under cultivation. Until 1860 the inhabitants confined themselves chiefly to mining, to the neglect of the more certain arts of husbandry; but of late years the State has made a magnificent advance in agriculture. The land is so rich and the climate so favorable that two crops per year are often secured from the same field, and with the adoption of a general system of irrigation, there can be no reasonable limit to the production of the cereals. There were raised in

STREET VIEW, SAN FRANCISCO.

1880, 45,760,000 bushels of wheat, and 3,537,600 bushels of corn. One-third of the barley crop of the United States is grown in California. The average value per acre of cleared land is $27.16. The following table shows the average annual value and other statistics of each principal crop of California from 1872 to 1879 inclusive:

Cror.	Amount of Crop.	Number of Acres.	Average Annual Value.	Yield per Acre.	Value of Crop.	Value per Acre.
Buckwheat	23,500	1,015	30,619	23.1	$ 1 25	$ 29 15
Rye	100,871	6,181	97,524	16.5	26	15 89
Corn	1,936,031	58,088	1,650,221	34.	89	30 73
Oats	2,813,762	91,608	2,015,728	30.6	73	22 30
Potatoes	3,339,187	31,415	2,946,483	107.	90	95 77
Barley	10,838,186	513,415	8,097,133	20.	77	15 28
Hay	822,325	564,152	11,134,170	1.45	14 12	20 19
Wheat	28,531,250	2,199,796	32,760,147	12.9	1 16	14 91

Every variety of fruit known to the temperate and semi-tropical zones grows luxuriantly. The peach, pear, apple, fig, grape, orange, olive, nectarine, pomegranate, pineapple, quince, banana, lemon and citron are all grown in great quantities and attain perfection. Walnuts, almonds, chestnuts and all kinds of berries also flourish. Mulberry trees grow well, affording sustenance for millions of silk-worms, and the production of silk is becoming an important industry. There are in the State five silk factories. * * * Within the past ten years the exportation of fruit to the Eastern States has grown to vast proportions. The markets of all the large cities are now supplied with pears, grapes and other delicious fruits, which command high prices, and the trade is constantly increasing. Thousands of car loads are annually shipped by the Pacific Railroads, and large packing and canning factories have been established in Sacramento and other cities. There were put up in 1880, 6,000 tons of fruit and 3,500 tons of vegetables. Of the fruit trees of temperate climates there are about 4,000,000, divided as follows· Apple, 2,446,000; peach, 835,000; pear, 356,000; plum, 243,000; cherry, 122,000. There are also about 250,000 almond, walnut, fig, orange, olive and lemon trees. The soil is admirably adapted to the culture of the grape, and a large area is devoted to vineyards. There were produced in 1880, 10,000,000 gallons of wine, 450,000 gallons of brandy, and raisins to the value of $100,000. The total yield from the culture of the grape was $3,500,000. Over 10,000 acres were planted in grape-vines in 1880. California is regarded as, next to Australia, the best sheep-raising country in the world. There were in 1880, 7,646,800 sheep in the State. There were also 64,720 cashmere goats, these animals having been introduced about fifteen years ago. The wool clip in 1879 was 46,903,360 pounds, and in 1880, 46,974,154 pounds." The tillable land of the State amounts to about 40,000,000 acres. The railway companies own about 3,000,000 acres of land, part of which is tillable and part not so. As has been said before, the great crops of California are the cereals, especially wheat. Of this grain every variety is raised—Club, Chile, Australian, Odessa, Red Mediterranean, Sonora and Egyptian. Of these kinds the Chile is considered the best. California raises very little winter wheat. All the grain produced in the State is, as a rule, of good quality, running in that respect considerably ahead of other States.

BURRO TRAIN.

One peculiarity of California wheat is that it is always white—red wheat turning white after two seasons. The average yield in California is from thirty to twenty-five bushels per acre.

California is in the current of a new and a substantial prosperity. Her old feverish, restless, mercurial condition, incident to the mining business, has passed away, and the steadier, better state which comes of agricultural, industrial and commercial development is at hand.

TOURIST ATTRACTIONS.

CITIES AND RESORTS OF CALIFORNIA — SAN FRANCISCO AND VICINITY — LOS ANGELES — SANTA BARBARA, SAN DIEGO AND MONTEREY — YOSEMITE VALLEY — BIG TREES, ETC.

HE Tourist who would see California at its best should visit it in the spring. In May or June the very dry season sets in, and vegetation becomes parched and dusty. In March or April the country is at its loveliest. It is then a realm of sunshine, flowers and beauty. All is fresh and gay. Men banish melancholy, while women and birds and flowers in an exuberance of beauty rival the rainbow. Responsibility takes to itself wings and flies away. The most worn and overburdened must yield to the magic of brilliant light and luxuriant blossom. The persistent uniformity of the days, one cloudless dawn succeeding another, deepens the soothing charm. Here at last is the land

"In which it seemeth always afternoon;
A land where all things always seem the same."

There is no rest under the stimulating skies of New England; endless activity is the demand on soul and body there. Duty stands sentinel at every gate. Every room is a laboratory. Everything must be analyzed before it can be enjoyed. Flying

VICINITY OF GEORGETOWN

(172)

from that whip of the sky across river and prairie to the great interior basin there is still something in the sweeping cyclone of the Mississippi and the Missouri valleys, in the sharp changes of the seasons, that exhausts and wearies. The summer heat is tropical, but the winter days may be arctic. But in California, on the further coast, the wanderer may stay his feet.

> "There is sweet music here that softer falls
> Than petals from blown roses on the grass."

Here, if anywhere in the New World, the song of the *Lotus Eaters* is not a discord.

> "Why should we toil alone,
> We only toil who are the first of things,
> And make perpetual moan,
> Still from one sorrow to another thrown :
> Nor ever fold our wings
> And cease from wanderings,
> Nor steep our brows in slumber's holy balm ;
> Nor harken what the inner spirit sings,
> 'There is no joy but calm!' "

What Paris is to France, San Francisco is to the Pacific coast of the United States; and the similarity does not end in the mere matter of size. The character of San Francisco as a city is like that of Paris. San Francisco is a gay city, the metropolis of a light-hearted people. It is a condensation of California. It is a city of sunshine, flowers, music, poetry, painting, literature, business activity and swift social currents—swift, if not deep. Two hundred and fifty thousand people, or thereabouts, are gathered together on the extremity of a tumulus, sandy, wave-washed point of land. The city on its many hills is like Rome, only more so; in its water-beleaguered condition is like Venice, only not quite so much so; in its Chinese quarter is like Pekin or Hong Kong; in its fog malady for half the year is like London; in its love for music, art and literature is like Boston; in its business mania is like New York or Chicago. Crossing the bay from Oakland the stranger lands in San Francisco, and at once realizes that he *is* a stranger. The street cars run without visible means of support; up hill and down they go with all the intelligence, steadiness and quiet of "the oldest inhabitant," the secret of their activity being a noiseless underground cable. The hotels, from the Palace and the Baldwin down to the What-cheer House are unusual and unprecedented. The Palace is a hollow square, seven stories high, covered with glass, having a conservatory or hanging garden on the top floor, and a band of music in the rotunda. Count Smith, chief clerk, is as remarkable as any other part of the institution. He knows everybody, and forgets nothing. The Grand Hotel is just across the street from the Palace, and is the handsomest hotel building in the city. The What-cheer House is the house where a guest's plate is filled with soup from a monster syringe. If the necessary five cents in payment is not at once forthcoming the syringe is again applied to the plate and the soup withdrawn. The theatres are large and handsome, though of late the theatrical business has considerably declined. The churches, from Mayor Kalloch's Tabernacle to the Chinese Joss Houses, are well built and well

VIEW IN THE YOSEMITE.

supported. The clubs—Bohemian and others—are conducted on the most "generous, gorgeous and gigantic" plan. Hospitality is the object of their every endeavor. The schools of the city are modern in every respect. The mint is an institution where the stranger should go to see how it seems to see gold and silver handled like corn and potatoes. Chinatown must be visited at night with a policeman or some other functionary as a guide.

Here you will see a Simon pure chunk of China, broken off and relocated in San Francisco. The stores with their queer commodities; the merchants with their counting machines; the theatres with their senseless performances—stale, flat and unprofitable; the Joss Houses, or churches, with their idols, symbols and magnificent specimens of carving; the restaurants,

IN THE GARDEN OF THE GODS.

where nimble-fingered Chinamen "eatee lice" (rice) with two small round sticks; the opium dens, where one comes as near getting a smell of Hell and a sight of the Devil as anywhere else in the world; the underground burrowings, where there are more Chinamen to the square yard than there are inhabitants in Kansas to the square mile; the narrow black alleys,

SNOWY RANGE, COLORADO.

where the only kind of Chinese women brought in any number to America, stand like cattle in the market place; the grand aggregation of crooked smells and noises, and, over and above all, the babblings of a strange and chilling tongue—these are the tints which compose the picture of Chinatown.

ON THE WESTERN SLOPE.

San Francisco jewelry stores, photographic establishments and Japanese importing houses should all be visited. "Nobb hill" is the place where much of the wealth of California has its place of residence. The grave of Starr King, the new City Hall, the wharfs and naval posts, all should be seen. Golden Gate Park, the Cliff House and Seal Rocks should be visited,

12

and then may come an endless variety of excursions—north, east, south—near at hand along the bay, or further off inland or along the coast. San Francisco is a wooden city, the peculiar climate making it advantageous to build of wood and finish with a cement which gives buildings the appearance of marble. The red-wood used does not burn rapidly, and altogether this system of building which at first seems shoddy and unsubstantial is really the best possible one. This is San Francisco. It must be seen to be appreciated.

If San Francisco itself has too much the stir of business, across the bay lies Oakland, with its 35,000 people, a city of green gardens and groves stretching out to the base of the mountains. It is a city of homes rather than of trade; and if ever the happy people there tire of its loveliness, there are romantic spots enough nearer the sea, for rest and change. There is Sancelito close by the Golden Gate, and other places within sound of the waves. Oakland has made itself comfortable with its macadamized streets, its different lines of horse and steam railroads; and ornamented itself with the State University, and the asylums for the deaf, the dumb and the blind. It is reaching out now for a harbor. It is proposed to construct one in San Antonio creek, which has a width of 300 yards and at its head two tide-water basins covering an area of 900 acres. Walls are to be built from the mouth of this creek to deep water, extending the creek out to ship channel, and avoiding the mud flat which now prevents ships from reaching Oakland. Such a harbor, nearly three miles long, with five miles of front, would be more commodious, secure and convenient of access than some harbors of considerable seaports in Europe. So we leave Oakland dreaming of the sea and the commerce that is coming, and wander down to the Santa Clara valley. Here we find ourselves surrounded by musical Spanish names and in the midst of orchards and groves and vineyards as old as the century. The town was laid out in about 1800, and still has many adobe houses. The long Alameda avenue extending three miles, lined with willow and cottonwood trees, is one of the charms of the town. And how can it be told what the humming of bees and the loaded fragrance of the air is, when 1,100 acres of fruit trees that surround the place are all in bloom?

Santa Clara is at the end of the Alameda avenue. Here is an old mission church, the Santa Clara Mission dating back as far as 1777. The church was built in a lovely laurel grove on the banks of Guadalupe creek. Ill fate pursued the mission, for the first building was swept away by a flood, and the new one which replaces it, an earthquake destroyed in 1818.

There is no better town in the southern part of California than Los Angeles, the town of the Queen of the Angels. Hittel, in describing it, says: "It was founded about 1780, and was a considerable town previous to the American conquest. The town is situated on the western bank of the Los

Angeles river, where that stream breaks through the range of low hills, twenty miles north of the bay of San Pedro. The streets are mostly of good width, but are not straight, do not cross each other at right angles, and are not graded or paved. All the old houses are adobes, and mostly one story, with flat roofs of asphaltum. The new houses are of wood or brick.

KNOB CAÑON.

On the northwestern side of the town, and very near to the most busy side of it, is a hill about sixty feet high, whence an excellent view of the whole town may be obtained. The vineyards and gardens are beautiful. There are 2,500 or 3,000 acres of brilliant green—the largest body of land in **vine**.

yard, orchard and garden in the State. The fences fix the attention of the
stranger. They are made of willow trees planted from nine inches to two
feet apart, the spaces between the trunks being filled with poles and brush.
After the fences the stranger's notice is attracted by the *aroyas* or irrigating
ditches which run through the town in every direction. These ditches vary
in size, but most of them have a body of water three feet wide and a foot
deep running through them at a speed of five miles an hour. They carry
the water from the river to the gardens, and are absolutely necessary to
secure the growth of the hedges, vines and fruit trees, at least when young.
One of the officers of the town is the Zarijero, whose duty it is to take care
of the entire system of irrigation. Entering the enclosures we are among
the vines, orange, lime, lemon, citron, pear, apple, peach, olive, fig and
walnut trees. Many of the vines are from ten to thirty years of age. The
population of the place may be described as consisting of three nearly
equal classes—Americans, Europeans, and Spanish Californians. The
Americans own most of the land and houses in the town; the Europeans do
most of the trade. The song of Mignon came vividly before me as I
walked through the gardens of the City of the Angels.

> "Knowst thou the land where the lemon trees bloom,
> Where the gold orange glows in the green thicket's gloom,
> Where the wind ever soft from the blue heaven blows,
> And groves are of myrtle and orange and rose?"

"Luscious fruits of many species and unnumbered varieties loaded the
trees. Gentle breezes came through the bowers. The water rippled
musically through many assequis. Delicious odors came from all the most
fragrant flowers of the temperate zone." The German writer, Froebel, in
writing of Los Angeles, says: "I could wish no better home for myself and
my friends than such a one as noble, sensible men could here make for
themselves. Nature has preserved here in its workings and phenomena
that medium between too much and too little, which was one of the great
conditions of high civilization in the classic regions of ancient times.
Indeed, when we seek in other lands for places like Los Angeles and
Southern California generally, we must turn our eyes to the Levant." Dr.
Hough, an oriental traveler, says of Los Angeles: "The general view of the
town from the Old Fort, more nearly resembles that of Damascus, the pearl
of the Orient, than any city I have elsewhere seen. The hills skirt it on
the north and west as the range of Anti-Lebanon does the eastern city;
while from them the eye sweeps over the same broad, brown plain in the
midst of which lies an island of verdure, with the city embowered in its
midst. True, there are no minarets rising from the modern town, and the
Los Angeles river is a poor substitute for the ancient Abana; nor are the
desert schooners, which take their departure for the Colorado river, much

like the caravans which leave for the Euphrates. But the vineyards have the same luxuriance, the pomegranates the same real blossom, and the orange trees the same ravishing beauty; while an occasional palm—stateliest of trees—gives a decidedly Oriental air to the scene. One misses the ocean view, and the mountains lie away on the horizon; the city itself is rather irregular, and has few fine buildings. The beauty is in the environs, where lovely cottages and lofty mansions peep out from amid bowers in which lemons and limes and apricots are mingled with oranges and walnuts and grapes."

CHICAGO LAKE.

It seems one might live forever in Los Angeles in content, but it is not the only town of California that rivals Southern France as a resort for invalids or pleasure seekers. It is suspected now that Florida is too warm, and Minnesota too cold for consumptives. California is becoming a rival to both.

The town of Santa Barbara, lying in latitude 34° 24' on the ocean shore, about forty miles east of Point Argüello, under the shelter of the Santa Inez ridge, which runs east and west, is at present highly in favor as a health resort. Dr. Logan, secretary of the State Board of Health, said of

VIEW OF COURT IN PALACE HOTEL, SAN FRANCISCO.

it: "Bounded on the north by the Coast range mountains, of an average height of 3,000 feet, which prove an insurmountable barrier to the peculiar harsh oceanic winds; and on the south by a channel formed by the Santa Cruz and other islands, some twenty miles distant, which serve as well to deflect the cold current that sweeps down from the Arctic seas as to afford protection from the concomitant cold fogs that roll in so uninterruptedly in other parts of the coast, this portion of California stands out pre-eminently, the land of promise to the weary, desponding invalid."

MOUNTAIN VIEW, COLORADO.

San Diego is a town on the borders of a fine bay. Its isolation is its chief disadvantage. When some railway pushes its way to tide water at this point, and settles definitely just where and how the town is to be built, then the era of "booms," new towns and new dead towns, will be passed.

To reach the Yosemite valley the railroad should be left at Madera, where all trains are met by first-class Concord coaches in charge of competent drivers. The distance to be traveled is about seventy-five miles each way, and a week should be devoted to the place, though less time may be made to answer.

Said Horace Greeley: "Of the sights I have enjoyed—Rome from the dome of St. Peter's—the Alps from the valley of lake Como—Mount Blanc

and her glaciers from Chamouny—Niagara—and the Yosemite—I judge
the last-named most unique and stupendous. It is a partially-wooded
gorge, 100 to 300 yards wide, and 3,000 to 4,000 feet deep, between almost
perpendicular walls of gray granite, and here and there a dark yellow pine
rooted in a crevice of either wall, and clinging with desperate tenacity to
its dizzy elevation. The isolation of the Yosemite—the absolute wilderness
of its sylvan solitudes, many miles from human settlement or cultivation—
its cascade 2,000 feet high, though the stream which makes this leap has
worn a channel in the hard bed-rock to a depth of 1,000 feet—renders it the
grandest marvel that ever met my gaze." Starr King said: "Nowhere
among the Alps, in no pass of the Andes, and in no cañon of the mighty
Oregon range, is there such stupendous rock scenery as the traveler now
lifts his eyes to." The Valley is 4,060 feet high where the Merced river
runs, and twelve or fifteen mountain peaks rise to a height of from 12,000
feet to 4,600 feet. At least a dozen cliffs are over 3,000 feet high, and of the
numerous cataracts one is 1,700 feet high. The Yosemite season lasts from
May until September. The provisions made for the comfort, safety and
convenience of visitors are ample. No one should fail to see the valley and
devote to it as much time as possible.

The big trees of Calaveras, the geysers of Sonoma, the petrified forest of
Calistoga, lake Tahoe, the Hetchhetchy valley, the charming resorts at
Santa Cruz and Monterey, the hydraulic mining regions, the beautiful
capital city, Sacramento, should enter into the tourist's experience.   At
Monterey, a few hours' ride from San Francisco by the Southern Pacific Railroad, northern division, the railroad company has prepared one of the most
charming resorts in America. A splendid hotel, standing in the midst of a
magnificent grove, within sound of the breaking waves and within reach
of the old mission of Monterey and a thousand beautiful resorts, is perhaps
the place of all others where a visitor may gain happy impressions of the
golden slope.

When California has been thoroughly "done," if one can voyage to
Oregon, Washington Territory and British Columbia, sail up the Columbia
river and cruise about Puget Sound, the sum of human happiness, so far as
traveling in America is concerned, will have been reached. The Oregon
Railway & Navigation Company and the Pacific Coast Steamship Company
are the carriers to be patronized.

HUNTING AND FISHING.

—

THE GAME BIRDS OF KANSAS — LARGE GAME IN NEW MEXICO — THE EARL
OF DUNRAVEN IN COLORADO — SHOOTING IN CALIFORNIA —
CAMP EQUIPAGES.

—

THE reputation of the great West rests, not only upon its wonderful agricultural resources, its mountains of precious minerals, its broad expanse of prairie and plateau, rich with nutritious grasses, upon which graze millions of sheep and cattle, but also upon the great attraction it offers to lovers of field sports. The great variety of game—birds, animals and fishes—found on the eastern slope of the Rocky mountains, among the foot-hills, on the mesas and along the valley of the great Arkansas river, has already attracted the attention of eminent naturalists and sportsmen in Great Britain and the Continent, as well as in our own land. And there are few, if any, other railway lines in the world along the line of which fur, fin and feather in such great variety and such vast numbers are found, as along the line of the Atchison, Topeka & Santa Fe Railroad and western connecting lines.

The pinnated grouse, or prairie chicken, affords the earliest shooting in autumn, breeding and rearing its young on every farm, prairie and slough from Topeka south to the Indian Territory, and west for 300 miles or more. They are found short distances from the towns, along the margin of the wheat stubbles or the ripening corn in coveys ranging in number from eight to twenty birds. The law permits their shooting from September 1st, and there can be no sport more enjoyable than to beat heather and stubble on a bright September day with a well-trained setter or pointer. A good shot usually gets all the birds he wants in a few hours, either morning or evening. A full grown cock-grouse will weigh about two and a half pounds. They are delicious as food and on account of their beautiful plumage are highly prized as ornithological specimens. Emporia, Florence, El Dorado, Winfield or Sterling are among the many favorable locations in Kansas for this charming sport.

The American quail or "Bob White" comes next in season. This acknowledged king of the partridge family, although found in nearly all the Eastern and Middle States, does not afford the shooting there that it has in earlier days. The increase of population, the advent of breech-loaders and trained dogs are death knells to pretty Bob White everywhere, excepting in

A VIEW NEAR SILVERTON.

a great State like Kansas, where there is "so much land to the acre" that our friend—so thoroughly protected by rigid game laws and the absence of deep snows and an arctic climate—will increase and multiply for generations to come. Never anywhere has there been so great a crop of quail as in Southern Kansas in 1881. The hunting season opens November 1st and closes January 1st, and from Topeka west and south they can be found by thousands. A good shot, with a well trained setter or pointer, can easily bag from forty to seventy-five quail in a day's tramp. The points mentioned as being good for prairie chicken shooting are equally good for quail shooting.

With the advent of fall weather, with its blizzards and frosts in the northwest, comes the wild fowl—not an occasional flock and of a few varieties but in countless thousands. They come early in November, feeding during the day in the prolific corn fields and on the growing winter wheat, and at night seek rest and water on the bosom of the beautiful Arkansas river and its many tributaries and neighboring lakelets. Of ducks we have the mallard, the widgeon, the wood-duck, the spring-tail, the canvas-back, the red-head, the blue-wing, the green-wing, the cinnamon teal and a dozen other minor vareities. Of the goose family we have the snow goose, (the most beautiful but not the largest of the family), the white-fronted and the Canadian goose. The vicinities of Nickerson, Sterling and Great Bend on the Arkansas are favorable for the shooting of wild fowl. The hotels, as a rule, charge three dollars per day, and good livery rigs cost from two dollars and a half to three dollars per day. Good shooting can be found within reasonable walking distance of the towns mentioned.

It is not practicable to enter into detail in the description of the resorts of the snipe, plover, curlew, squirrels, cotton-tails, jack-rabbits and the like, except to say that they abound everywhere where the land is suited to their tastes and habits.

Further west we come to the great plains in a great degree yet uncultivated. Here is the home of the buffalo, (so far as he now has a home on earth), the antelope and the broncho or wild horse. The antelope are numerous from Dodge City west to La Junta, and thence south throughout New Mexico, in bands ranging from five or six to thirty. To successfully hunt the antelope one must be willing to devote more than a day to it. We would advise going as far as Springer, New Mexico, only twenty-four hours' ride by rail from the locality for quail shooting. Mr. Robert Stepp, a merchant at Springer, will tell you what to do. The southern band of buffalo are in the "Pan-Handle" region of Texas. In New Mexico the enthusiastic sportsman can find adventure and big game—Virginia or red deer, black-tailed deer, elk, mountain sheep, grizzly bear, cinnamon bear, frosty or range bear, (a cross between the grizzly and the cinnamon, and the most ferocious of the tribe), the common black bear, wild turkey, mountain grouse, plumed quail, wild cat, mountain lion and mountain trout. All of these are found in large numbers—particularly the deer, wild turkey, bear and mountain lion. Mountain sheep or big-horn are never found in great numbers anywhere. A band of considerable size is said to exist on the top of "Old Baldy." Elk are found in great numbers in the Black Range, the wonderful new mining district in Southwestern New

Mexico. The black-tailed deer are abundant almost everywhere in the mountains.

As to where to go, among other good points or localities for a beginning are Trinidad, Raton, Cimarron, Glorietta pass, Albuquerque, the Cañons of the Red, the Canadian, the Cimarron and the Pecos rivers. The Maxwell

MOUNTAIN FALLS.

grant, covering a territory of nearly 2,000,000 of acres, embracing mountain and valley, offers shooting and fishing unsurpassed on the American continent. Sportsmen who are not market or hide hunters can always get permission to camp in the beautiful parks of the mountain ranges where they may shoot and fish to their hearts' content. The black-tailed deer go in bands and are always still-hunted. The grizzly and other bear are numerous enough to give one any amount of exciting adventure while a mountain lion is liable to drop in at any time, just to "encourage the game." Hunters should go armed with a good breech-loading shot gun, a repeating rifle, (the larger the bore and the heavier the charge of powder the better,) a Colt's forty-five calibre pistol, and a good hunting knife. For a camp outfit there should be a good wall tent, two pairs of heavy blankets for each man, and a frying pan and coffee pot. Buy provisions and hire burros and a guide, and stay in the mountains as long as possible between August and November. The results will be more than satisfactory.

In the valley of the Rio Grande river, from Albuquerque south, snipe and wood-cock are found in great numbers. Ducks and geese winter in this valley. The plumed quail, the Messena quail and the sage hen are abundant. The climate is perfectly charming. From first to last the scenery is of a varied and interesting character—changeable, grand, sublime. The naturalist will find many strange and varied birds, insects and a few reptiles, though the latter are comparatively scarce.

In California, for the sportsman's attention, there are chiefly the black-tailed deer, the California quail and fishing of many sorts. In all the mountain streams, not too near the centres of civilization, trout abound and may always be taken by the skillful angler.

In this connection the reader will enjoy the narrative published in the September (1880) number of the *Nineteenth Century*, by the Earl of Dunraven. The Earl gives in his article the following clever description of hunting in Colorado:

"It was sport—or, as it would be called in the States, hunting—that led me first to visit Estes Park. Some friends and I visited Denver at Christmas to pay our proper devotions to the good things of this earth at that festive season, and hearing rumors of much game at Estes Park, we determined to go there. We spent a day or two laying in supplies, purchasing many of the necessaries and a few of the luxuries of life, and wound up our sojourn in Denver with a very pleasant dinner at an excellent restaurant, not inaptly styled the "Delmonico" of the West. During dinner one of those sudden and violent storms peculiar to that region came on. When we sat down the stars were shining clear and hard with the brilliancy that is so beautiful in those high altiudes on a cold, dry, mid-winter night, and not a breath of wind disturbed the stillness of the air; but before we had half satisfied the appetites engendered by the keen, frosty atmosphere the stars were all shrouded in cloud, the gale was howling through the streets, and snow was whirling in the air, piling up in drifts wherever it found a lodgment, and sifting in fine powder through every chink and cranny in the door. It did not last long. Before morning the sky was clear, cloudless, steely, star-bespangled as before, and when we left by an early train for Longmont Station the sun was shining undimmed upon the fields of freshly-fallen snow.

The next morning we loaded up a wagon with stores, and started on our toilsome expedition to the Park. It is very easy work—it is not work at all, in fact—to get into the Park nowadays. It was a very different affair at that time. There are two good stage roads now; there was no road at all then—only a rough track going straight up hill and down dale, and over rocks and through trees, and along nearly perpendicular slopes, with the glorious determination to go straight forward of an old Roman road, but without any of the engineering skill and labor expended upon the latter. It was a hard road to travel, covered with snow, and slippery with ice; but by dint of literally putting our shoulders to the wheel up-hill, by chaining the wheels down-hill, and by holding up the wagon by ropes and main strength on precipitous hill-sides, we got to our destination very late at night, with only one serious accident—the fracture of a bottle containing medical comforts.

A log-house is comfortable enough at any time; and on that particular night it appeared eminently so to us, as, cold and wearied, we passed the hospitable threshold. What a supper we devoured, and what logs we heaped upon the fire, till we made the flames leap and roar on the open hearth and then lay down on mattresses on the floor, and listened to the howling of the wind, till the noise of the tempest, confusedly mingling with our dreams, was finally hushed in deep unbroken sleep

In spring and summer the scene and climate are very different. Ice and snow and withered grass have passed away, and everything is basking and glowing under a blazing sun, hot, but always tempered with a cool breeze. Cattle wander about the plain—or try to wander, for they are so fat they can scarcely move.

The whole earth is green, and the margins of the streams are luxuriant with a profuse growth of wild flowers and rich herbage. The air is scented with the sweet-smelling sap of the pines, whose branches welcome many feathered visitors from Southern climes; an occasional humming-bird whirs among the shrubs, trout leap in the creeks, insects buzz in the air; all nature is active and exuberant with life.

I and a Scotch gillie, who had accompanied me from home, took up our abode in a little log shanty close to the ranch-house, and made ourselves very cozy. There was not much elegance or luxury in our domicile, but plenty of comfort. Two rough rooms—a huge fire-place in one of them— two beds, and no other furniture of any kind whatever, completed our establishment. But what on earth did we want with furniture? We were up before daylight, out hunting or fishing all day, had our food at the ranch, sat on the ground and smoked our pipes, and went to bed early. One's rest is a good deal broken in winter time, and it is necessary to go to bed early in order to get enough sleep, because in very cold weather it is highly advisable to keep a fire burning all night; and, as yet, hunters have not evolved the faculty of putting on logs in their sleep. It would be most useful if they could do so; and, according to the law of evolution, some of them by this time ought to have done it. However, I was not much troubled; for Sandie, who slept by the fire, was very wakeful. I would generally awake about two or three in the morning to find the logs blazing and cracking merrily, and Sandie sitting in the ingle smoking his pipe, plunged in deep thought.

"Well, Sandie," I would say, "what kind of a night is it, and what are you thinking of?"

"Oh, well, it's a fine night, just a wee bit cheely outside," (thermometer about 25° below zero); "and I'm thinking we did not make that stalk after the big stag just right yesterday; and I'm thinking where we'll go to-day to find him." Then we would smoke a little—*haver* a little, as Sandie would call it—and discuss the vexed question of how we made the mistake with the big stag; and having come to a satisfactory conclusion, and agreed that the stag had the biggest antlers that ever were seen—which is always the case with the deer you *don't* get—would put out our pipes, and sleep till daylight warned us to set about our appointed task, which was to find a deer somehow, for the larder wanted replenishing.

In those days you had not far to seek for game, and you could scarcely go wrong in any direction at any season of the year. In winter and spring the park still swarms with game; but it is necessary in summer to know where to look for it, to understand its manners and customs, to go further and to work harder than formerly, for Estes Park is civilized. In summer time beautiful but dangerous creatures roam the park. The tracks of tiny little shoes are more frequent than the less interesting, but harmless, footprints of mountain sheep. You are more likely to catch a glimpse of the flicker of the hem of a white petticoat in the distance than of the glancing form of a deer. The marks of carriage wheels are more plentiful than elk signs, and you are not now so likely to be scared by the human-like track of a gigantic bear as by the appalling impress of a number eleven boot. That is as it should be. There is plenty of room elsewhere for wild beasts, and nature's beauties should be enjoyed by man. I well remember the commencement of civilization. I was sitting on the stoop of the log shanty one fine hot summer's evening, when to me appeared the strange apparition of an aged gentleman on a diminutive donkey. He was the first stranger I had ever seen in the park. After surveying me in silence for some moments, he observed, "Say, is this a pretty good place to drink whisky in?" I replied "Yes," naturally, for I have never heard of a spot that was not favorable for the consumption of whisky, the State of Maine not excepted. "Well, have you any to sell?" he continued. "No," I answered, "got none." After gazing at me in melancholy silence for some moments, evidently puzzled at the idea of a man and a house,

but no whisky, he went slowly and sadly on his way, and I saw him no
more.

On the morning that Sandie and I went out it was not necessary to go far
from the house. We had not ridden long before we came to likely-looking
country, got off, unsaddled and tethered our horses, and started on foot,
carefully scanning the ground for fresh sign. Soon we came upon it—
quite recently formed tracks of three or four deer. Then we had to decide
upon the plan of operations in a long and whispered conversation; and,
finally having settled where the deer were likely to be, and how to get at
them, we made a long circuit, so as to be down wind of the game, and went
to work. The ground to which I am referring is very rough. It slopes
precipitously toward the river. Huge masses of rock lie littered about on
a surface pierced by many perpendicular, jagged crags, hundreds of feet
high, and long ridges and spurs strike downward from the sheer scarp that
crowns the cañon of the river, forming beautiful little glades—sheltered,
sunny, clothed with sweet grass—on which the deer love to feed.

In such a country there is no chance of seeing game at any distance; so
we had to go very cautiously, examining every sign, crawling up to every
little ridge, and inch by inch craning our heads over and peering into every
bush and under every tree. In looking over a rise of ground it is advisable
for the hunter to take off his head-covering unless he wears a tight-fitting
cap. I have often laughed to see great hunters (great in their own esti-
mation) raising their heads most carefully, forgetting that a tall felt hat,
some six inches above the eyes, had already been for some time in view of
the deer. Many hunters seem to think that the deer cannot see them till
they see the deer.

The sportsman can not go too slowly, and it is better to hunt out one little
gully thoroughly, than to cover miles of ground in the day. If he walks
rapidly he will scare heaps of deer, hear lots of crashing in the trees and
scattering of stones, and perhaps see the whisk of a white tail, or the glance
of a dark form, through the trees, but never get a shot for his pains. We
pursued a different plan—took each little gulch separately, and carefully
crept up it, searching every inch of ground, using redoubled caution toward
the end where the bush is thickest, and especially scanning the north side;
for, strange to say, deer prefer lying on the north side of the valleys, in the
snow, even during the coldest weather, to resting on the warm, sunny grass
on the southern slopes. Patiently we worked; but our patience was not
well rewarded, for not a sign of anything did we see until our entirely
foodless stomachs and the nearly shadowless tree indicated that it was past
noon. So we sat us down in a nice little sheltered nook, from whence we
commanded a good view of the precipitous cliffs and gullies that led down
to the tortuous and ice-bound creek some thousands of feet below us, as
well as of the face of the mountain that reared itself on the opposite side,

and betook ourselves to food and reflection. It is very pleasant to lie comfortably stretched out with nothing to do but to gaze with idle pleasure and complete content upon grand and varied scenery. The eye, now plunging into the abyss of blue, crossed at intervals by swiftly-moving clouds, now lowered and resting on the earth, pauses for a minute on the dazzling, snow-white summits, then travels down through dark green pine woods, wanders over little open glades or valleys gray with withered grass, glances at steep cliffs and great riven masses of rock which time and weather have detached and hurled down the mountain side, and falls at last upon the pale green belt of aspens that fringes the river, white with snow where spanned with ice, but black as ink where a rapid torrent has defied the frost. Nor is the eye wearied with its journey; for mountain, valley, cliff and glade are so mingled, and are so constantly changing with light and shade, that one could look for hours without a wish to move. The mind goes half asleep, and wonders lazily whether its body is really there in the heart of of the Rocky mountains, leading a hunter's life, or whether it is not all a dream—a dream of school-boy days which seemed at one time so little likely to be realized, and yet which is at length fulfilled.

It must not be supposed that, because we were half asleep and wholly dreaming, we were not also keeping a sharp lookout; for in a man who is very much accustomed to take note of every unusual object, of every moving thing, and of the slightest sign of any living creature—more especially if he has roamed much on the prairies, where hostile redskins lurk and creep—the faculty of observation is so constantly exercised that it becomes a habit unconsciously used, and he is all the time seeing sights, and hearing sounds, and smelling smells, and noting them down, and receiving all kinds of impressions from all external objects, without being the least aware of it himself. However, none of our senses were gratified by anything that betokened the presence of game, and after resting a little while, we picked up our rifles and stole quietly on again. So we crept and hunted, and hunted and crept, and peered and whispered, and wondered we saw nothing, till the pine trees were casting long shadows to the east, when suddenly Sandie, who was a pace or two in front of me, became rigid, changed into a man of stone, and then, almost imperceptibly, a hair's-breadth at a time, stooped his head and sank down. If you come suddenly in sight of game you should remain perfectly motionless for a time, and sink out of sight gradually; for if you drop down quickly the movement will startle it. Deer seem to be short-sighted. They do not notice a man, even close by, unless he moves. I never saw a man so excited at the sight of game, and yet so quiet, as Sandie. It seemed as if he would fly to pieces; he seized my arm with a grip like a vise, and whispered, "Oh, a great stag within easy shot from the big rock yonder! He has not seen me!" So, prone upon the earth, I crawled up to the rock, cocked the

13

rifle, drew a long breath, raised myself into a sitting position, got a good sight on the deer, pulled, and had the satisfaction of seeing him tumbling headlong down the gulch, till he stopped stone dead, jammed between two trees.

Leaving Sandie to prepare the stag for transportation, I started off as fast as I could and brought one of the ponies down to the carcass. It was pretty bad going for a four-footed animal; but Colorado horses, if used in the mountains, will go almost anywhere. The way they will climb up places, and slither down places, and pick their way through "windfalls," is marvelous. They seem to be possessed of any number of feet, and to put them down always exactly at the right moment in the right place. I do not suppose they like it, for they groan and grunt the while in a most piteous manner. My pony was sure-footed and willing, and moreover, was used to pack game, so we had little trouble with him, and before long had the deer firmly secured on the saddle, and were well on our way home. It was well for us that we killed the deer in a comparatively accessible place, or we should not have got him in that night or next day. It was almost dark when we topped the ridge, and could look down into the park and see the range beyond, and there were plenty of signs there to show that a storm was at hand. Right overhead the stars were shining, but all the sky to the west was one huge wall of cloud. Black cañon, the cañon of the river, and all the great rents in the range were filled with vapor, and all the mountains were wrapped in cloud.

When we left the ranch that night, after a good supper, a game of euchre, and sundry pipes, it was pitch-dark, and light flakes of snow were noiselessly floating down to the earth; and when we got up the next morning, behold! there was not a thing to be seen. Mountains, ranch-house, and everything else were blotted out by a densely falling, white, bewildering mass of snow. Toward noon it lightened up a little, and great gray shapes of mountains loomed out now and then, a shade darker than the white wall that almost hid them; but the weather was not fit for hunting, and as there was nothing else to be done out-of-doors, we made a *fete* of it, as a French-Canadian would say, and devoted ourselves to gun-cleaning and spinning yarns."

THE MINING LAWS.

UNITED STATES MINING LAWS — REPEAL PROVISIONS — REGULATIONS
UNDER UNITED STATES LAWS — MINING LAWS OF COLORADO,
ARIZONA, AND NEW MEXICO.

THE mining laws of the United States are, of course, supreme in all the States and Territories, and any laws made by other corporate bodies must keep within those boundaries. A State or Territory can make its own laws, but not to conflict with a national law. All valuable mineral deposits of lands belonging to the United States are free and open to exploration and purchase, and the lands in which they are found, to occupation and purchase by citizens of the United States and those who have declared their intention to become such, under regulations prescribed by law and according to the local customs or rules of miners, so far as they are applicable and not inconsistent with the laws of the United States. A mining claim, whether located by one or more persons, may equal, but shall not exceed, one thousand five hundred feet in length along the vein or lode, and no claim shall extend over three hundred feet on each side of the middle of the vein on the surface, nor shall any claim be limited by any mining regulations to less than twenty five feet on each side of the middle of the vein on the surface. No location of a mining claim shall be made until the discovery of a vein or lode within the limits of the claim located. The locators, so long as they comply with the laws, and State, Territorial and local regulations, have the exclusive right of possession and enjoyment of all the surface included within the lines of their locations, and of all veins, lodes and ledges throughout their entire depth, the top or apex of which lies inside of such surface lines extended downward vertically, although such veins, lodes or ledges may so far depart from a perpendicular in their course downward as to extend outside the vertical side-lines of said surface locations; provided that their right of possession to such outside parts of such veins or ledges shall be confined to such portions thereof as lie between vertical planes drawn downward through the the end-lines of their locations, so continued in their own direction that they will intersect such exterior parts of said veins or ledges. Where a vein or lode is known to exist within the boundaries of a placer claim, an application for a patent, which does not include an application for the vein or lode claim, is construed as a conclusive declaration that the claimant of the placer claim has no right of possession of the vein or lode claim; but where the existence of a vein or lode in a placer claim is not known, a patent for the latter includes all valuable mineral or ore deposit within the boundaries thereof. Where two or more veins intersect, priority of title governs, and the prior location is entitled to all ore or mineral contained within the space of intersection. Where a tunnel is run for the development of a vein or lode, or for the discovery of mines, the owner of such tunnel has the right of possession of all veins or lodes within three thousand feet from the face of such tunnel or the line thereof, not previously known to exist and discovered in the tunnel, to the same extent as if discovered from the surface; and locations on the line of such a tunnel, of veins or lodes not appearing on the surface, made by other parties after the commencement of the tunnel, and while the same is being prosecuted with reasonable diligence, are invalid. Any three miners, in a part of the country which has not been districted, can form a mining district, and make such laws as the circumstances of the mineral and the district require. They can enact that the size of claims, located after the formation of the district, shall be less than six hundred by fifteen hundred feet, but they cannot reduce the width to less than twenty-five feet, nor can they alter the size of claims located prior to the formation of the district. When they form, they place on file in the county recorder's office, a description of the territory intended to be included in the district. Each claim must have $100 worth of work done on it every year to entitle the owner to its possession, and one man may hold as many claims as he can do on each $100 worth of work. This work is called the "assessment." The question as to whether the same man may take up more than one claim on the same vein is an unsettled one, and different views are held. As a matter of fact, men do take more than one claim on the same lode, and hold them. In New Mexico, Chief Justice Prince has decided, in the first judicial district, which includes the northern half of that Territory, that one man can not take more than one claim on the same vein; but that he can take one on each new vein that he discovers, and in that way he can have as many claims as he finds veins. The Supreme Court of the Territory has not yet been asked to pass on the question, and neither, of course, has the Supreme Court of the United States, so that the question is still undecided. In the second and third districts of New Mexico, the southern half of the Territory, the question has never been ruled on, and there men take as many extensions as they can perform their assessment work on. The reader will find it profitable to study the mining laws in detail, and therefore the laws and regulations of the United States, and also the laws of Colorado, New Mexico and Arizona, are given below in full:

UNITED STATES MINING LAWS.

TITLE XXXII., CHAPTER 6.

MINERAL LANDS RESERVED.

SECTION 2318. In all cases lands valuable for minerals shall be reserved from sale, except as otherwise expressly directed by law.

MINERAL LANDS OPEN TO PURCHASE BY CITIZENS.

SEC. 2319. All valuable mineral deposits in lands belonging to the United States, both surveyed and unsurveyed, are hereby declared to be free and open to exploration and purchase, and the lands in which they are found to occupation and purchase, by citizens of the United States and those who have declared their intention to become such, under regulations prescribed by law, and according to the local customs or rules of miners in the several mining districts, so far as the same are applicable and not inconsistent with the laws of the United States

LENGTH OF MINING-CLAIMS UPON VEINS OR LODES.

SEC. 2320. Mining-claims upon veins or lodes of quartz or other rock in place bearing gold, silver, cinnabar, lead, tin, copper, or other valuable deposits, heretofore located, shall be governed as to length along the vein or lode by the customs, regulations, and laws in force at the date of their location. A mining-claim located after the tenth day of May, eighteen hundred and seventy-two, whether located by one or more persons, may equal, but shall not exceed, one thousand five hundred feet in length along the vein or lode; but no location of a mining-claim shall be made until the discovery of the vein or lode within the limits of the claim located. No claim shall extend more than three hundred feet on each side of the middle of the vein at the surface, nor shall any claim be limited by any mining regulation to less than twenty-five feet on each side of the middle of the vein at the surface, except where adverse rights existing on the tenth day of May, eighteen hundred and seventy-two, render such limitation necessary. The end-lines of each claim shall be parallel to each other.

PROOF OF CITIZENSHIP.

SEC. 2321. Proof of citizenship, under this chapter, may consist, in the case of an individual of his own affidavit thereof; in the case of an association of persons unincorporated, of the affidavit of their authorized agent, made on his own knowledge, or upon information and belief; and in the case of a corporation organized under the laws of the United States, or of any State or Territory thereof, by the filing of a certified copy of their charter or certificate of incorporation.

LOCATOR'S RIGHTS OF POSSESSION AND ENJOYMENT.

SEC. 2322. The locators of all mining locations heretofore made, or which shall hereafter be made, on any mineral vein, lode, or ledge, situated on the public domain, their heirs and assigns, where no adverse claim exists on the tenth day of May, eighteen hundred and seventy-two, so long as they comply with the laws of the United States, and with State, Territorial and local regulations not in conflict with the laws of the United States governing their possessory title, shall have the exclusive right of possession and enjoyment of all the surface included within the lines of their locations, and of all veins, lodes and ledges throughout their entire depth, the top or apex of which lies inside of such surface-lines extended downward vertically, although such veins, lodes, or ledges may so far depart from a perpendicular in their course downward as to extend outside the vertical side-lines of such surface locations. But their right of possession to such outside parts of such veins or ledges should be confined to such portions thereof as lie between vertical planes drawn downward as above described, through the end-lines of their locations, so continued in their own direction that such planes will intersect such exterior parts of such veins or ledges. And nothing in this section shall authorize the locator or possessor of a vein or lode which extends in its downward course beyond the vertical lines of his claim to enter upon the surface of a claim owned or possessed by another.

RIGHTS OF OWNERS OF TUNNELS.

Sec. 2323. Where a tunnel is run for the development of a vein or lode, or for the discovery of mines, the owners of such tunnel shall have the right of possession of all veins or lodes within three thousand feet from the face of such tunnel on the line thereof, not previously known to exist, discovered in such tunnel, to the same extent as if discovered from the surface; and locations on the line of such tunnel or veins or lodes not appearing on the surface, made by other parties after the commencement of the tunnel, and while the same is being prosecuted with reasonable diligence, shall be invalid; but failure to prosecute the work on the tunnel for six months shall be considered as an abandonment of the right to all undiscovered veins on the line of such tunnel.

REGULATIONS MADE BY MINERS.

Sec. 2324. The miners of each mining district may make regulations not in conflict with the laws of the United States or with the laws of the State or Territory in which the district is situated, governing the location, manner of recording, amount of work necessary to hold possession of a mining-claim, subject to the following requirements: The location must be distinctly marked on the ground so that its boundaries can be readily traced. All records of mining-claims hereafter made shall contain the name or names of the locators, the date of the location, and such a description of the claim or claims located by reference to some natural object or permanent monument as will identify the claim. On each claim located after the tenth day of May, eighteen hundred and seventy-two, and until a patent has been issued therefor, not less than one hundred dollars' worth of labor shall be performed or improvements made during each year. On all claims located prior to the tenth day of May, eighteen hundred and seventy-two, ten dollars' worth of labor shall be performed or improvements made, by the tenth day of June, eighteen hundred and seventy-four, and each year thereafter, for each one hundred feet in length along the vein until a patent has been issued therefor; but where such claims are held in common, such expenditure may be made upon any one claim; and upon a failure to comply with these conditions, the claim or mine upon which such failure occurred shall be open to relocation in the same manner as if no location of the same had ever been made, provided that the original locators, their heirs, assigns, or legal representatives, have not resumed work upon the claim after failure and before such location. Upon the failure of any one of several co-owners, to contribute his proportion of the expenditures required hereby, the co-owners who have performed the labor or made the improvements may, at the expiration of the year, give such delinquent co-owner personal notice in writing, or notice by publication in the newspaper published nearest the claim, for at least once a week for ninety days, and if at the expiration of ninety days after such notice in writing or by publication such delinquent should fail or refuse to contribute his proportion of the expenditure required by this section, his interest in the claim shall become the property of his co-owners who have made the required expenditures. *Provided,* that the period within which the work required to be done annually on all unpatented mineral claims shall commence the first day of January succeeding the date of location of such claim, and this section shall apply to all claims located since the tenth day of May, A. D. eighteen hundred and seventy-two.

PATENTS FOR MINERAL LANDS, HOW OBTAINED.

SEC. 2325. A patent for any land claimed and located for valuable deposits may be obtained in the following manner: Any person, association, or corporation authorized to locate a claim under this chapter, having claimed and located a piece of land for such purposes, who has, or have, complied with the terms of this chapter, may file in the proper land office an application for a patent, under oath, showing such compliance, together with a plat and field-notes of the claim or claims in common, made by or under the direction of the United States surveyor-general, showing accurately the boundaries of the claim or claims, which shall be distinctly marked by monuments on the ground, and shall post a copy of such plat, together with a notice of such application for a patent, in a conspicuous place on the land embraced in such plat previous to the filing of the application for a patent, and shall file an affidavit of at least two persons that such notice has been duly posted, and shall file a copy of the notice in such land-office, and shall thereupon be entitled to a patent for the land, in the manner following: The register of the land-office, upon the filing of such application, plat, field-notes, notices, and affidavits, shall publish a notice that such application has been made, for the period of sixty days, in a newspaper to be by him designated as published nearest to such claim; and he shall also post such notice in his office for the same period. The claimant at the time of filing this application, or at any time thereafter, within the sixty days of publication, shall file with the register a certificate of the United States surveyor-general that five hundred dollars' worth of labor has been expended or improvements made, upon the claim by himself or grantors; that the plat is correct, with such further description by such reference to natural objects or permanent monuments as shall identify the claim, and furnish an accurate description, to be incorporated in the patent. At the expiration of the sixty days of publication the claimant shall file his affidavit, showing that the plat and notice have been posted in a conspicuous place on the claim during such period of publication. If no adverse claim shall have been filed with the register and the receiver of the proper land-office at the expiration of the sixty days of publication, it shall be assumed that the applicant is entitled to a patent, upon the payment to the proper officer of five dollars per acre, and that no adverse claim exists; and thereafter no objection from third parties to the issuance of a patent shall be heard, except it be shown that the applicant has failed to comply with the terms of this chapter. *Provided*, that where the claimant of a patent is not a resident of or within the land district wherein the vein, lode, ledge, or deposit sought to be patented is located, the application for patent and the affidavits required to be made in this section by the claimant for such patent may be made by his, her or its authorized agent, where said agent is conversant with the facts sought to be established by said affidavits: And *provided*, that this section shall apply to all applications now pending for patents to mineral lands.

ADVERSE CLAIM, PROCEEDINGS ON.

SEC. 2326. Where an adverse claim is filed during the period of publication, it shall be upon oath of the person or persons making the same, and shall show the nature, boundaries, and extent of such adverse claim, and all proceedings, except the publication of notice and making and filing of the affidavit thereof, shall be stayed until the controversy shall have been settled or decided by a court of competent jurisdiction, or the adverse claim waived. It shall be the duty of the adverse claimant, within thirty days after filing his claim, to commence proceedings in a court of competent jurisdiction, to determine the question of the right of possession, and prosecute the same with reasonable diligence to final judgment; and a failure so to do shall be a waiver of his adverse claim. After such judgment shall have been rendered, the party entitled to the possession of the claim, or any portion thereof, may, without giving further notice, file a certified copy of the judgment-roll with the register of the land-office, together with the certificate of the surveyor-general that the requisite amount of labor has been expended or improvements made thereon, and the description required in other cases, and shall pay to the receiver five dollars per acre for his claim, together with the proper fees, whereupon the whole proceedings and the judgment-roll shall be certified by the register to the commissioner of the general land-office, and a patent shall issue thereon for the claim, or such portion thereof as the applicant shall appear, from the decision of the court, to rightly possess. If it appears from the decision of the court that several parties are entitled to separate and different portions of the claim, each party may pay for his portion of the claim, with the proper fees, and file the certificate and description by the surveyor-general, whereupon the register shall certify the proceedings and judgment-roll to the commissioner of the general land-office, as in the preceding case, and patents shall issue to the several parties according to their respective rights. Nothing herein contained shall be construed to prevent the alienation of the title conveyed by a patent for a mining-claim to any person whatever.

DESCRIPTION OF VEIN-CLAIMS ON SURVEYED AND UNSURVEYED LANDS.

SEC. 2327. The description of vein or lode claims, upon surveyed lands, shall designate the location of the claim with reference to the lines of the public surveys, but need not conform therewith; but where a patent shall be issued for claims upon unsurveyed lands, the surveyor-general, in extending the surveys, shall adjust the same to the boundaries of such patented claim, according to the plat or description thereof, but so as in no case to interfere with or change the location of any such patented claim.

PENDING APPLICATIONS—EXISTING RIGHTS.

SEC. 2328. Applications for patents for mining-claims under former laws now pending may be prosecuted to a final decision in the general land-office; but in such cases, where adverse rights are not affected thereby, patents may issue in pursuance of the provisions of this chapter; and all patents for mining-claims upon veins or lodes heretofore issued shall convey all the rights and privileges conferred by this chapter where no adverse rights existed on the tenth day of May, eighteen hundred and seventy-two.

CONFORMITY OF PLACER-CLAIMS TO SURVEYS, LIMIT OF.

SEC. 2329. Claims usually called "placers," including all forms of deposit, excepting veins of quartz or other rock in place, shall be subject to entry and patent, under like circumstances and conditions, and upon similar proceedings, as are provided for vein or lode claims; but where the lands have been previously surveyed by the United States, the entry in its exterior limits shall conform to the legal subdivisions of the public lands.

SUBDIVISIONS OF TEN-ACRE TRACTS—MAXIMUM OF PLACER LOCATIONS.

SEC. 2330. Legal subdivisions of forty acres may be subdivided into ten-acre tracts; and two or more persons, or associations of persons, having contiguous claims of any size, although such claims may be less than ten acres each, may make joint entry thereof; but no location of a placer-claim, made after the ninth day of July, eighteen hundred and seventy, shall exceed one hundred and sixty acres for any one person or association of persons, which location shall conform to the United States surveys; and nothing in this section contained shall defeat or impair any bona fide pre-emption or homestead claim upon agricultural lands, or authorize the sale of the improvements of any bona fide settler to any purchaser.

CONFORMITY OF PLACER-CLAIMS TO SURVEYS—LIMITATION OF CLAIMS.

SEC. 2331. Where placer-claims are upon surveyed lands, and conform to legal subdivisions, no further survey or plat shall be required, and all placer-mining claims located after the tenth day of May, eighteen hundred and seventy-two, shall conform as near as practicable with the United States system of public-land surveys, and the rectangular subdivisions of such surveys, and no location shall include more than twenty acres for each individual claimant; but where placer-claims can not be conformed to legal subdivisions, survey and plat shall be made as on unsurveyed lands ; and where by the segregation of mineral lands in any legal subdivision a quantity of agricultural land less than forty acres remains, such fractional portion of agricultural land may be entered, by any party qualified by law, for homestead or pre-emption purposes.

WHAT EVIDENCE OF POSSESSION, ETC., TO ESTABLISH RIGHT TO A PATENT.

SEC. 2332. Where such person or association, they and their grantors, have held and worked their claims for a period equal to the time prescribed by the statute of limitations for mining-claims of the State or Territory where the same may be situated, evidence of such possession and working of the claims for such period shall be sufficient to establish a right to a patent thereto under this chapter, in the absence of any adverse claim; but nothing in this chapter shall be deemed to impair any lien which may have attached in any way whatever to any mining-claim or property thereto attached prior to the issuance of a patent.

PROCEEDINGS FOR PATENT FOR PLACER-CLAIM, ETC.

SEC. 2333. Where the same person, association, or corporation is in possession of a placer-claim, and also a vein or lode included within the boundaries thereof, application shall be made for a patent for the placer-claim, with the statement that it includes such vein or lode, and in such case a patent shall issue for the placer-claim, subject to the provisions of this chapter, including such vein or lode, upon the payment of five dollars per acre for such vein or lode claim, and twenty-five feet of surface on each side thereof. The remainder of the placer-claim, or any placer-claim not embracing any vein or lode claim, shall be paid for at the rate of two dollars and fifty cents per acre, together with all costs of proceedings; and when a vein or lode, such as is described in section twenty-three hundred and twenty, is known to exist within the boundaries of a placer-claim, an application for a patent for such placer-claim which does not include an application for the vein or lode claim shall be construed as a conclusive declaration that the claimant of the placer-claim has no right of possession of the vein or lode claim; but where the existence of a vein or lode in a placer-claim is not known, a patent for the placer-claim shall convey all valuable mineral and other deposits within the boundaries thereof.

SURVEYOR-GENERAL TO APPOINT SURVEYORS OF MINING-CLAIMS, ETC.

SEC. 2334. The surveyor-general of the United States may appoint in each land-district containing mineral lands as many competent surveyors as shall apply for appointment to survey mining-claims. The expenses of the survey of vein or lode claims, and the survey and subdivision of placer-claims into smaller quantities than one hundred and sixty acres, together with the cost of publication of notices, shall be paid by the applicants, and they shall be at liberty to obtain the same at the most reasonable rates, and they shall also be at liberty to employ any United States deputy surveyor to make the survey. The commissioner of the general land-office shall also have power to establish the maximum charges for surveys and publication of notices under this chapter; and, in case of excessive charges for publication, he may designate any newspaper published in a land-district where mines are situated for the publication of mining-notices in such district, and fix the rates to be charged by such paper; and, to the end that the commissioner may be fully informed on the subject, each applicant shall file with the register a sworn statement of all charges and fees paid by such applicant for publication and surveys, together with all fees and money paid the register and the receiver of the land-office, which statement shall be transmitted, with the other papers in the case, to the commissioner of the general land-office.

VERIFICATION OF AFFIDAVITS, ETC.

Sec. 2335. All affidavits required to be made under this chapter may be verified before any officer authorized to administer oaths within the land-district where the claims may be situated, and all testimony and proofs may be taken before any such officer, and, when duly certified by the officer taking the same, shall have the same force and effect as if taken before the register and receiver of the land-office. In cases of contest as to the mineral or agricultural character of the land, the testimony and proofs may be taken as herein provided on personal notice of at least ten days to the opposing party; or if such party can not be found, then by publication of at least once a week for thirty days in a newspaper, to be designated by the register of the land-office as published nearest to the location of such land; and the register shall require proof that such notice has been given.

WHERE VEINS INTERSECT, ETC.

Sec. 2336. Where two or more veins intersect or cross each other, priority of title shall govern; and such prior location shall be entitled to all ore or mineral contained within the space of intersection; but the subsequent location shall have the right of way through the space of intersection for the purposes of the convenient working of the mine. And where two or more veins unite, the oldest or prior location shall take the vein below the point of union, including all the space of intersection.

PATENTS FOR NON-MINERAL LANDS, ETC.

Sec. 2337. Where non-mineral land not contiguous to the vein or lode is used or occupied by the proprietor of such vein or lode for mining or milling purposes, such non-adjacent surface-ground may be embraced and included in an application for a patent for such vein or lode, and the same may be patented therewith, subject to the same preliminary requirements as to survey and notice as are applicable to veins or lodes; but no location hereafter made of such non-adjacent land shall exceed five acres, and payment for the same must be made at the same rate as fixed by this chapter for the superficies of the lode. The owner of a quartz-mill or reduction-works, not owning a mine in connection therewith, may also receive a patent for his mill-site, as provided in this section.

WHAT CONDITIONS OF SALE MAY BE MADE BY LOCAL LEGISLATURE.

Sec. 2338. As a condition of sale, in the absence of necessary legislation by congress, the local legislature of any State or Territory may provide rules for working mines, involving easements, drainage, and other necessary means to their complete development; and those conditions shall be fully expressed in the patent.

VESTED RIGHTS TO USE OF WATER FOR MINING, ETC.—RIGHT OF WAY FOR CANALS.

Sec. 2339. Whenever, by priority of possession, rights to the use of water for mining, agricultural, manufacturing, or other purposes, have vested and accrued, and the same are recognized and acknowledged by the local customs, laws, and the decisions of courts, the possessors and owners of such vested rights shall be maintained and protected in the same; and the right of way for the construction of ditches and canals for the purposes herein specified is acknowledged and confirmed; but whenever any person, in the construction of any ditch or canal, injures or damages the possession of any settler on the public domain, the party committing such injury or damage shall be liable to the party injured for such injury or damage.

PATENTS, PRE-EMPTIONS, AND HOMESTEADS SUBJECT TO VESTED AND ACCRUED WATER-RIGHTS.

Sec. 2340. All patents granted, or pre-emption or homesteads allowed, shall be subject to any vested and accrued water-rights, or rights to ditches and reservoirs used in connection with such water-rights, as may have been acquired under or recognized by the preceding section.

MINERAL LANDS IN WHICH NO VALUABLE MINES ARE DISCOVERED, OPEN TO HOMESTEADS.

Sec. 2341. Wherever, upon the lands heretofore designated as mineral lands, which have been excluded from survey and sale, there have been homesteads made by citizens of the United States, or persons who have declared their intention to become citizens, which homesteads have been made, improved, and used for agricultural purposes, and upon which there have been no valuable mines of gold, silver, cinnabar, or copper discovered, and which are properly agricultural lands, the settlers or owners of such homesteads shall have a right of pre-emption thereto, and shall be entitled to purchase the same at the price of one dollar and twenty-five cents per acre, and in quantity not to exceed one hundred and sixty acres; or they may avail themselves of the provisions of chapter five of this title, relating to "HOMESTEADS."

MINERAL LANDS—HOW SET APART AS AGRICULTURAL LANDS.

Sec. 2342. Upon the survey of the lands described in the preceding section, the secretary of the Interior may designate and set apart such portions of the same as are clearly agricultural lands, which lands shall thereafter be subject to pre-emption and sale as other public lands, and be subject to all the laws and regulations applicable to the same.

ADDITIONAL LAND-DISTRICTS AND OFFICERS—POWER OF THE PRESIDENT TO PROVIDE.

Sec. 2343. The president is authorized to establish additional land-districts, and to appoint the necessary officers under existing laws, wherever he may deem the same necessary for the public convenience in executing the provisions of this chapter.

PROVISIONS OF THIS CHAPTER NOT TO AFFECT CERTAIN RIGHTS.

Sec. 2344. Nothing contained in this chapter shall be construed to impair, in any way, rights or interests in mining property acquired under existing laws; nor to affect the provisions of the act entitled "An act granting to A. Sutro the right of way and other privileges to aid in the construction of a draining and exploring tunnel to the Comstock lode, in the State of Nevada," approved July 25th, eighteen hundred and sixty-six.

MINERAL LANDS IN CERTAIN STATES EXCEPTED.

Sec. 2345. The provisions of the preceding sections of this chapter shall not apply to the mineral lands situated in the States of Michigan, Wisconsin, and Minnesota, which are declared free and open to exploration and purchase, according to legal subdivisions, in like manner as before the tenth day of May, eighteen hundred and seventy-two. And any *bona fide* entries of such lands within the States named since the tenth of May, eighteen hundred and seventy-two, may be patented without reference to any of the foregoing provisions of this chapter. Such lands shall be offered for public sale in the same manner, at the same minimum price, and under the same rights of pre-emption as other public lands.

GRANTS OF LANDS TO STATES OR CORPORATIONS NOT TO INCLUDE MINERAL LANDS.

Sec. 2346. No act passed at the first session of the thirty-eighth congress, granting lands to States or corporations to aid in the construction of roads, or for other purposes, or to extend the time of grants made prior to the thirtieth day of January, eighteen hundred and sixty-five, shall be so construed as to embrace mineral lands, which in all cases are reserved exclusively to the United States, unless otherwise specially provided in the act or acts making the grant.

REPEAL PROVISIONS.

TITLE LXXIV.

WHAT REVISED STATUTES EMBRACE.

Sec. 5595. The foregoing seventy-three titles embrace the statutes of the United States general and permanent in their nature, in force on the first day of December, one thousand eight hundred and seventy-three, as revised and consolidated by commissioners appointed under an act of congress, and the same shall be designated and cited as the revised statutes of the United States.

REPEAL OF ACTS EMBRACED IN REVISION.

Sec. 5596. All acts of congress passed prior to said first day of December, one thousand eight hundred and seventy-three, any portion of which is embraced in any section of said revision, are hereby repealed, and the section applicable thereto shall be in force in lieu thereof; all parts of such acts not contained in such revision, having been repealed or superseded by subsequent acts, or not being general and permanent in their nature: *Provided*, That the incorporation into such revision of any general and permanent provision, taken from an act making appropriations, or from an act containing other provisions of a private, local, or temporary character, shall not repeal, or in any way affect any appropriation, or any provision of a private, local, or temporary character, contained in any of said acts, but the same shall remain in force; and all acts of congress passed prior to said last-named day no part of which are embraced in said revision, shall not be affected or changed by its enactments.

ACCRUED RIGHTS RESERVED.

Sec. 5597. The repeal of the several acts embraced in said revision, shall not affect any act done, or any right accruing or accrued, or any suit or proceeding had or commenced in any civil cause before the said repeal, but all rights and liabilities under said acts shall continue, and may be enforced in the same manner, as if said repeal had not been made: nor shall said repeal, in any manner affect the right to any office, or change the term or tenure thereof.

PROSECUTIONS AND PUNISHMENTS.

Sec. 5598. All offenses committed, and all penalties or forfeitures incurred under any statute embraced in said revision prior to said repeal, may be prosecuted and punished in the same manner and with the same effect, as if said repeal had not been made.

ACTS OF LIMITATION.

Sec. 5599. All acts of limitation, whether applicable to civil causes and proceedings, or to the prosecution of offenses, or for the recovery of penalties or forfeitures, embraced in said revision and covered by said repeal, shall not be affected thereby, but all suits, proceedings or prosecutions, whether civil or criminal, for causes arising, or acts done or committed prior to said repeal, may be commenced and prosecuted within the same time as if said repeal had not been made.

ARRANGEMENT AND CLASSIFICATION OF SECTIONS.

Sec. 5600. The arrangement and classification of the several sections of the revision have been made for the purpose of a more convenient and orderly arrangement of the same, and therefore no inference or presumption of a legislative construction is to be drawn by reason of the title under which any particular section is placed.

ACTS PASSED SINCE DECEMBER 1, 1873, NOT AFFECTED.

Sec. 5601. The enactment of the said revision is not to affect or repeal any act of congress passed since the first day of December, one thousand eight hundred and seventy-

three, and all acts passed since that date are to have full effect as if passed after the enactment of this revision, and so far as such acts vary from, or conflict with any provision contained in said revision, they are to have effect as subsequent statutes, and as repealing any
portion of the revision inconsistent therewith.

Approved June 22, 1874.

The following is an act of congress approved June 6, 1874:

AN ACT to amend the act entitled "An act to promote the development of the mining
resources of the United States," passed May tenth, eighteen hundred and seventy-two.

*Be it enacted by the Senate and House of Representatives of the United States of
America in congress assembled*, That the provisions of the fifth section of the act entitled
"An act to promote the development of the mining resources of the United States," passed
May tenth, eighteen hundred and seventy-two, which requires expenditures of labor and
improvements on claims located prior to the passage of said act, are hereby so amended
that the time for the first annual expenditure on claims located prior to the passage of
said act shall be extended to the first day of January, eighteen hundred and seventy-five.

The following is an act of congress approved February 11, 1875:

AN ACT to amend section two thousand three hundred and twenty-four of the revised
statutes, relating to the development of the mining resources of the United States.

*Be it enacted by the Senate and House of Representatives of the United States of
America in congress assembled*, That section two thousand three hundred and twenty-
four of the revised statutes be, and the same is hereby amended so that where a person or
company has or may run a tunnel for the purpose of developing a lode or lodes, owned by
said person or company, the money so expended in said tunnel shall be taken and considered as expended on said lode or lodes, whether located prior to or since the passage of
said act, and such person or company shall not be required to perform work on the surface of said lode or lodes in order to hold the same as required by said act.

The following is an act of congress approved May 5, 1876:

AN ACT to exclude the States of Missouri and Kansas from the provisions of the act of
congress entitled "An act to promote the development of the mining resources of the
United States," approved May tenth, eighteen hundred and seventy-two.

*Be it enacted by the Senate and House of Representatives of the United States of America
in congress assembled*, That within the States of Missouri and Kansas deposits of coal,
iron, lead, or other mineral be, and they are hereby, excluded from the operation of the act
entitled "An act to promote the development of the mining resources of the United
States," approved May tenth, eighteen hundred and seventy-two, and all lands in said
States shall be subject to disposal as agricultural lands.

AN ACT authorizing the citizens of Colorado, Nevada, and the Territories to fell and remove timber on the public domain for mining and domestic purposes.

*Be it enacted by the Senate and House of Representatives of the United States of Amer-
ica in congress assembled*, That all citizens of the United States and other persons, *bona
fide* residents of the State of Colorado or Nevada, or either of the Territories of New Mex-
co, Arizona, Utah, Wyoming, Dakota, Idaho, or Montana, and all other mineral districts
of the United States, shall be, and are hereby, authorized and permitted to fell and remove,
for building, agricultural, mining or other domestic purposes, any timber or other trees
growing or being on the public lands, said lands being mineral, and not subject to entry
under existing laws of the United States, except for mineral entry, in either of said States,
Territories or districts of which such citizens or persons may at the time be *bona fide* residents, subject to such rules and regulations as the secretary of the interior may prescribe

for the protection of the timber and of the undergrowth growing upon such lands, and for
other purposes: *Provided*, The provisions of this act shall not extend to railroad corporations.

SEC. 2. That it shall be the duty of the register and the receiver of any local land-office
in whose district any mineral land may be situated to ascertain from time to time whether
any timber is being cut or used upon any such lands, except for the purposes authorized
by this act, within their respective land districts; and, if so, they shall immediately notify
the commissioner of the general land-office of that fact; and all necessary expenses
incurred in making such proper examinations shall be paid and allowed such register and
receiver in making up their next quarterly accounts.

SEC. 3. Any person or persons who shall violate the provisions of this act, or any
rules and regulations in pursuance thereof made by the secretary of the interior, shall be
deemed guilty of a misdemeanor, and upon conviction shall be fined in any sum not
exceeding five hundred dollars, and to which may be added imprisonment for any term not
exceeding six months.

Approved June 3, 1878.

REGULATIONS UNDER UNITED STATES LAWS.

MINERAL LANDS OPEN TO EXPLORATION, OCCUPATION, AND PURCHASE.

1. It will be perceived that, by the foregoing provisions of law the mineral lands in
the public domain, surveyed or unsurveyed, are open to exploration, occupation, and purchase, by all citizens of the United States and all those who have declared their intention
to become such.

STATUS OF LODE-CLAIMS LOCATED PRIOR TO MAY 10, 1872.

2. By an examination of the several sections of the revised statutes it will be seen
that the *status* of lode-claims located *previous* to the tenth of May, 1872, is not changed
with regard to their *extent along the lode or width of surface*.

3. Mining rights acquired under such previous locations are, however, enlarged by said
revised statutes in the following respect, viz.: The locators of all such previously taken
veins or lodes, their heirs and assigns, so long as they comply with the laws of congress
and with State, Territorial, or local regulations not in conflict therewith, governing
mining-claims, are invested with the exclusive possessory right of all the surface included
within the lines of their locations, and of all veins, lodes, or ledges, throughout their entire
depth, the top or apex of which lies inside of such surface-lines extended downward vertically, although such veins, lodes, or ledges may so far depart from a perpendicular in
their course downward as to extend outside the vertical side-lines of such locations at the
surface, it being expressly provided, however, that the right of possession to such outside
parts of said veins or ledges shall be confined to such portions thereof as lie between
vertical planes drawn downward as aforesaid, through the end-lines of their locations, so
continued in their own direction that such planes will intersect such exterior parts of
such veins, lodes, or ledges; no right being granted, however, to the claimant of such
outside portion of a vein or ledge to enter upon the surface location of another claimant.

4. It is to be distinctly understood, however, that the law limits the possessory right
to veins, lodes, or ledges, *other* than the one named in the original location, to such as
were not *adversely claimed on May 10, 1872*, and that where such other vein or ledge was
so adversely claimed at that date, the right of the party so adversely claiming is in no
way impaired by the provisions of the revised statutes.

5. In order to hold the possessory title to a mining-claim located prior to May 10, 1872,
and for which a patent has not been issued, the law requires that *ten dollars* shall be
expended annually in labor or improvements on each claim of *one hundred feet* on the

course of the vein or lode until a patent shall have been issued therefor; but where a number of such claims are held in common upon the same vein or lode the aggregate expenditure that would be necessary to hold all the claims, at the rate of ten dollars per one hundred feet, may be made upon any one claim; a failure to comply with this requirement in any one year subjecting the claim upon which such failure occurred to relocation by other parties, the same as if no previous location thereof had ever been made, unless the claimants under the original location shall have resumed work thereon after such failure and before such relocation. The first annual expenditure upon claims of this class should have been performed subsequent to May 10, 1872, and prior to January 1, 1875. From and after January 1, 1875, the required amount must be expended *annually* until patent issues. By decision of the honorable secretary of the interior, dated March 4, 1879, such annual expenditures are not required subsequent to entry, the date of issuing the patent certificate being the date contemplated by the statute.

6. Upon the failure of any one of several co-owners of a vein, lode, or ledge, which has not been entered, to contribute his proportion of the expenditures necessary to hold the claim or claims so held in ownership in common, the co-owners who have performed the labor, or made the improvements, as required by said revised statutes, may, at the expiration of the year, give such delinquent co-owner personal notice in writing, or notice by publication in the newspaper published nearest the claim, for at least once a week for ninety days; and if upon the expiration of ninety days after such notice in writing, or upon the expiration of one hundred and eighty days after the first newspaper publication of notice, the delinquent co-owner shall have failed to contribute his proportion to meet such expenditure or improvements, his interest in the claim by law passes to his co-owners, who have made the expenditures or improvements as aforesaid.

PATENTS FOR VEINS OR LODES HERETOFORE ISSUED.

7. Rights under patents for veins or lodes heretofore granted under previous legislation of congress are enlarged by the revised statutes so as to invest the patentee, his heirs or assigns, with title to all veins, lodes, or ledges, throughout their entire depth, the top or apex of which lies within the end and side boundary-lines of his claim on the surface, as patented, extended downward vertically, although such veins, lodes, or ledges may so far depart from a perpendicular in their course downward as to extend outside the vertical side-lines of the claim at the surface. The right of possession to such outside parts of such veins or ledges to be confined to such portions thereof as lie between vertical planes drawn downward through the end-lines of the claims at the surface, so continued in their own direction that such planes will intersect such exterior parts of such veins or ledges, it being expressly provided, however, that all veins, lodes, or ledges, the top or apex of which lies inside such surface locations, *other* than the one named in the patent, which were *adversely claimed on the* 10th *day of May*, 1872, are excluded from such conveyance by patent.

8. Applications for patents for mining-claims pending at the date of the act of May 10, 1872, may be prosecuted to final decision in the general land-office, and where no adverse rights are affected thereby, patents will be issued in pursuance of the provisions of the revised statutes.

MANNER OF LOCATING CLAIMS ON VEINS OR LODES AFTER MAY 10, 1872.

9. From and after the 10th of May, 1872, any person who is a citizen of the United States or who has declared his intention to become a citizen, may locate, record, and hold a mining-claim, *of fifteen hundred linear feet* along the course of any mineral vein or lode subject to location; or an association of persons, severally qualified as above, may make joint location of such claim *of fifteen hundred feet*, but in no event can a location of a vein or lode made subsequent to May 10, 1872, exceed fifteen hundred feet along the course thereof, whatever may be the number of persons composing the association.

10. With regard to the extent of surface-ground adjoining a vein or lode, and claimed for the convenient working thereof, the revised statutes provide that the lateral extent of locations of veins or lodes made after May 10, 1875, shall in no case *exceed three hundred feet on each side of the middle of the vein at the surface,* and that no such surface-rights shall be limited by any mining regulations to less than twenty-five feet one each side of the middle of the vein at the surface, except where adverse rights existing on the 10th of May, 1872, may render such limitation necessary; the end-lines of such claims to be in all cases parallel to each other. Said lateral measurements can not extend beyond three hundred feet on *either* side of the middle of the vein at the surface, or such distance as is allowed by local laws. For example: four hundred feet can not be taken on one side and two hundred feet on the other. If, however, three hundred feet on each side are allowed, and by reason of prior claims but one hundred feet can be taken on one side, the locator will not be restricted to less than three hundred feet on the other side; and when the locator does not determine by exploration *where* the middle of the vein at the surface is, his discovery shaft must be assumed to mark such point.

11. By the foregoing it will be perceived that no lole-claim located after the 10th of May, 1872, can exceed a parallelogram fifteen hundred feet in length by six hundred feet in width, but whether surface-ground of that width can be taken, depends upon the local regulations or State or Territorial laws, in force in the several mining districts; and that no such local regulations or State or Territorial laws shall limit a vein or lode claim to less than fifteen hundred feet along the course thereof, whether the location is made by one or more persons, nor can surface-rights be limited to less than fifty feet in width, unless adverse claims existing on the 10th day of May, 1872, render such lateral limitation necessary.

12. It is provided by the revised statutes that the miners of each district may make rules and regulations not in conflict with the laws of the United States, or of the State or Territory in which such districts are respectively situated, governing the location, manner of recording, and amount of work necessary to hold possession of a claim. They likewise require that the location shall be so distinctly marked on the ground that its boundaries may be readily traced. This is a very important matter, and locators can not exercise too much care in defining their locations at the outset, inasmuch as the law requires that all records of mining locations made subsequent to May 10, 1872, shall contain the name or names of the locators, the date of the location, and such a *description of the claim or claims* located, by reference to some natural object or permanent monument, as will identify the claim.

13. The statutes provide that no lode-claim shall be recorded until after the discovery of a vein or lode within the limits of the ground claimed; the object of which provision is evidently to prevent the encumbering of the district mining records with useless locations before sufficient work has been done thereon, to determine whether a vein or lode has really been discovered or not.

14. The claimant should therefore, prior to recording his claim, unless the vein can be traced upon the surface, sink a shaft, or run a tunnel or drift, to a sufficient depth therein to discover and develop a mineral-bearing vein, lode, or crevice; should determine, if possible, the general course of such vein in either direction from the point of discovery, by which direction he will be governed in marking the boundaries of his claim on the surface, and should give the course and distance as nearly as practicable from the discovery-shaft on the claim to some permanent, well-known points or objects, such, for instance, as stone monuments, blazed trees, the confluence of streams, points of intersection of well-known gulches, ravines or roads, prominent buttes, hills, &c., which may be in the immediate vicinity, and which will serve to perpetuate and fix the *locus* of the claim, and render it susceptible of identification from the description thereof given in the record of locations in the district.

15 In addition to the foregoing data, the claimant should state the names of adjoining claims, or, if none adjoin, the relative positions of the nearest claims; should drive a

post or erect a monument of stones at each corner of his surface-ground, and at the point of discovery or discovery-shaft should fix a post, stake, or board, upon which should be designated the name of the lode, the name or names of the locators, the number of feet claimed, and in which direction from the point of discovery; it being essential that the location notice filed for record, in addition to the foregoing description, should state whether the entire claim of fifteen hundred feet is taken on one side of the point of discovery, or whether it is partly upon one and partly upon the other side thereof, and in the latter case, how many feet are claimed upon each side of such discovery-point.

16. Within a reasonable time, say twenty days after the location shall have been marked on the ground, or such time as is allowed by the local laws, notice thereof, accurately describing the claim in manner aforesaid, should be filed for record with the proper recorder of the district, who will thereupon issue the usual certificate of location.

17. In order to hold the possessory right to a location made since May 10, 1872, not less than one hundred dollars' worth of labor must be performed, or improvements made thereon, within one year from the date of such location, and annually thereafter; in default of which the claim will be subject to relocation by any other party having the necessary qualifications, unless the original locator, his heirs, assigns, or legal representatives, have resumed work thereon after such failure and before such relocation.

18. The expenditures required upon mining-claims may be made from the surface or in running a tunnel for the development of such claims, the act of February 11, 1875, providing that where a person or company has, or may, run a tunnel for the purpose of developing a lode or lodes owned by said person or company, the money so expended in said tunnel shall be taken and considered as expended on said lode or lodes, and such person or company shall not be required to perform work on the surface of said lode or lodes in order to hold the same.

19. The importance of attending to these details in the matter of location, labor, and expenditure will be more readily perceived when it is understood that a failure to give the subject proper attention may invalidate the claim.

TUNNEL RIGHTS.

20. Section 2323 provides that where a tunnel is run for the development of a vein or lode, or for the discovery of mines, the owners of such tunnel shall have the right of possession of all veins or lodes within three thousand feet from the face of such tunnel on the line thereof, not previously known to exist, discovered in such tunnel, to the same extent as if discovered from the surface; and locations on the line of such tunnel or veins or lodes not appearing on the surface, made by other parties after the commencement of the tunnel, and while the same is being prosecuted with reasonable diligence, shall be invalid; but failure to prosecute the work on the tunnel for six months shall be considered as an abandonment of the right to all undiscovered veins or lodes on the line of said tunnel.

21. The effect of this is simply to give the proprietors of a mining-tunnel run in good faith the possessory right to fifteen hundred feet of any blind-lodes cut, discovered or intersected by such tunnel, which were not previously known to exist, within three thousand feet from the face or point of commencement of such tunnel, and to prohibit other parties, after the commencement of the tunnel, from prospecting for and making locations of lodes on the *line thereof* and within said distance of three thousand feet, unless such lodes appear upon the surface or were previously known to exist.

22. The term "face," as used in said section, is construed and held to mean the first working-face formed in the tunnel, and to signify the point at which the tunnel actually enters cover; it being from this point that the three thousand feet are to be counted, upon which prospecting is prohibited as aforesaid.

23. To avail themselves of the benefits of this provision of law, the proprietors of a mining-tunnel will be required, at the time they enter cover as aforesaid, to give proper

14

notice of their tunnel location, by erecting a substantial post, board, or monument at the face or point of commencement thereof, upon which should be posted a good and sufficient notice, giving the names of the parties or company claiming the tunnel-right; the actual or proposed course or direction of the tunnel; the height and width thereof, and the course and distance from such face or point of commencement to some permanent well-known objects in the vicinity by which to fix and determine the *locus* in manner heretofore set forth applicable to locations of veins or lodes, and at the time of posting such notice they shall, in order that miners or prospectors may be enabled to determine whether or not they are within the lines of the tunnel, establish the boundary lines thereof, by stakes or monuments placed along such lines at proper intervals, to the terminus of the three thousand feet from the face or point of commencement of the tunnel, and the lines so marked will define and govern as to the specific boundaries within which prospecting for lodes not previously known to exist is prohibited while work on the tunnel is being prosecuted with reasonable diligence.

24. At the time of posting notice and marking out the lines of the tunnel as aforesaid, a full and correct copy of such notice of location defining the tunnel-claim must be filed for record with the mining recorder of the district, to which notice must be attached the sworn statement or declaration of the owners, claimants, or projectors of such tunnel, setting forth the facts in the case; stating the amount expended by themselves and their predecessors in interest in prosecuting work thereon; the extent of the work performed, and that it is *bona fide* their intention to prosecute work on the tunnel so located and described with reasonable diligence for the development of a vein or lode, or for the discovery of mines, or both, as the case may be.

This notice of location must be duly recorded, and with the said sworn statement attached, kept on the recorder's files for future reference.

25. By a compliance with the foregoing, much needless difficulty will be avoided, and the way for the adjustment of legal rights acquired in virtue of said section 2323 will be made much more easy and certain.

26. This office will take particular care that no improper advantage is taken of this provision of law by parties making or professing to make tunnel locations, ostensibly for the purposes named in the statute, but really for the purpose of monopolizing the lands lying in front of their tunnels to the detriment of the mining interests and to the exclusion of *bona fide* prospectors or miners, but will hold such tunnel claimants to a strict compliance with the terms of the statutes; and a *reasonable diligence* on their part in prosecuting the work is one of the essential conditions of their implied contract. Negligence or want of due diligence will be construed as working a forfeiture of their right to all undiscovered veins on the line of such tunnel.

MANNER OF PROCEEDING TO OBTAIN GOVERNMENT TITLE TO VEIN OR LODE CLAIMS.

27. By section 2325 authority is given for granting titles for mines by patent from the government to any person, association, or corporation, having the necessary qualifications as to citizenship and holding the right of possession to a claim in compliance with law.

28. The claimant is required in the first place to have a correct survey of his claim made under authority of the surveyor-general of the State or Territory in which the claim lies; such survey to show with accuracy the exterior surface boundaries of the claim, which boundaries are required to be distinctly marked by monuments on the ground. Four plats and one copy of the original field-notes, in each case, will be prepared by the surveyor-general; one plat and the original field-notes to be retained in the office of the surveyor-general, one copy of the plat to be given the claimant for posting upon the claim, one plat and a copy of the field-notes to be given the claimant for filing with the proper register, to be finally transmitted by that officer, with other papers in the case, to

this office, and one plat to be sent by the surveyor-general to the register of the proper land-district to be retained on his files for future reference.

29. The claimant is then required to post a copy of the plat of such survey in a conspicuous place upon the claim, together with notice of his intention to apply for a patent therefor, which notice will give the date of posting, the name of the claimant, the name of the claim, mine, or lode; the mining district and county; whether the location is of record, and, if so, where the record may be found; the number of feet claimed along the vein and the presumed direction thereof; the number of feet claimed on the lode in each direction from the point of discovery, or other well-defined place on the claim; the name or names of adjoining claimants on the same or other lodes; or, if none adjoin, the names of the nearest claims, &c.

30. After posting the said plat and notice upon the premises, the claimant will file with the proper register and receiver a copy of such plat, and the field-notes of survey of the claim, accompanied by the affidavit of at least two credible witnesses that such plat and notice are posted conspicuously upon the claim, giving the date and place of such posting; a copy of the *notice* so posted to be attached to, and form a part of, said affidavit.

31. Attached to the field-notes so filed must be the sworn statement of the claimant that he has the possessory right to the premises therein described, in virtue of a compliance by himself (and by his grantors, if he claims by purchase) with the mining rules, regulations, and customs of the mining-district, State, or Territory in which the claim lies, and with the mining laws of congress; such sworn statement to narrate briefly, but as clearly as possible, the facts constituting such compliance, the origin of his possession, and the basis of his claim to a patent.

32. This affidavit should be supported by appropriate evidence from the mining recorder's office as to his possessory right, as follows, viz.: Where he claims to be a locator, a full, true and correct copy of such location should be furnished, as the same appears upon the mining records; such copy to be attested by the seal of the recorder, or if he has no seal, then he should make oath to the same being correct, as shown by his records; where the applicant claims as a locator in company with others who have since conveyed their interests in the lode to him, a copy of the original record of location should be filed, together with an abstract of title from the proper recorder, under seal or upon oath as aforesaid, tracing the co-locator's possessory rights in the claim to such applicant for patent; where the applicant claims only as a purchaser for valuable consideration, a copy of the location record must be filed, under seal or upon oath as aforesaid, with an abstract of title certified as above by the proper recorder, tracing the right of possession by a continuous chain of conveyance from the original locators to the applicant.

33. In the event of the mining records in any case having been destroyed by fire or otherwise lost, affidavit of the fact should be made, and secondary evidence of possessory title will be received, which may consist of the affidavit of the claimant, supported by those of any other parties cognizant of the facts relative to his location, occupancy, possession, improvements, &c.; and in such case of lost records, any deeds, certificates of location or purchase, or other evidence which may be in the claimant's possession, and tend to establish his claim, should be filed.

34. Upon the receipt of these papers the register will, at the expense of the claimant (who must furnish the agreement of the publisher to hold applicant for patent alone responsible for charges of publication), publish a notice of such application for the period of sixty days, in a newspaper published nearest to the claim; and will post a copy of such notice in his office for the same period. In all cases sixty days must intervene between the first and the last insertion of the notice in such newspaper. When the notice is published in a *weekly* newspaper ten consecutive insertions are necessary; when in a *daily* newspaper the notice must appear in each issue for the required period.

35.   The notices so published and posted must be as full and complete as possible, and embrace all the *data* given in the notice posted upon the claim.

36.   Too much care can not be exercised in the preparation of these notices, inasmuch as upon their accuracy and completeness will depend, in a great measure, the regularity and validity of the whole proceeding.

37.   The claimant, either at the time of filing these papers with the register, or at any time during the sixty days' publication, is required to file a certificate of the surveyor-general that not less than five hundred dollars' worth of labor has been expended or improvements made upon the claim by the applicant or his grantors; that the plat filed by the claimant is correct; that the field-notes of the survey, as filed, furnish such an accurate description of the claim as will, if incorporated into a patent, serve to fully identify the premises, and that such reference is made therein to natural objects or permanent monuments as will perpetuate and fix the *locus* thereof.

38.   It will be the more convenient way to have this certificate indorsed by the surveyor-general, both upon the plat and field-notes of survey filed by the claimant as aforesaid.

39.   After the sixty days' period of newspaper publication has expired, the claimant will file his affidavit, showing that the plat and notice aforesaid remained conspicuously posted upon the claim sought to be patented during said sixty days' publication, giving the dates.

40.   Upon the filing of this affidavit the register will, if no adverse claim was filed in his office during the period of publication, permit the claimant to pay for the land according to the area given in the plat and field-notes of survey aforesaid, at the rate of five dollars for each acre and five dollars for each fractional part of an acre, the receiver issuing the usual duplicate receipt therefor. The claimant will also make a sworn statement of all charges and fees paid by him for publication and surveys, together with all fees and money paid the register and receiver of the land-office; after which the whole matter will be forwarded to the commissioner of the general land-office and a patent issued thereon if found regular.

41.   In sending up the papers in the case, the register must not omit certifying to the fact that the notice was posted in his office for the full period of sixty days, such certificate to state distinctly when such posting was done and how long continued.

42.   The consecutive series of numbers of mineral entries must be continued, whether the same are of lode or placer-claims.

43.   The surveyor-general must continue to designate all surveyed mineral claims as heretofore by a progressive series of numbers, beginning with lot No. 37 in each township; the claim to be so designated at date of filing the plat, field-notes, &c., in addition to the local designation of the claim; it being required in all cases that the plat and field-notes of the survey of a claim must, in addition to the reference to permanent objects in the neighborhood, describe the *locus* of the claim with reference to the lines of public surveys by a line connecting a corner of the claim with the nearest public corner of the United States surveys, unless such claim be on unsurveyed lands at a remote distance from such public corner, in which latter case the reference by course and distance to permanent objects in the neighborhood will be a sufficient designation by which to fix the *locus* until the public surveys shall have been closed upon its boundaries.

ADVERSE CLAIMS.

44.   Section 2326 provides for adverse claims, fixes the time within which they shall be filed to have legal effect, and prescribes the manner of their adjustment.

45.   Said section requires that the adverse claim shall be filed during the period of publication of notice; that it must be on the oath of the adverse claimant; and that it must show the "*nature*," the "*boundaries*," and the "*extent*" of the adverse claim.

46.   In order that this section of law may be properly carried into effect, the following is communicated for the information of all concerned:

47. An adverse mining-claim must be filed with the register of the same land-office with whom the application for patent was filed, or in his absence with the receiver, and within the sixty days' period of newspaper publication of notice.

48. The adverse notice must be duly sworn to by the person or persons making the same before an officer authorized to administer oaths within the land district, or before the register or receiver: it will fully set forth the nature and extent of the interference or conflict; whether the adverse party claims as a purchaser for valuable consideration or as a locator; if the former, a certified copy of the original location, the original conveyance, a duly certified copy thereof, or an abstract of title from the office of the proper recorder should be furnished, or if the transaction was a mere verbal one he will narrate the circumstances attending the purchase, the date thereof, and the amount paid, which facts should be supported by the affidavit of one or more witnesses, if any were present at the time, and if he claims as a locator he must file a duly certified copy of the location from the office of the proper recorder.

49. In order that the "*boundaries*" and "*extent*" of the claim may be shown, it will be incumbent upon the adverse claimant to file a plat showing his entire claim, its relative situation or position with the one against which he claims, and the extent of the conflict. This plat must be made from an actual survey by a United States deputy-surveyor, who will officially certify thereon to its correctness; and in addition there must be attached to such plat of survey a certificate or sworn statement by the surveyor as to the approximate value of the labor performed or improvements made upon the claim by the adverse party or his predecessors in interest, and the plat must indicate the position of any shafts, tunnels, or other improvements, if any such exist, upon the claim of the party opposing the application, and by which party said improvements were made.

50. Upon the foregoing being filed within the sixty days as aforesaid, the register, or in his absence the receiver, will give notice in writing to *both parties* to the contest that such adverse claim has been filed, informing them that the party who filed the adverse claim will be required within thirty days from the date of such filing to commence proceedings in a court of competent jurisdiction to determine the question of right of possession, and to prosecute the same with reasonable diligence to final judgment, and that should such adverse claimant fail to do so, his adverse claim will be considered waived, and the application for patent be allowed to proceed upon its merits.

51. When an adverse claim is filed as aforesaid, the register or receiver will indorse upon the same the precise date of filing, and preserve a record of the date of notification issued thereon; and thereafter all proceedings on the application for patent will be suspended, with the exception of the completion of the publication and posting of notices and plat, and the filing of the necessary proof thereof, until the controversy shall have been adjudicated in court, or the adverse claim waived or withdrawn.

52. The proceedings after rendition of judgment by the court in such case are so clearly defined by the act itself as to render it unnecessary to enlarge thereon in this place.

PLACER CLAIMS.

53. The proceedings to obtain patents for claims usually called placers, including all forms of deposit, are similar to the proceedings prescribed for obtaining patents for vein or lode claims; but where said placer-claim shall be upon surveyed lands, and conform to legal subdivisions, no further survey or plat will be required, and all placer-mining claims located after May 10, 1872, shall conform as nearly as practicable with the United States system of public-land surveys and the rectangular subdivisions of such surveys, and no such location shall include more than twenty acres for each individual claimant; but where placer-claims can not be conformed to legal subdivisions, survey and plat shall be made as on unsurveyed lands. But where such claims are located previous to the public surveys and do not conform to legal subdivisions, survey, plat, and entry thereof may be made according to the boundaries thereof, provided the location is in all respects legal.

54. The proceedings for obtaining patents for veins or lodes having already been fully given, it will not be necessary to repeat them here; it being thought that careful attention thereto by applicants and the local officers will enable them to act understandingly in the matter and make such slight modifications in the notice, or otherwise, as may be necessary in view of the different nature of the two classes of claims, placer-claims being fixed, however, at two dollars and fifty cents per acre, or fractional part of an acre.

55. By section 2330 authority is given for the subdivision of forty-acre legal subdivisions into *ten-acre* lots, which is intended for the greater convenience of miners in segregating their claims both from one another and from intervening agricultural lands.

56. It is held, therefore, that under a proper construction of the law these ten-acre lots in mining districts should be considered and dealt with, to all intents and purposes, as legal subdivisions, and that an applicant having a legal claim which conforms to one or more of these ten-acre lots, either adjoining or cornering, may make entry thereof after the usual proceedings, without further survey or plat.

57. In cases of this kind, however, the notice given of the application must be very specific and accurate in description, and as the forty-acre tracts may be subdivided into ten-acre lots, either in the form of squares of ten by ten chains, or of parallelograms five by twenty chains, so long as the lines are parallel and at right angles with the lines of the public surveys, it will be necessary that the notice and application state specifically what ten-acre lots are sought to be patented, in addition to the other *data* required in the notice.

58. Where the ten-acre subdivision is in the form of a square it may be described, for instance, as the "S. E. ¼ of the the S. W. ½ of N. W. ¼," or, if in the form of a parallelogram as aforesaid, it may be described as the " W. ½ of the W. ½ of the S. W. ¼ of the N. W. ¼ (or the N. ½ of the S. ½ of the N. E. ¼ of the S. E. ¼) of section ——, township ——, range ——." as the case may be: but, in addition to this description of the land, the notice must give all the other *data* that is required in a mineral application, by which parties may be put on inquiry as to the premises sought to be patented. The proof submittee with applications for claims of this kind must show clearly the character and the extent of the improvements upon the premises.

59. Applicants for patent to a placer-claim, who are also in possession of a known vein or lode included therein, must state in their application that the placer includes such vein or lode. The published and posted notices must also include such statement; and the vein or lode must be surveyed and marked upon the plat; the field-notes and plat giving the area of the lode claim or claims and the area of the placer separately. If veins or lodes lying within a placer location are owned by other parties, the fact should be distinctly stated in the application for patent, and in all the notices. It should be remembered that an application which omits to include an application for a known vein or lode therein, must be construed as a conclusive declaration that the applicant has no right of possession to the vein or lode. Where there is no known lode or vein, the fact must appear by the affidavit of claimant and one or more witnesses.

60. When an adverse claim is filed to a placer application, the proceedings are the same as in the case of vein or lode claims, already described.

QUANTITY OF PLACER GROUND SUBJECT TO LOCATION.

61. By section 2330 it is declared that no location of a placer-claim, made after July 9, 1870, shall exceed one hundred and sixty acres for any one person or association of persons, which location shall conform to the United States surveys.

62. Section 2331 provides that all placer-mining claims located after May 10, 1872, shall conform as nearly as practicable with the United States system of public surveys and the subdivisions of such surveys, and no such locations shall include more than twenty acres for each individual claimant.

63. The foregoing provisions of law are construed to mean that after the 9th day of July, 1870, no location of a placer-claim can be made to exceed one hundred and sixty acres, whatever may be the number of locators associated together, or whatever the local regulations of the district may allow; and that from and after May 10, 1872, no location made by an individual can exceed twenty acres, and no location made by an association of individuals can exceed one hundred and sixty acres, which location of one hundred and sixty acres can not be made by a less number than eight *bona fide* locators; and no local laws or mining regulations can restrict a placer location to less than twenty acres, although the locator is not compelled to take so much.

64. The regulations hereinbefore given as to the manner of marking locations on the ground and placing the same on record, must be observed in the case of placer locations, so far as the same are applicable; the law requiring, however, that where placer-claims are upon *surveyed* public lands the locations must hereafter be made to conform to legal subdivisions thereof as near as practicable.

65. With regard to the proofs necessary to establish the possessory right to a placer-claim, section 2332 provides that "where such person or association, they and their grantors, have held and worked their claims for a period equal to the time prescribed by the statute of limitations for mining-claims of the State or Territory where the same may be situated, evidence of such possession and working of the claims for such period shall be sufficient to establish a right to a patent thereto under this chapter, in the absence of any adverse claim."

66. This provision of law will greatly lessen the burden of proof, more especially in the case of old claims located many years since, the records of which, in many cases, have been destroyed by fire, or lost in other ways during the lapse of time, but concerning the possessory right to which all controversy or litigation has long been settled.

67. When an applicant desires to make his proof of possessory right in accordance with this provision of law, you will not require him to produce evidence of location, copies of conveyances, or abstracts of title, as in other cases, but will require him to furnish a duly certified copy of the statute of limitations of mining-claims for the State or Territory, together with his sworn statement giving a clear and succinct narration of the facts as to the origin of his title, and likewise as to the continuation of his possession of the mining-ground covered by his application, the area thereof, the nature and extent of the mining that has been done thereon; whether there has been any opposition to his possession, or litigation with regard to his claim, and, if so, when the same ceased; whether such cessation was caused by compromise or by judicial decree, and any additional facts within the claimant's knowledge having a direct bearing upon his possession and *bona fides* which he may desire to submit in support of his claim.

68. There should likewise be filed a certificate, under seal of the court having jurisdiction of mining cases within the judicial district embracing the claim, that no suit or action of any character whatever involving the right of possession to any portion of the claim applied for is pending, and that there has been no litigation before said court affecting the title to said claim or any part thereof for a period equal to the time fixed by the statute of limitations for mining-claims in the State or Territory as aforesaid, other than that which has been finally decided in favor of the claimant.

69. The claimant should support his narrative of facts relative to his possession, occupancy, and improvements by corroborative testimony of any disinterested person or persons of credibility who may be cognizant of the facts in the case and are capable of testifying understandingly in the premises.

70. It will be to the advantage of claimants to make their proofs as full and complete as practicable.

71. Section 2337 provides that, "where non-mineral land not contiguous to the vein or lode is used or occupied by the proprietor of such vein or lode for mining or milling purposes, such non-adjacent surface-ground may be embraced and included in an application for a patent for such vein or lode, and the same may be patented therewith, subject to the same preliminary requirements as to survey and notice as are applicable to veins or lodes; but no location hereafter made of such non-adjacent land shall exceed five acres, and payment for the same must be made at the same rate as fixed by this chapter for the superficies of the lode. The owner of a quartz-mill or reduction-works, not owning a mine in connection therewith, may also receive a patent for his mill-site, as provided in this section."

72. To avail themselves of this provision of law, parties holding the possessory right to a vein or lode, and to a piece of non-mineral land not contiguous thereto, for mining or milling purposes, not exceeding the quantity allowed for such purpose by section 2337 United States revised statutes, or prior laws, under which the land was appropriated, the proprietors of such vein or lode may file in the proper land-office their application for a patent, under oath, in manner already set forth herein, which application, together with the plat and field-notes, may include, embrace, and describe, in addition to the vein or lode, such non-contiguous mill-site, and after due proceedings as to notice, &c., a patent will be issued conveying the same as one claim.

73. In making the survey in a case of this kind, the lode-claim should be described in the plat and field-notes as "Lot No. 37, A." and the mill-site as "Lot No. 37, B," or whatever may be its appropriate numerical designation; the course and distance from a corner of the mill-site to a corner of the lode-claim to be invariably given in such plat and field-notes, and a copy of the plat and notice of application for patent must be conspicuously posted upon the mill-site as well as upon the vein or lode for the statutory period of sixty days. In making the entry no separate receipt or certificate need be issued for the mill-site, but the whole area of both lode and mill-site will be embraced in one entry, the price being five dollars for each acre and fractional part of an acre embraced by such lode and mill-site claim.

74. In case the owner of a quartz-mill or reduction-works is not the owner or claimant of a vein or lode, the law permits him to make application therefor in the same manner prescribed herein for mining-claims, and after due notice and proceedings, in the absence of a valid adverse filing, to enter and receive a patent for his mill-site at said price per acre.

75. In every case there must be satisfactory proof that the land claimed as a mill-site is not mineral in character, which proof may, where the matter is unquestioned, consist of the sworn statement of the claimant, supported by that of one or more disinterested persons capable from acquaintance with the land to testify understandingly.

76. The law expressly limits mill-site locations made from and after its passage to *five acres*.

77. The registers and receivers will preserve an unbroken consecutive series of numbers for all mineral entries.

PROOF OF CITIZENSHIP OF MINING CLAIMANTS.

78. The proof necessary to establish the citizenship of applicants for mining patents must be made in the following manner: In case of an incorporated company, a certified copy of their charter or certificate of incorporation must be filed. In case of an association of persons unincorporated, the affidavit of their duly authorized agent, made upon his own knowledge, or upon information and belief, setting forth the residence of each person forming such association, must be submitted. This affidavit must be accompanied by a power of attorney from the parties forming such association, authorizing the person

who makes the affidavit of citizenship to act for them in the matter of their application for patent.

79. In case of an individual or an association of individuals who do not appear by their duly authorized agent, you will require the affidavit of each applicant, showing whether he is a native or naturalized citizen, when and where born, and his residence.

80. In case an applicant has declared his intention to become a citizen, or has been naturalized, his affidavit must show the date, place, and the court before which he declared his intention, or from which his certificate of citizenship issued, and present residence.

81. The affidavit of citizenship may be taken before the register and receiver, or any other officer authorized to administer oaths within the district.

APPOINTMENT OF DEPUTY SURVEYORS OF MINING CLAIMS—CHARGES FOR SURVEYS AND PUBLICATIONS—FEES OF REGISTERS AND RECEIVERS, &C.

82. Section 2334 provides for the appointment of surveyors of mineral claims, authorizes the commissioner of the general land-office to establish the rates to be charged for surveys and for newspaper publications, prescribes the fees allowed to the local officers for receiving and acting upon applications for mining patents, and for adverse claims thereto, &c.

83. The surveyors-general of the several districts will, in pursuance of said law, appoint in each land-district as many *competent* deputies for the survey of mining-claims as may seek such appointment; it being distinctly understood that all expenses of these notices and surveys are to be borne by the mining-claimants and not by the United States; the system of making *deposits* for mineral surveys, as required by previous instructions, being hereby revoked as regards *field-work ;* the claimant having the option of employing *any* deputy surveyor within such district to do his work in the field.

84. With regard to the *platting* of the claim and other *office-work* in the surveyor-general's office, that officer will make an estimate of the cost thereof, which amount the claimant will deposit with any assistant United States treasurer, or designated depository, in favor of the United States treasurer, to be passed to the credit of the fund created by "individual depositors for surveys of the public lands," and file with the surveyor-general duplicate certificates of such deposit in the usual manner.

85. The surveyors-general will endeavor to appoint mineral deputy surveyors so that one or more may be located in each mining district for the greater convenience of miners.

86. The usual oaths will be required of these deputies and their assistants as to the correctness of each survey executed by them.

87. The law requires that each applicant shall file with the register and receiver a sworn statement of all charges and fees paid by him for publication of notice and for survey, together with all fees and money paid the register and receiver, which sworn statement is required to be transmitted to this office, for the information of the commissioner.

88. Should it appear that excessive or exorbitant charges have been made by any surveyor or any publisher, prompt action will be taken with the view of correcting the abuse.

89. The fees payable to the register and receiver for filing and acting upon applications for mineral-land patents are five dollars to each officer, to be paid by the applicant for patent at the time of filing, and the like sum of five dollars is payable to each officer by an adverse claimant at the time of filing his adverse claim.

90. All fees or charges under this law may be paid in United States currency.

91. The register and receiver will, at the close of each month, forward to this office an abstract of mining applications filed, and a register of receipts, accompanied with an abstract of mineral lands sold, and an abstract of adverse claims filed.

92. The fees and purchase money received by registers and receivers must be placed to the credit of the United States in the receiver's monthly and quarterly account, charging up in the disbursing account the sums to which the register and receiver may be respectively entitled as fees and commissions, with limitations in regard to the legal maximum.

HEARINGS TO ESTABLISH THE CHARACTER OF LANDS.

93. Section 2335 provides that all affidavits required under this chapter may be verified before *any* officer authorized to administer oaths within the land-district where the claims may be situated, and all testimony and proofs may be taken before any such officer, and when duly certified by the officer taking the same shall have the same force and effect as if taken before the register and receiver of the land-office.

94. Hearings of this character, as practically distinguished, are of two kinds.

1st. Where lands which are sought to be entered and patented as agricultural are alleged by affidavit to be mineral, or when sought as mineral their non-mineral character is alleged.

The proceedings relative to this class are in the nature of a contest between two or more known parties, and the testimony may be taken on personal notice of at least ten days, duly served on all parties, or, if they can not be found, then by publication, for thirty days in a newspaper of general circulation, to be designated by the register of the land-office as published nearest to the land in controversy. If publication is made in a weekly newspaper, the notice must be inserted in five consecutive issues thereof.

2d. When lands are returned as mineral by the surveyor-general, or are withdrawn as mineral by direction of this office.

When such lands are sought to be entered as agricultural, notice must be given by publication for thirty days, as aforesaid, and also by posting in a conspicuous place on each forty-acre subdivision of the land claimed, for the same period.

95. All notices must describe the land, give the name and address of the claimant, the character of his claim, and the time, place, and purpose of the hearing.

Proof of service of notice, when personal, must consist of either acknowledgment of service indorsed on the citation, (which is always desirable,) or the affidavit of the party serving the same, giving date, place, and manner of service, indorsed as aforesaid.

Proof of publication must be the affidavit of the publisher of the newspaper, stating the period of publication, giving dates, stating whether in a daily or weekly issue, and a copy of the notice so published must be attached to, and form a part of, the affidavit.

Proof of posting on the claim must be made by the affidavits of two or more persons who state when and where the notice was posted; that it remained so posted during the prescribed period, giving dates, and a copy of the notice so posted must be attached to, and form a part of, the affidavits.

Proof of notice is indispensable to the regularity of proceedings, and must accompany the record in every case.

The expense of notice must in every case be paid by the parties thereto.

96. At the hearing there must be filed the affidavit of the publisher of the paper that the said notice was published for the required time, stating when and for how long such publication was made, a printed copy thereof to be attached and made a part of the affidavit. In every case where practicable, in addition to the foregoing, *personal* notice must be served upon the mineral affiants, and upon any parties who may be mining upon or claiming the land.

97. At the hearing the claimants and witnesses will be thoroughly examined with regard to the character of the land; whether the same has been thoroughly prospected; whether or not there exists within the tract or tracts claimed any lode or vein of quartz or other rock in place, bearing gold, silver, cinnabar, lead, tin, or copper, or other valuable deposit which has ever been claimed, located, recorded, or worked; whether such work is entirely abandoned, or whether occasionally resumed; if such lode does exist, by whom claimed, under what designation, and in which subdivision of the land it lies; whether any placer-mine or mines exist upon the land; if so, what is the character thereof—whether of the shallow-surface description, or of the deep cement, blue lead, or gravel deposits; to what extent mining is carried on when water can be obtained, and what the facilities are for

obtaining water for mining purposes; upon what particular ten-acre subdivisions mining has been done, and at what time the land was abandoned for mining purposes, if abandoned at all.

98. The testimony should also show the agricultural capacities of the land, what kind of crops are raised thereon, and the value thereof; the number of acres actually cultivated for crops of cereals or vegetables, and within which particular ten-acre subdivisions such crops are raised; also which of these subdivisions embrace his improvements, giving in detail the extent and value of his improvements, such as house, barn, vineyard, orchard, fencing, etc.

99. It is thought that *bona fide* settlers upon lands really agricultural will be able to show, by a clear, logical, and succinct chain of evidence, that their claims are founded upon law and justice; while parties who have made little or no permanent agricultural improvements, and who only seek title for speculative purposes, on account of the mineral deposits known to themselves to be contained in the land, will be defeated in their intentions.

100. The testimony should be as full and complete as possible; and, in addition to the leading points indicated above, everything of importance bearing upon the question of the character of the land should be elicited at the hearing.

101. Where the testimony is taken before an officer who does not use a seal, other than the register and receiver, the official character of such officer must be attested by a clerk of a court of record, and the testimony transmitted to the register and receiver, who will thereupon examine and forward the same to this office, with their joint opinion as to the character of the land as shown by the testimony.

102. When the case comes before this office, such an award of the land will be made as the law and the facts may justify; and in cases where a survey is necessary to set apart the mineral from the agricultural land in any forty-acre tract, the necessary instructions will be issued to enable the agricultural claimant, *at his own expense,* to have the work done, at his option, either by United States deputy, county, or other local surveyor; the survey in such case may be executed in such manner as will segregate the portion of land actually containing the mine, and used as surface-ground for the convenient working thereof, from the remainder of the tract, which remainder will be patented to the agriculturist to whom the same may have been awarded, subject, however, to the condition that the land may be entered upon by the proprietor of any vein or lode for which a patent has been issued by the United States for the purpose of extracting and removing the ore from the same, where found to penetrate or intersect the land so patented as agricultural, as stipulated by the mining act.

103. Such survey when executed must be properly sworn to by the surveyor, either before a notary public, officer of a court of record, or before the register or receiver, the deponent's character and credibility to be properly certified to by the officer administering the oath.

104. Upon the filing of the plat and field-notes of such survey, duly sworn to as aforesaid, you will transmit the same to the surveyor-general for his verification and approval; who, if he finds the work correctly performed, will properly mark out the same upon the original township plat in his office, and furnish authenticated copies of such plat and description both to the proper local land-office and to this office, to be affixed to the duplicate and triplicate township plats respectively.

105. In cases where a portion of a forty-acre tract is awarded to an agricultural claimant and he causes the segregation thereof from the mineral portion, as aforesaid, such agricultural portion will not be given a numerical designation as in the case of surveyed mineral claims, but will simply be described as the "Fractional —— quarter of the —— quarter of section ——, in township ——, of range ——, meridian, containing —— acres, the same being exclusive of the land adjudged to be mineral in said forty-acre tract."

106. The surveyor must correctly compute the area of such agricultural portion, which computation will be verified by the surveyor-general.

107. After the authenticated plat and field-notes of the survey have been received from the surveyor-general, this office will issue the necessary order for the entry of the land, and in issuing the receiver's receipt and the register's patent certificate you will invariably be governed by the description of the land given in the order from this office.

108. The fees for taking testimony and reducing the same to writing in these cases will have to be defrayed by the parties in interest. Where such testimony is taken before any other officer than the register and receiver, the register and receiver will be entitled to no fees.

109. If, upon a review of the testimony at this office, a ten-acre tract should be found to be properly mineral in character, that fact will be no bar to the execution of the settler's legal right to the remaining *non-mineral* portion of his claim, if contiguous.

110. No fear need be entertained that miners will be permitted to make entries of tracts ostensibly as mining claims, which are not mineral, simply for the purpose of obtaining possession and defrauding settlers out of their valuable agricultural improvements; it being almost an impossibility for such a fraud to be consummated under the laws and regulations applicable to obtaining patents for mining-claims.

111. The fact that a certain tract of land is decided upon testimony to be mineral in character is by no means equivalent to an award of the land to a miner. A miner is compelled by law to give sixty days' publication of notice, and posting of diagrams and notices, as a preliminary step; and then, before he can enter the land, he must show that the land yields mineral; that he is entitled to the possessory right thereto in virtue of compliance with local customs or rules of miners or by virtue of the statute of limitations; that he or his grantors have expended, in actual labor and improvements, an amount of not less than five hundred dollars thereon, and that the claim is one in regard to which there is no controversy or opposing claim. After all these proofs are met, he is entitled to have a survey made at his own cost where a survey is required, after which he can enter and pay for the land embraced by his claim.

J. A. WILLIAMSON,

Commissioner

MINING LAWS OF COLORADO.

AN ACT CONCERNING MINES.

Be it enacted by the Council and House of Representatives of Colorado.

EXTENT OF LODE-CLAIM.

Section 1. The length of any lode-claim hereafter located may equal but not exceed fifteen hundred feet along the vein.

DIMENSIONS.

Sec. 2. The width of lode-claims hereafter located in Gilpin, Clear Creek, Boulder and Summit counties, shall be seventy-five feet on each side of the centre of the vein or crevice; and in all other counties the width of the same shall be one hundred and fifty feet on each side of the centre of the vein or crevice: *Provided*, That hereafter any county may, at any general election, determine on a greater width, not exceeding three hundred feet on each side of the centre of the vein or lode, by a majority of the legal votes cast at said election; and any county, by such vote at such election, may determine upon a less width than above specified.

CERTIFICATE OF LOCATION.

Sec. 3. The discoverer of a lode shall, within three months from the date of discovery, record his claim in the office of the recorder of the county in which such lode is situated by a location certificate, which shall contain: 1st, the name of the lode; 2nd, the name of the locator: 3d, the date of location: 4th. the number of feet in length claimed on each side of the centre of the discovery shaft; 5th, the general course of the lode, as near as may be.

WHEN VOID.

Sec. 4. Any location certificate of a lode-claim which shall not contain the name of the lode, the name of the locator, the date of location, the number of lineal feet claimed on each side of the discovery shaft, the general course of the lode, and such description as shall identify the claim with reasonable certainty, shall be void.

DISCOVERY SHAFT.

Sec. 5. Before filing such location certificate the discoverer shall locate his claim by first sinking a discovery shaft upon the lode to the depth of at least ten feet from the lowest part of the rim of such shaft at the surface, or deeper, if necessary to show a well-defined crevice. *Second*, by posting at the point of discovery on the surface, a plain sign or notice containing the name of the lode, the name of the locator, and the date of discovery. *Third*, by marking the surface boundaries of the claim.

STAKING.

Sec. 6. Such surface boundaries shall be marked by six substantial posts, hewed or marked on the side or sides which are in toward the claim, and sunk in the ground, to wit: One at each corner and one at the centre of each side line. Where it is practically impossible on account of bedrock or precipitous ground to sink such posts, they may be placed in a pile of stones.

OPEN CUTS, ETC.

Sec. 7. Any open cut, cross cut or tunnel which shall cut a lode at the depth of ten feet below the surface, shall hold such lode the same as if a discovery shaft were sunk thereon; or an adit of at least ten feet along the lode, from the point where the lode may be in any manner discovered, shall be equivalent to a discovery shaft.

TIME.

Sec. 8. The disoverer shall have sixty days from the time of uncovering or disclosing a lode to sink a discovery shaft thereon.

CONSTRUCTION OF CERTIFICATE.

Sec. 9. The location or location certificate of any lode-claim shall be construed to include all surface ground within the surface lines thereof and all lodes and ledges throughout their entire depth, the top or apex of which lies inside of such lines extended downward, vertically, with such parts of all lodes or ledges as continue to dip beyond the side lines of the claim, but shall not include any portion of such lodes or ledges beyond the end lines of the claim, or at the end lines continued, whether by dip or otherwise, or beyond the side lines in any other manner than by the dip of the lode.

CAN NOT BE FOLLOWED.

Sec. 10. If the top or apex of a lode in its longitudinal course extends beyond the exterior lines of the claim at any point on the surface, or as extended vertically downward, such lode may not be followed in its longitudinal course beyond the point where it is intersected by the exterior lines.

RIGHT OF WAY AND RIGHT OF SURFACE.

Sec. 11. All mining claims now located, or which may hereafter be located, shall be subject to the right of way of any ditch or flume for mining purposes, or any tramway or pack-trail, whether now in use or which may be hereafter laid out across any such location: *Provided, always,* That such right of way shall not be exercised against any location duly made and recorded and not abandoned prior to the establishment of the ditch or flume, tramway, or pack-trail, without consent of the owner, except by condemnation, as in case of land taken for public highways. Parol consent to the location of any such easement, accompanied by the completion of the same over the claim, shall be sufficient without writings. *And provided further,* That such ditch or flume shall be so constructed that the water from such ditch or flume shall not injure vested rights by flooding or otherwise.

Sec. 12. When the right to mine is in any case separate from the ownership or right of occupancy to the surface, the owner or rightful occupant of the surface may demand satisfactory security from the miner, and if it be refused, may enjoin such miner from working until such security is given. The order for injunction shall fix the amount of the bond.

RELOCATION OF CLAIMS.

Sec. 13. If at any time the locator of any mining-claim heretofore or hereafter located, or his assigns, shall apprehend that his original certificate was defective, erroneous, or that the requirements of the law had not been complied with before filing; or shall be desirous of changing his surface boundaries; or of taking in any part of an overlapping claim which has been abandoned; or in case the original certificate was made prior to the passage of this law, and he shall be desirous of securing the benefits of this act, such locator or his assigns may file an additional certificate, subject to the provisions of this act: *Provided,* That such relocation does not interfere with the existing rights of others, at the time of such relocation; and no such relocation, or the record thereof, shall preclude the claimant or claimants from proving any such title or titles as he or they may have held under previous location.

PROOF OF DEVELOPMENT.

Sec. 14. The amount of work done, or improvements made during each year, shall be that prescribed by the laws of the United States.

FORM OF AFFIDAVIT.

Sec. 15. Within six months after any set time, or annual period herein allowed for the performance of labor or making improvements upon any lode-claim, the person on whose behalf such outlay was made, or some person for him, shall make and record an affidavit in substance as follows:

State of Colorado, } ss.
  County of......... }

Before me, the subscriber, personally appeared.................who, being duly sworn, saith that at least.... ....dollars' worth of work or improvements were performed or made upon [here describe the claim or part of claim] situate in....................... mining-district, county of...........State of Colorado. Such expenditure was made by or at the expense of.............. ...owners of said claim, for the purpose of said claim.
[Jurat.]   ....(Signature.)

And such signature shall be *prima facie* evidence of the performance of such labor.

WORKING OVER OLD CLAIMS.

Sec. 16. The relocation of abandoned lode-claims shall be by sinking a new discovery shaft and fixing new boundaries in the same manner as if it were the location of a new claim; or the relocator may sink the original discovery shaft ten feet deeper than it was at

the time of abandonment, and erect new or adopt the old boundaries, renewing the posts
it removed or destroyed. In either case a new location stake shall be erected. In any
case, whether the whole or part of an abandoned claim is taken, the location certificate
may state that the whole or any part of the new location is located as abandoned property.

RECORD FOR CLAIM.

SEC. 17. No location certificate shall claim more than one location, whether the location be made by one or several locators. And if it purport to claim more than one
location, it shall be absolutely void, except as to the first location therein described.
And if they are described together, so that it can not be told which location is first
described, the certificate shall be void as to all.

SEC. 18. All acts or parts of acts in conflict with this act are hereby repealed.

SEC. 19. This act shall be in force from and after June 15, 1874.

Approved February 13, 1874.

SUPPLEMENTARY ACT.

Be it enacted by the Council and House of Representatives of Colorado:

JURISDICTION OF AUTHORITIES.

SECTION 1. In all actions pending in any district court of this Territory, wherein the
title or right of possession to any mining-claim shall be in dispute, the said court, or the
judge thereof, may, upon application of any of the parties to such suit, enter an order for
the underground as well as the surface survey of such part of the property in dispute as
may be necessary to a just determination of the question involved. Such order shall
designate some competent surveyor, not related to any of the parties to such suit, or in
anywise interested in the result of the same; and upon the application of the party
adverse to such application, the court may also appoint some competent surveyor, to be
selected by such adverse applicant, whose duty it shall be to attend upon such survey,
and observe the method of making the same; said second surveyor to be at the cost of
the party asking therefor. It shall also be lawful in such order to specify the names of
witnesses named by either party, not exceeding three on each side, to examine such
property, who shall hereupon be allowed to enter into such property and examine the
same; said court, or the judge thereof, may also cause the removal of any rock, debris, or
other obstacle in any of the drifts or shafts of said property, when such removal is shown
to be necessary to a just determination of the questions involved: *Provided, however,*
That no such order shall be made for survey and inspection, except in open court or in
chambers, upon notice of application for such order of at least six days, and not then
except by agreement of parties or upon the affidavit of two or more persons that such
survey and inspection is necessary to the just determination of the suit, which affidavit
shall state the facts in such case, and wherein the necessity for survey exists: nor
shall such order be made unless it appears that the party asking therefor has been refused
the privilege of survey and inspection by the adverse party.

WRITS RESTORING POSSESSION.

SEC. 2. The said district courts of this State, or any judge thereof, sitting in chancery,
shall have, in addition to the power already possessed, power to issue writs of injunction
for affirmative relief, having the force and effect of a writ of restitution, restoring any person or persons to the possession of any mining property from which he or they may have
been ousted, by force and violence, or by fraud, or from which they are kept out of possession by threats, or whenever such possession was taken from him or them by entry of

the adverse party on Sunday or a legal holiday, or while the party in possession was temporarily absent therefrom. The granting of such writ to extend only to the right of possession under the facts of the case in respect to the manner in which the possession was obtained, leaving the parties to their legal rights on all other questions as though no such writ had issued.

PENALTIES FOLLOWING UNLAWFUL ENTRY.

SEC. 3. In all cases where two or more persons shall associate themselves together for the purpose of obtaining the possession of any lode, gulch or placer-claim, then in the actual possession of another, by force and violence, or threats of violence, or by stealth, and shall proceed to carry out such purpose by making threats against the party or parties in possession, or who shall enter upon such lode or mining-claim for the purpose aforesaid, or who shall enter upon or into any lode, gulch, placer-claim, quartz-mill, or other mining property, or, not being upon such property, but within hearing of the same, shall make any threats, or make use of any language, signs or gestures, calculated to intimidate any person or persons at work on said property, from continuing to work thereon or therein, or to intimidate others from engaging to work thereon or therein, every such person so offending shall, on conviction thereof, be fined in a sum not to exceed two hundred and fifty dollars, and be imprisoned in the county jail not less than thirty days nor more than six months; such fine to be discharged either by payment or by confinement in said jail until such fine is discharged at the rate of two dollars and fifty cents ($2.50) per day. On trials under this section, proof of a common purpose of two or more persons to obtain possession of property, as aforesaid, or to intimidate laborers as above set forth, accompanied or followed by any of the acts above specified by any of them, shall be sufficient evidence to convict any one committing such acts, although the parties may not be associated together at the time of committing the same.

FORCE OR VIOLENCE.

SEC. 4. If any person or persons shall associate and agree to enter or attempt to enter by force of numbers, and the terror such numbers are calculated to inspire, or by force and violence, or by threats of violence against any person or persons in the actual possession of any lode, gulch or placer-claim, and upon such entry or attempted entry, any person or persons shall be killed, said persons, and all and each of them so entering or attempting to enter, shall be deemed guilty of murder in the first degree, and punished accordingly. Upon the trial of such cases, any person or parties cognizant of such entry, or attempted entry, who shall be present, aiding, assisting, or in anywise encouraging such entry, or attempted entry, shall be deemed a principal in the commission of said offense.

SEC. 5. This act shall take effect and be in force from and after its passage.

Approved February 13, 1874.

THE ACT OF 1877.

AN ACT to provide for the Drainage of Mines, and to regulate the Liabilities of Miners, Mine-Owners and Mill-Men in certain cases, and to repeal all Territorial Acts on the Subject.

Be it enacted by the General Assembly of the State of Colorado:

DRAINAGE.

1830—SECTION 1. Whenever contiguous or adjacent mines upon the same or upon separate lodes have a common ingress of water, or from subterraneous communication of the water have a common drainage, it shall be the duty of the owners, lessees or occupants of each mine so related to provide for their proportionate share of the drainage thereof.

PENALTY FOR NON-COMPLIANCE.

1831—Sec. 2. Any parties so related failing to provide as aforesaid for the drainage of the mines owned or occupied by them, thereby imposing an unjust burden upon neighboring mines, whether owned or occupied by them, shall pay respectively to those performing the work of drainage their proportion of the actual and necessary cost and expense of doing such drainage, to be recovered by an action in any court of competent jurisdiction.

COMMON INTERESTS.

1832—Sec. 3. It shall be lawful for all mining corporations or companies, and all individuals engaged in mining, who have thus a common interest in draining such mines, to unite for the purpose of effecting the same, under such common name and upon such terms and conditions as may be agreed upon; and every such association having filed a certificate of incorporation, as provided by law, shall be deemed a corporation, with all the rights, incidents and liabilities of a body corporate, so far as the same may be applicable.

SUBJECT TO ACTION.

1833—Sec. 4. Failing to mutually agree, as indicated in the preceding section for drainage, jointly, one or more of the said parties may undertake the work of drainage, after giving reasonable notice; and should the remaining parties then fail, neglect or refuse to unite in equitable arrangements for doing the work, or sharing the expense thereof, they shall be subject to an action therefor as already specified, to be enforced in any court of competent jurisdiction.

ACTION TO RECOVER.

1834—Sec. 5. When an action is commenced to recover the cost and expenses for draining a lode or mine, it shall be lawful for the plaintiff to apply to the court, if in session, or to the judge thereof in vacation, for an order to inspect and examine the lodes or mines claimed to have been drained by the plaintiff; or some one for him shall make affidavit that such inspection or examination is necessary for a proper preparation of the case for trial; and the court or judge shall grant an order for the underground inspection and examination of the lode or mines described in the petition. Such order shall designate the number of persons, not exceeding three, besides the plaintiff or his representative, to examine and inspect such lode and mines, and take the measurements thereof, relating to the amount of water drained from the lode or mine, or the number of fathoms of ground mined and worked out of the lode or mines claimed to have been drained, the cost of such examination and inspection to be borne by the party applying therefor. The court or judge shall have power to cause the removal of any rock, debris, or other obstacles in any lode or vein, when such removal is shown to be necessary to a just determination of the question involved: *Provided,* That no such order for inspection and examination shall be made, except in open court or in chambers, upon notice of application for such order of at least three days, and not then except by agreement of parties, nor unless it appears that the plaintiff has been refused the privilege of making the inspection and examination by the defendant or defendants, his or their agent.

WATER RIGHTS.

1835—Sec. 6. That hereafter, when any person or persons, or corporation, shall be engaged in mining or milling, and in the prosecution of such business shall hoist or raise water from mines or natural channels, and the same shall flow away from the premises of such persons or corporations to any natural channel or gulch, the same shall be considered beyond the control of the parties so hoisting or raising the same, and may be taken and used by other parties the same as that of natural water-courses.

15

1836—SEC. 7. After any such water shall have been so raised, and the same shall have flown into any such natural channel, gulch or draw, the party so hoisting or raising the same shall only be liable for injury caused thereby, in the same manner as riparian owners along natural water-courses.

EXPLANATORY.

1837—SEC. 8. The provisions of this act shall not be construed to apply to incipient or undeveloped mines, but to those only which shall have been opened, and shall clearly derive a benefit from being drained.

EVIDENCE.

1838—SEC. 9. In trial of cases arising under this act the court shall admit evidence of the normal stand or position of the water while at rest in an idle mine, also the observed prevalence of a common water-level or a standing water-line in the same or separate lodes; also the effect, if any, the elevating or depressing the water by natural or mechanical means in any given lode has upon elevating or depressing the water in the same, contiguous or separate lodes or mines; also the effect which draining or ceasing to drain any given lode or mine had upon the water in the same or contiguous or separate lodes or mines, and all other evidence which tends to prove the common ingress or subterraneous communication of water into the same lode or mine, or contiguous or separate lodes or mines.

Approved March 16, 1877.

TAXES.

Section 3, Article 10, of the Constitution of the State of Colorado, reads as follows:

"All taxes shall be uniform upon the same class of subjects within the territorial limits of the authority levying the tax, and shall be levied and collected under general laws, which shall prescribe such regulations as shall secure a just valuation for taxation of all property, real and personal: *Provided,* That mines and mining claims bearing gold, silver, and other precious metals, (except the net proceeds and surface improvements thereof,) shall be exempt from taxation for the period of ten years from the date of the adoption of this constitution, and thereafter may be taxed as provided by law. Ditches, canals, and flumes owned and used by individuals or corporations for irrigating lands owned by such individuals or corporations, or the individual members thereof, shall not be separately taxed, so long as they shall be owned and used exclusively for such purpose."

MINING LAWS OF ARIZONA.

ACTS RELATING TO MINES.*

AN ACT ALLOWING PERSONS IN THE MILITARY SERVICE OF THE UNITED STATES AND OF THIS TERRITORY TO HOLD MINING CLAIMS.

[Approved November 9, 1864.]

3109—SECTION 1. All persons in the military service of the United States or this Territory shall be allowed to locate claims on mineral lodes or veins in the limits of this

* This chapter is in place of chapter fifty of the Howell code, which has been repealed.

Territory, subject to the requirements of the mining laws of this Territory, and shall be protected in the possession of the same, and shall have the same rights in all respects, in regard to such claims, as like persons not in the military service.

3110—SEC. 2. All the laws of any mining district contrary to the spirit and provisions of this act are declared to be null and void, and shall not be evidence in any court having jurisdiction of mining suits in this Territory.

SEC. 3. This act shall take effect and be in force from and after its passage.

AN ACT OF PLACER MINES AND MINING.

[*Approved December 30, 1865.*]

3111—SECTION 1. It shall be lawful for any person, company, or association who shall place upon the mineral lands of this Territory commonly called placer-mining grounds, a pump or pumps, having a capacity sufficient to raise at least one hundred gallons of water per minute, with an engine or other power attached thereto, of sufficient power to work the same, with the *bona fide* intention of working the said placer grounds for the purpose of extracting the gold therefrom, to locate an amount of said placer grounds equal in extent to one quarter section, in such form and direction as he or they may elect: *Provided*, That said location shall in no case be more than one mile in length, nor less than one-quarter of a mile in width: and, *Provided*, That said machinery shall be used at least three months in each year for raising water to extract the gold from said grounds, and the presence of said machinery upon said grounds shall be the only evidence of title to said grounds; but in no case shall this act be so construed as to mean placer grounds which can be worked by water brought in ditches or flumes from any stream or other deposit of water; and said locations shall not in any case be made upon any grounds in the possession of any miner or miners at the time of location.

3112—SEC. 2. This act shall only apply to the county of Yuma.

SEC. 3. This act shall take effect and be in force from and after its passage.

AN ACT PROVIDING FOR THE LOCATION AND REGISTRATION OF MINES AND MINERAL DEPOSITS, AND FOR OTHER PURPOSES.

[*Approved November 5, 1866.*]

3113—SECTION 1. The mining districts heretofore created in the several counties of this Territory are hereby authorized and empowered to make all necessary rules and regulations for the location, registry and working of mines therein: *Provided*, That all locations and registrations of mines and mineral deposits hereafter made in any of the said districts shall be transmitted to the county recorder for record within sixty days after the same shall have been located.

3114—SEC. 2. The county recorders of the several counties are authorized and required to procure suitable books in which the records of all mines and mineral deposits shall be kept, which said books shall be paid for out of the county treasury, and they shall receive for their services herein the following fees: For recording and indexing each claim not exceeding one folio, one dollar; and for each additional folio, twenty cents.

3115—SEC. 3. Nothing in this act shall be so construed as to affect the claims to mines and mineral deposits heretofore located and duly recorded.

3116—SEC. 4. The claim of the Territory to all mining-claims heretofore located is hereby abandoned, and the same are hereby declared open to relocation and registry*

Provided, That nothing herein contained shall be so construed as to affect mining-claims heretofore sold and disposed of by the Territory.

3117 - SEC. 5. Nothing in this act shall be construed to apply to placer mines or mining, or other mineral deposits other than those commonly called veins or lode mines.

3118—SEC. 6. Chapter fifty, of the Howell code, entitled, "Of the registration and government of mines and mineral deposits," as well as all other acts or parts of acts in conflict with the provisions of this act, are hereby repealed.

SEC. 7. This act shall take effect and be in force from and after the first day of January, A. D. eighteen hundred and sixty-seven.

AN ACT TO PROVIDE FOR THE SEGREGATION OF MINING CLAIMS.

[Approved September 30, 1867.]

3119—SECTION 1. Whenever any one or more joint owners or tenants in common of gold, silver, copper, or mineral-bearing ledges or claims may desire to work or develop such ledges or claims, and any other owner or owners thereof shall fail or refuse to join in said work, after due notice of at least thirty days, given by publication in one newspaper printed in the county in which such ledges or claims are located, and if none be printed in said county, then in any newspaper printed in the Territory, said notice to have publication in four successive weeks of said paper, said other owner or owners may, upon application to the district court of the district wherein the ledge or claim is situated, cause the interests of said parties so refusing to be set off or segregated as hereinafter set forth.

3120—SEC. 2. The owner or owners of any mineral-bearing ledge or claim, after the expiration of said thirty days' notice having been given, may, if the party or parties notified fail or refuse to join in the working or developing said ledge or claim, apply to the district court of the district wherein the ledge or claim may be situated, for a partition or segregation of the interest or interests of the party or parties so failing or refusing to join.

3121—SEC. 3. The party or parties so applying shall set forth the fact that the said parties have been duly notified, in accordance with section one of this act, and that said party or parties have failed or refused to join in said work; all of which shall be sustained by the oath or affirmation of one or more of the parties applying; and, upon such application being made, the clerk of the said court shall post a notice at the office of the county recorder, and in two other conspicuous places within the district, stating the application, and notifying the parties interested that unless they appear within sixty days, and show good cause why the prayer of the petitioner should not be granted, that the same will be granted if good cause can be shown.

3122—SEC. 4. At the expiration of said sixty days, if the party or parties notified do not appear and show good cause why the prayer of the petitioner should not be granted, the court shall appoint two commissioners to go upon the ground and segregate the claims of the parties refusing to join; and in case they do not agree, they to choose a third party; and said commissioners shall make a report in writing to said court, who shall issue a decree in conformity with said report, which shall be final, except appeal be taken to the supreme court within thirty days after issuance thereof.

3123—SEC. 5. The provisions of this act shall not apply to the counties of Yavapai and Pima, and the county of Yuma.

3124—SEC. 6. All acts and parts of acts in conflict with the provisions of this act are hereby repealed.

SEC. 7. This act shall take effect and be in force from and after its passage.

AN ACT SUPPLEMENTARY TO CHAPTER XXXV., HOWELL CODE, "OF THE LIMITATION OF ACTIONS."

[Approved November 5, 1866.]

2111—SECTION 1. No action for the recovery of property in mining claims, or for the recovery of possession thereof, shall be maintained unless it appear that the plaintiff, his ancestor, predecessor, or grantor was seized or possessed of the premises in question within two years before the commencement of the action.

2112—SEC. 2. No cause of action or defense to an action, founded upon the title to property in mining claims, or to the rents or profits out of the same, shall be effectual unless it appear that the person prosecuting the action, or making the defense, or under whose title the action is prosecuted or the defense is made, or the ancestor, predecessor, or grantor of such person, was seized or possessed of the premises in question within two years before the commencement of the act in respect to which such action is prosecuted or defense made.

2113—SEC. 3. All acts or parts of acts in conflict with this act are hereby repealed.

SEC. 4. This act shall take effect and be in force from and after its passage.

AN ACT CONFERRING JURISDICTION OF ALL MINING CLAIMS ON THE DISTRICT COURT.

[Approved December 30, 1865.]

Be it enacted, etc. :

2366—SECTION 1. The district courts of said Territory shall have exclusive original jurisdiction of all suits and proceedings relating to mines and mineral and auxiliary lands, and the registry, and denouncement of the same, and all the jurisdiction, power, and authority conferred upon the probate courts and probate judges by chapter fifty of the Howell code, entitled, "Of the Registry and Government of Mines and Mineral Deposits," or otherwise, are hereby conferred upon the district courts and district judges respectively.

2367—SEC. 2. That section two of title one of said chapter is hereby repealed, and also all the other provisions of said chapter, conferring jurisdiction upon the probate courts and probate judges, over suits and proceedings relating to mines, mineral, and auxiliary lands, as well as other acts and parts of acts inconsistent with the provisions of this act.

2368—SEC. 3. All suits and other proceedings in said probate courts, now pending therein, and over which said probate courts have jurisdiction, are hereby transferred to, and shall be continued in, the district court of the county in which said suits and proceedings are now pending.

2369—SEC. 4. The clerks of the probate courts shall, within thirty days after the publication of this act, transfer to and file in the office of the district courts of their respective counties, all records and papers in suits and proceedings relating to mines, mineral, and auxiliary lands, which records and papers shall be kept and filed by the clerks of said district courts, and when so transferred and filed, said suits and proceedings shall be proceeded with as though commenced in said district courts: *Provided,* That in counties where there shall be no clerks of the district courts, the records and papers shall be transferred and filed as aforesaid within thirty days after the appointment of said clerks and their acceptance thereof.

SEC. 5. This act shall take effect and be in force from and after its passage.

A JUSTICE OF THE PEACE HAS NOT JURISDICTION IN MINING CASES.

3059—Sec. 623.   No action in regard to mining claims shall be maintained before any justice of the peace.

MINING LAWS OF NEW MEXICO.

The mining laws of New Mexico are simpler than those of any other State or Territory in the Union. By them only one record is necessary. If the claim is filed in the recorder's office of the county in which the property is situated, the title is perfect, and to learn all about the claims in a county a man has but to go to the recorder's office.

GENERAL LAWS OF 1876; CHAPTER XXXVIII.

AN ACT TO REGULATE THE MANNER OF LOCATING MINING CLAIMS AND FOR OTHER PURPOSES.

CONTENTS.

SEC. 1.   Location—bounds to be marked; notice of name of locator; make record in three months.
SEC. 2.   Record books must be provided.
SEC. 3.   Value of labor on mining claims defined.
SEC. 4.   Locations heretofore made, there being no adverse claims, may file claim within six months.
SEC. 5.   Ejectment in mining claims and real estate.
SEC. 6.   Repeals former acts.

Be it enacted by the Legislative Assembly of the Territory of New Mexico:

SECTION 1.   That any person or persons desiring to locate a mining claim upon a vein or lode of quartz or other rock in place bearing gold, silver, cinnabar, lead, tin, copper or other valuable deposit, must distinctly mark the location on the ground so that its boundaries may be readily traced; and post in some conspicuous place on such location, a notice in writing stating thereon the name or names of the locator or locators, his or their intention to locate the mining claim, giving a description thereof, by reference to some natural object or permanent monument as will identify the claim; and also within three months after posting such notice, cause to be recorded a copy thereof in the office of the recorder of the county in which the notice is posted; and provided no other record of such notice shall be necessary.

SEC. 2.   In order to carry out the intent of the preceding section, it is hereby made the duty of the probate judges of the several counties of this Territory, and they are hereby required to provide at the expense of their respective counties, such book or books as may be necessary and suitable in which to enter the record hereinbefore provided for. The fees for recording such notices shall be ten cents for every one hundred words.

SEC. 3.   That in estimating the worth of labor required to be performed upon any mining claim, to hold the same by the laws of the United States, in the regulation of mines, the value of a day's labor is hereby fixed at the sum of four dollars: *Provided, however,* That in the sense of this statute, eight hours of labor actually performed upon the mining claim shall constitute a day's labor.

SEC. 4. All locations heretofore made in good faith, to which there shall be no adverse claims, the certificate of which locations have been or may be filed for record and recorded in the recorder's office of the county where the location is made within six months after the passage of this act, are hereby confirmed and made valid. But where there may appear to be any such adverse claim, the said locations shall be held to be the property of the person having the superior title or claim, according to the laws in force at the time of the making of the said locations.

SEC. 5. An action of ejectment will lie for the recovery of the possession of a mining claim, as well also of any real estate, where the party suing has been wrongfully ousted from the possession thereof, and the possession wrongfully detained.

SEC. 6. That "An act concerning mining claims," approved January 18th, 1865, and an act amendatory thereof, approved January 3d, 1866: also, "An act entitled An act to amend certain acts concerning mining claims in the Territory of New Mexico," approved January 1st, 1872; be and the same are hereby repealed: *Provided*, That no locations completed or commenced under said acts shall be invalidated or in anywise affected by such repeal.

SEC. 7. That this act shall take effect and be in full force from and after its passage.

Approved January 11, 1876.

STOCK LAWS OF COLORADO.

CHAPTER LIX.

LIENS UPON PERSONAL PROPERTY.

SECTION 1. Any ranchman, farmer, agistor or herder of cattle, tavern-keeper or livery-stable keeper, to whom any horses, mules, asses, cattle or sheep, shall be entrusted for the purpose of feeding, herding, pasturing or ranching, shall have a lien upon said horses, mules, asses, cattle or sheep, for the amount that may be due for such feeding, herding, pasturing or ranching, and shall be authorized to retain possession of such horses, mules, asses, cattle or sheep, until the said amount is paid; and every hotel, tavern and boarding-house keeper shall have a lien upon the baggage of his or her patrons, boarders and guests, for the amount that may be due from such patrons, boarders and guests, for boarding and lodging, or either, and they are hereby authorized to hold and retain possession of such baggage until the amount so due for board or lodging, or either, is paid: *Provided*, That the provisions of this section shall not be construed to apply to stolen stock.

CHAPTER XXIII.

PUNISHMENT FOR BRANDING OR DEFACING BRAND OF STOCK.

SECTION 62. Every person who shall mark or brand, alter or deface the mark or brand of any horse, mare, colt, jack, jennet, mule, or any one or more head of neat cattle, or sheep, goat, hog, shoat or pig, not his or her own property, but belonging to some other person, with the intent thereby to steal the same, or to prevent identification thereof by the true owner, shall, on conviction thereof, be punished by confinement in the penitentiary for a term not less than one year nor more than five years: *Provided*, That no person shall be condemned to the penitentiary under this section unless the value of the property affected shall amount to twenty dollars. And in case the value of the property affected by the offenses herein described, or by larceny, or by buying or receiving goods, or other property obtained by larceny, burglary or robbery, shall not amount to five dollars, then the offender shall be punished by imprisonment in the county jail for a term not exceeding six months, or fined not exceeding one hundred dollars.

CHAPTER XCIII.

AN ACT to Provide for the Appointment of Sheep Inspectors.

SECTION 1. The county commissioners shall appoint a sheep inspector, who shall be a citizen of the county for which he is appointed, for each county containing two thousand sheep, who shall hold his office for two years, unless sooner removed; and any inspector may act in an adjoining county having no inspector, on request of the commissioners thereof.

Sec. 2. It shall be the duty of the sheep inspector, upon information by affidavit filed before a justice of the peace, that any flock of sheep within his jurisdiction has the scab or any other malignant contagious disease, upon two days' notice in writing to the owner or agent or person in custody of said flock, if owner or agent be absent from the county, to inspect said flock and report in writing the result of his inspection; and if so diseased, once every two weeks thereafter to re-inspect said flock and report in writing the result and treatment, if any, and the result until said disease is reported cured: *Provided*, That in case of the removal of the flock six miles from the range of any other sheep, as hereinafter provided, he shall only make one inspection every three months.

Sec. 3. And upon the arrival of any flock of sheep into the State, the owner or agent shall immediately report them to the inspector of the county for inspection, and the inspector shall inspect and report as provided in section two; and in case of failure, from any cause, of owner or agent to report for inspection, the inspector having knowledge of the arrival shall make an inspection of said flock and proceed as provided in section two.

Sec. 4. The owner or his agent of any flock reported by the inspector to be so diseased, shall immediately herd them so that they can not range upon or within one mile of any grounds accustomed to be ranged upon by any other sheep, and shall restrain them from passing over or traveling upon or within one mile of any public highway or road, and in case this can not be done he shall immediately remove said sheep to a locality where they shall not be permitted to range within less than six miles of any other flock of sheep, and said sheep shall continue to be herded under the above restrictions until, upon inspection, they shall be reported free from such disease.

Sec. 5. The owner or his agent or employes of any flock of sheep requiring or about to be inspected, shall afford the inspector all reasonable facilities for making the inspection; and for every violation of the provisions of this act, said owner or his agent or his employes shall be fined not less than ten dollars nor more than three hundred dollars, and every separate day's offense shall constitute a separate offense, and the written report of an offense made by an inspector under oath, shall be *prima facie* evidence of the commission of said offense, and any justice of the peace of the county in which the offense is committed shall have jurisdiction thereof, and the inspector shall *ex officio* report all violations of the provisions of this act of which he has knowledge.

Sec. 6. Every inspector, before entering upon the duties of his office, shall take the oath of office prescribed by law, and shall give bond to the State of Colorado in the sum of one thousand dollars, with good sureties, conditioned that he will faithfully perform the duties of his office; such bond shall be approved by the county clerk, who shall endorse upon every bond he shall approve as follows: " I am acquainted with the sureties herein, and believe them to be worth the amount of the sum of the within bond, over and above their just debts and liabilities."

Sec. 7. Such bond, with the oath endorsed thereon, shall be recorded in the office of the register of deeds for the county in which the inspector shall reside, and may be sued on by any person injured on account of the unfaithful performance of said inspector's duties: *Provided*, That no suit shall be so instituted after twelve months have elapsed from the time the cause of action accrued.

Sec. 8. Every inspector shall keep a fair and correct record of all his official acts, and, if required, give a certified copy of any record, upon payment of the fees therefor, and in case of inspector's death, resignation or removal, said record shall be deposited with the register of deeds.

Sec. 9. The inspector shall receive for his services five dollars per day whilst necessarily employed in inspecting; and for the first inspection an additional fee of one cent for every sheep, when the flock inspected is five hundred or less; and for inspecting larger flocks, five dollars for the first five hundred, and one-half cent each for the remainder of said flock, to be paid by the owner or his agent, and fifty cents for service of notice, and fifty cents for each copy, and two cents per line of ten words for any other official copies: *Provided*, That when an inspection is made upon information by affidavit, before a justice of the peace, and the inspector shall report, in substance, "no such disease," the party giving the information shall pay the inspector's fees; and the inspector shall receive ten per cent. of all fines and penalties in cases in which he gives information of the offense, and his interest in the result shall only go to his credibility, and not affect his competency as a witness. Remainder of fines shall be appropriated to the common school fund of the county.

SEC. 10. The notices herein shall be served by the inspector. or the sheriff, or any constable of the county.

SEC. 11. That the counties of Las Animas, Huerfano, Costilla and Conejos, are hereby excepted from the provisions of this act.

SEC. 12. No sheep inspector shall be appointed by the county commissioners of the counties of Pueblo, Douglas, Bent or Arapahoe, until they have been petitioned to make such appointment by the majority of the sheep owners of said counties, respectively.

AN ACT to prohibit the Herding of Sheep in the Neighborhood of Cities and Towns, and to repeal all Acts in relation thereto.

SECTION 1. No person shall keep or herd sheep to the number of ten (10) or more at or within two (2) miles of any city, town or village in this State: *Provided*, This act shall not prevent any one from driving sheep to market or from passing through any city, town or village, with such animals. or from keeping the same in any enclosure, or from herding for threshing purposes in any city, town or village: *Provided, further*, That this act shall not apply to any person who owns a stock ranch or farm within the above described limits.

SEC. 2. Whoever shall offend against the prohibitions of this act shall pay a fine of twenty-five dollars for each day in which the offense may be continued, and such fine may be recovered by action of debt in the name of the people, before a justice of the peace or in the district court of the proper county. All acts or parts of acts in conflict with this act are hereby repealed.

AN ACT regulating the Branding, Herding and Care of Stock.

SECTION 1. No person shall take up an estray animal, except in the county where he resides, and is a householder, nor unless the same be found in the vicinity of his residence. When any person shall take up an estray, he or she shall, within five days after taking up such estray, make out a written description of such animal, or animals, as the case may be, setting forth all marks and brands apparent and other marks of identity, such as color, age, or size, and present the same to the county clerk of the proper county. who shall endorse thereon the date of presentation of the same, and return one copy to the taker-up, and the other copy he shall place on record in the estray book. After filing said notice it shall be lawful for said taker-up to herd and take charge of said stock until the same shall be claimed and proved, and taken in charge by the owner thereof, or his duly authorized agent. The county clerk shall be entitled to twenty-five cents from the party presenting the same, for recording each certificate of estray, and five cents per head for each additional number more than one, contained in said certificate; and the taker-up of said estray shall be entitled to twenty-five cents for each original certificate, and mileage to and from the clerk's office at the rate of ten cents per mile.

SEC. 2. Before the owner of any estray so taken up and posted, shall be entitled to the possession of the same, he shall notify the taker-up of the time and place before the most convenient magistrate, county judge or justice of the peace, as the case may be, when and where he will prove his right to said property, and shall procure an order in writing from said magistrate to the taker-up to deliver the same over into the possession of the owner, upon payment to said taker-up of all the costs of taking up and ranching the said stock, at the rate of fifty cents per head per month: *Provided*, That where the taker-up is fully satisfied that said estray or estrays are the property of the claimant and that he is entitled to the possession of the same, he may, upon payment to him of his legal costs and charges, deliver the same to the claimant, and take his receipt therefor for the stock so delivered; but the taker-up shall be held liable for the value of said stock, if he shall deliver the same to any one not the owner or entitled to the same. At the expiration of twelve months from date of filing description of any estrays, and before the taker-up or other person not the rightful owner thereof shall gain any title to said estrays, it shall be the duty of the taker-up to file a notice with the county clerk, which shall be placed upon record in the estray book, setting forth a minute description of the estrays to be offered, and the time and place, when and where the same will be offered at public sale to the highest bidder for cash in hand, and shall put up a copy of the same at the court house door and in three other conspicuous places in the county, and one at the residence of the taker-up; said notice to be posted up for ten days before the day of sale. The sale shall be at public auction, to the highest bidder for cash in hand, and the proceeds of the same, after deducting all legal costs, fees, and charges, shall be paid into the hands of the county treasurer for the benefit and use of the school fund of the school district in which the said estray stock was taken up. If the said district shall not be organized, then the same shall be paid into the general school fund of the county: *Provided*, That no one shall have the right, for twelve months after the appearance of said stock, to advertise any animal which is branded with a brand recorded in the county where animal is running. Any justice of the peace of the county who is duly satisfied that the provisions of this act have been complied with by the taker-up, in all substantial parts, may, by order under his hand and seal, authorize the sale to be conducted by any constable or disinterested householder of the county, who shall execute and deliver to the purchaser a bill of sale of said stock, setting forth a description of the same and the price paid, and that the same was estray stock, which certificate shall vest a good and perfect title in the purchaser.

SEC. 3. If any person shall conceal, or attempt to conceal, any estray, or lost goods, found or taken up by such person, or shall efface or change any mark or brand thereon, or carry the same beyond the limits of the county where found, or knowingly permit the same to be done, or shall neglect to notify, or give information of estray animals to the county clerk of his county, every such person so offending shall be deemed guilty of larceny, and may be fined in any sum, at the discretion of the court.

SEC. 4. No mustang or other inferior stallion over the age of one year, nor any Texan, Mexican or Cherokee bull or other inferior bull over the age of one year, nor any Mexican or other inferior ram over the age of two months, shall be permitted to run at large in this State; and no stallion of any kind over the age of one year, shall be permitted to run at large in Boulder and Wells counties; nor shall any stallion over the age of one year be permitted to run at large in said State, except with a band of mares not less than ten in number. The owner or person in charge of such animal or animals as are prohibited from running at large by this section, who shall permit such animal or animals to run at large, may be fined for each offense not less than fifty dollars nor more than two hundred dollars. And it shall be lawful for any stock grower to castrate or cause to be castrated any such animal found running at large: *Provided*, That if any person shall castrate any stallion, bull or ram, and it shall, on proper evidence before any competent court, be proven to the satisfaction of said court that such animal was not of a class of stock prohibited from running at large by this act, said person shall be liable to damages to treble the value of said animal so castrated and costs of suit: *Provided, also,* That for the purposes of this act, any stallion possessing one-quarter of Mustang blood, shall be deemed a Mustang stallion; any bull possessing one-quarter Texan, Mexican or Cherokee blood, shall be deemed a Texan, Mexican or Cherokee bull, as the case may be; and any ram possessing one-quarter Mexican blood shall be deemed a Mexican ram: *And Provided, further,* That this section shall not take effect and be in force within the counties of Huerfano, Las Animas, Costilla and Conejos.

———

AN ACT to provide for the Branding, Herding and Care of Stock, and to repeal certain Acts in relation thereto.

SECTION 1. Any person or persons not being the owner or owners, or having the right of possession of any animal or animals, who shall be found driving or leading any such animal or animals from its or their usual range, such person or persons may be arrested by any constable, officer, or other person specially deputed for such purpose by a judge or justice of the peace, and such person or persons may be taken before any court of competent jurisdiction for examination and trial, and if found guilty, shall be punished as for larceny. In prosecutions for a violation of the provisions of this section, it shall not be necessary, in order to warrant a conviction, for the people to prove that the offense was committed knowingly, or willfully, or to show an intent, purpose or motive on the part of the accused; but if it shall be shown that the accused had had in his possession, or under his control or supervision, any animal so being wrongfully led or driven from its usual range, as aforesaid, or that the accused assisted in so leading or driving away any such animal without having the right of possession thereof as aforesaid, such showing shall be sufficient to warrant a conviction, unless the accused shall, by testimony in his behalf, explain the case made against him in such manner as to show good faith and an innocent purpose on his part.

SEC. 2. Any dog found worrying, running or injuring sheep or cattle, may be killed, and the owner or harborer of such dog shall be liable for all damages done by it.

SEC. 3. Any person or persons owning or keeping any flock or herd of sheep, any portion of which flock or herd may be diseased with the scab or any other contagious disease to which sheep are subject, shall be liable in the full amount of damage that may be incurred by other sheep owners or holders by reason of such diseased flock or herd of sheep being moved while in such condition.

SEC. 4. Animals such as are usually branded may be branded on either side with the owner's brand. All brands shall be recorded in the county where the owners reside. No evidence of ownership by brands shall be permitted in any court in this State unless the brands shall have been recorded as provided in this act. Each drove of cattle or sheep which may be driven into or through any county of this State shall be plainly branded or marked with one uniform brand or mark. The cattle shall be so branded with the distinguishing ranch or road brand of the owner as to show distinctly in such place or places as the owner may adopt. Sheep shall be marked distinctly with such mark or device as may be sufficient to distinguish the same readily, should they become intermixed with other flocks of sheep owned in the State. Any such owner or owners, or person in charge of such drove, which may be driven into or through the State, who shall fail to comply with the provisions of this act, shall be fined not less than fifty (50) nor more than three hundred (300) dollars, at the discretion of the court.

SEC. 5. Any person desiring to use any brand, shall make and sign a certificate setting forth a *fac simile* and description of the brand which he desires to use, and shall file the same for record in the office of the county clerk of the county wherein he resides, which clerk shall record the same in a book kept by him for that purpose, and from and after the filing of such certificate the person filing the same shall have the exclusive right to use such brand within such county for the purposes aforesaid. And any person or persons so desiring may, in the manner and with like effect, as herein provided, record his brand or mark in any county in this State into which his stock are liable to stray: *Provided*, That such mark or brand has not been heretofore recorded in such county by some other person, and if the clerk and recorder of any county shall, for any persons, record a brand, there being at the time of such recording a similar living mark or brand upon the records of his county, such clerk and recorder shall be liable to pay a fine of not less than twenty (20) nor more than one hundred (100) dollars: *And Provided, further,* When two or more similar marks or brands have been heretofore recorded in any county, the oldest record shall entitle the owner to the exclusive use thereof in such county.

SEC. 6. If any person shall brand or mark, or cause to be branded or marked, with his, her or their brand, or any other not the recorded brand of the owner, any animal being the property of another, or shall efface, deface or obliterate any brand or mark upon any animal, any such person so offending shall be deemed guilty of larceny, and on conviction thereof shall be confined in the penitentiary not less than one year nor more than five, as the court may direct, and shall also be liable to the owner thereof for three times the value of the animal so branded or marked, or upon which the brand or mark shall have been so effaced, defaced or obliterated, and in no case shall the payment of the forfeiture herein mentioned entitle the person so branding, effacing, defacing or obliterating a brand, to the property in the animal so branded or upon which the brand was effaced, defaced or obliterated, but such animal shall be surrendered to the proper owner.

SEC. 7. All neat stock over the age of one year found running at large in this State, without a mother, and upon which there is neither ear mark nor brand, shall be deemed a "Mavorick," and may be taken in charge by the captain or foreman of a legal round-up, and sold at such times and places and in such manner as shall be determined by the board of commissioners of the county in which they were taken up. The proceeds arising from such sales shall be paid into the county treasury of such county, and if any stock so sold shall, within the period of twelve months immediately following such sale, be claimed, identified and proven by the rightful owner, to the satisfaction of the board of county commissioners, it shall be their duty to issue a warrant against such fund in his favor, for the market value of such stock. At the expiration of such twelve months, the balance remaining of such fund shall be for the use and benefit of the cattle growers' association of the county in which such stock was found, if such an association then exists in such county; if not, it shall go into the general county fund for the benefit of the county. The captain or foreman of a legal round-up who shall sell any stock under the provisions of this section shall, within thirty days after such sale, pay all the proceeds of such sale into the county treasury, and he shall, as soon as convenient after coming into possession of said "Mavoricks," brand them with a brand adopted by the county commissioners for such "Mavoricks." Any person purchasing a "Mavorick" as aforesaid, shall receive from the captain or foreman of such legal round-up selling the same, a bill of sale signed by him as captain of such round-up, giving a description of the brand aforesaid and price paid. And such bill of sale shall entitle the purchaser to the legal ownership of such stock.

SEC. 8. Any captain or foreman of round-up who shall refuse or neglect to deliver to the county treasury all moneys received from the sale of "Mavoricks" or unbranded stock sold by him, or shall give a false or incorrect bill of sale of any stock sold, or shall refuse to give a bill of sale of any stock sold by him, shall be guilty of a misdemeanor, and on conviction thereof shall be fined or imprisoned, or both, at the discretion of the court.

SEC. 9. Any person who shall mark or brand, or cause to be marked or branded, or in any way convert to his or her use, or allow the same to be done by his employe or agent in his behalf, any animal known as a "Maverick," or any other animal not lawfully in possession of such person, except as otherwise provided in this act, shall be deemed guilty of larceny, and on conviction thereof shall be imprisoned not less than one month nor more than one year, as the court may determine.

SEC. 10. Any stock grower of this State may adopt and use an ear mark, and such ear mark shall be taken in evidence in connection with the owner's recorded brand, in all suits at law or in equity in which the title to stock is involved. Such ear mark shall be made by cutting or shaping the ear or ears of the animal so marked, but in no case shall the person so marking an animal cut off more than one-half of the ear so marked; neither shall any one mark by cutting an ear on both sides to a point. No county clerk or recorder shall record the same ear mark to more than one person.

SEC. 11. In all suits at law or in equity, or in any criminal proceedings, when the title to any stock is involved, the brand on an animal shall be *prima facie* evidence of the ownership of the person whose brand it may be: *Provided*, That such brand has been duly recorded as provided by law. Proof of the right of any person to use such brand shall be made by a copy of the record of the same, certified to by the county clerk of that county or any county in which the same is recorded under the hand and seal of office of such clerk.

SEC. 12. When the stock of any resident shall intermix with any drove of animals, it shall be the duty of any drovers or persons in charge to cut out and separate such stock from said drove immediately, except in the case of sheep and horses, when they shall be driven to the nearest suitable corral to be separated. Any person, either owner or driver, or otherwise connected with the management of such drove, who shall neglect to comply with the provisions of this section, shall be fined in any sum not exceeding five hundred (500) dollars for every offense, and shall be liable to indictment for larceny.

SEC. 13. When the stock of any person in Colorado shall be driven off its range without the owner's consent, by the drover of any herd or drove, every person engaged as drover of such stock, or otherwise engaged in the care and management thereof, shall be liable to indictment and punishment as for larceny, and shall be liable for damages to the amount of two hundred (200) dollars for each animal so driven off, together with all costs accruing in the trial of said cause, and said herd of stock or a sufficient number to cover all damages and costs, shall be held liable for the same.

SEC. 14. Any person owning or having in charge any drove of cattle, horses or sheep, who shall drive the same into or through any county of Colorado, of which the owner is not a resident or land owner, and where the land in such county is occupied and improved by settlers and ranchers, it shall be the duty of such owner or person in charge of such cattle, horses or sheep, to prevent the same from mixing with the cattle, horses or sheep belonging to the actual settlers, and also to prevent said drove of cattle, horses or sheep from trespassing on such land as may be the property or be in the possession of the actual settler and used by him for the grazing of animals or the growing of hay or other crops, or from doing injury to ditches. If any owner or person in charge of any said drove of stock shall willfully injure any resident of the State, by driving such drove of stock from the public highway, and herding the same on lands occupied and improved by settlers in possession of the same, it shall constitute a misdemeanor, and shall be punished by a fine of not less than twenty-five nor more than one hundred dollars, at the discretion of the court, and render the owner or person in charge of the drove so trespassing liable for the damages done to such settler.

SEC. 15. No hog or swine shall be permitted to run at large, and the owner of any hog or swine trespassing on the property of any person shall be liable in treble the damages occasioned by such trespass, and a fine of not less than five nor more than ten (10) dollars for each offense.

Sec. 16. The county commissioners of the several counties in this State shall have power or on request or ample notice given, to order that cattle be gathered together or rounded up at such time and places as shall be convenient and desirable to stock owners, in their respective counties, under such rules and regulations as the said county commissioners shall provide, and under their care and supervision: *Provided*, That such round-up shall not occur oftener than once in each year: *And Provided*, That no round-up shall be held within four miles of the line of any county in which no round-up is authorized by the county commissioners.

Sec. 17. Any person or persons who may skin or remove from the carcass any part of the skin, hide or pelt, of any neat cattle or sheep found dead, without permission from the owner, shall be deemed guilty of larceny, and on conviction thereof shall be punished in the manner provided by law for the punishment of larceny: *Provided*, Nothing herein shall be deemed to prevent the skinning of animals killed by railroad companies, by the employes of any company by which such stock may have been killed.

Sec. 18. No person or persons, whether as principal or agent, shall hereafter sell or otherwise dispose of any neat stock, nor shall any person, whether as principal or agent, buy, purchase or otherwise receive any such stock, unless the person or persons so selling or disposing of any such stock, shall give and the person or persons buying, purchasing or otherwise receiving any such stock shall take a bill of sale in writing, of the stock so sold, or disposed of, or so bought, purchased, or otherwise received as the case may be, in any of the following cases, viz.:

First. When such stock or any part thereof is to be shipped from the State, or slaughtered by the purchaser, or when the said stock or any part thereof is to be, by any such purchaser, sold to any other person or persons for shipment or slaughtering, or is to be by any such other person or persons offered for shipment or slaughtering.

Second. When any such stock is to be driven, led, taken or shipped to any market, range or other place more than ten miles distant from the place of delivery thereof, upon any such sale or purchase, or when any such stock is to be led, driven, taken or shipped to any market, range or other place more than ten miles distant from the place where such stock may be herded, or kept, or permitted to range at the time of the sale or purchase thereof, or to any market, range or other place more than ten miles distant from the place where such stock may have been herded, or kept, or permitted to range, for any portion of the three months next preceding such sale or purchase.

Third. When any such stock so sold or purchased, is at the time of such sale or purchase, or for any part of the sixty days next prior thereto, has been running at large upon an unenclosed range; but this provision shall not apply to sales of stock when the persons who sell are selling stock of which they have had actual and personal control and supervision, daily, for the said period of sixty days next prior to the sale thereof, and are rightfully entitled, either as principal or agent, to sell and dispose of the same.

Sec. 19. Any person who shall violate or fail to comply with any of the provisions of the last foregoing section, shall be deemed guilty of a misdemeanor, and upon conviction shall be fined in a sum not less than twenty-five dollars nor more than five hundred dollars, or imprisoned in the county jail not less than thirty days nor exceeding six months, or may be punished by both fine and imprisonment, in the discretion of the court.

Sec. 20. It shall be the duty of any person who may have purchased or received, or have in his possession any such stock, either for himself or for another, to exhibit, on reasonable request to any person inquiring therefor, the bill of sale of such stock, if in his power to do so, and if not in his power so to do, to state and give the reason therefor, and any person violating or failing to comply with the provisions of this section shall be deemed guilty and liable to punishment as provided in the next preceding section.

SEC. 21. The provisions of the last three sections shall be liberally construed in favor of the people, and, in order to convict of any offense made punishable in any of the said sections, it shall not be necessary for the prosecution to prove knowledge, intent, purpose or motive on the part of accused, but such knowledge, intent, purpose and motive may be presumed when the wrongful act of the accused has been shown, and shall justify a conviction, unless the testimony in the case shall satisfactorily show the good faith and innocent purpose of the accused.

SEC. 22. Any person who shall steal, embezzle, or knowingly kill, sell, drive, lead or ride away, or in any manner deprive the owner of the immediate possession of any neat cattle, horse, mule, sheep, goat, swine or ass, or any person who shall steal, embezzle, or knowingly kill, sell, drive, lead or ride away, or in any manner apply to his own use any neat cattle, horse, mule, goat, sheep, ass or swine, the owner of which is unknown, or any person who shall knowingly purchase from any one not having the lawful right to sell and dispose of the same, any neat cattle, horse, mule, sheep, swine or ass, shall be deemed guilty of a felony, and on conviction thereof in any court of competent jurisdiction, shall be punished by imprisonment not exceeding six years, or by a fine not exceeding five thousand (5,000) dollars, at the discretion of the court.

SEC. 23. All cases which are by this act declared to be larceny, and in all cases of felonious taking, stealing, riding, driving, leading and carrying away of any animal or animals herein referred to, the same shall be deemed, and taken to be, and the courts of this State shall construe the same to be grand larceny, subjecting the offender or offenders to be condemned to the penitentiary for a term of not less than one year nor more than ten years, except as otherwise provided for in this act, notwithstanding the value of such animals may be less than twenty dollars.

SEC. 24. Any person or persons who may sell or offer for sale or trade any neat stock upon which such persons have not their recorded mark or brand, or for which the person so offering has neither bill of sale nor power of attorney from the owner of such stock, authorizing such sale, every person so offering shall be deemed guilty of larceny, unless such person upon trial shall establish and prove that he was at the time the actual owner of the stock so sold or traded, or offered for sale or trade, or that he acted by the direction of one shown and proved to be the actual owner of such stock; and in prosecutions for a violation of this section it shall not be necessary, in order to warrant a conviction for the people, to prove motive, intent or purpose on the part of the accused, or that the accused knew that the stock sold or traded, or offered for sale or trade, was so sold, traded or offered in violation hereof, but the fact of such selling, trading, or offering for sale or trade contrary to the provisions hereof, when proved, shall be sufficient to authorize a conviction, unless the accused shall by testimony explain the case made by the people in a manner consistent with good faith and an innocent purpose.

Approved March 22, 1877.

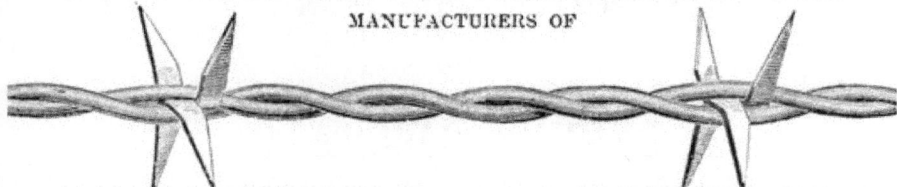

ARIZONA STAR.

DAILY AND WEEKLY.

The ARIZONA STAR, published in Tucson, Arizona Territory, is acknowledged as the best authority on the great silver mining and stock interests of Arizona, and especially of Pima county and Southern Arizona.

The STAR has reliable correspondents in every mining district of any importance, who report all developments and new discoveries, so that its readers are always informed as to what is going on.

To advertisers the STAR offers the best medium in the Territory. Its circulation is more than double that of any other journal published in Arizona. It circulates in every settlement in the Territory, Sonora and Southern New Mexico

The progress of Arizona has been marvelous during the past two years. The bullion output has increased in that time from $500,000 to $12,000,000. This is almost all produced in Southern Arizona. Population of the Territory has increased 22,000 during 1881. The mercantile tonnage delivered at Tucson has increased in two years from 12,500,000 lbs. per year, to 160,000,000 lbs., and several hundred millions for Southern Arizona. Agriculture and stock raising are flourishing as well as mining.

For mill men, manufacturers of all kinds, and wholesale merchants, Arizona opens a new field. The railroad has pierced our Territory. Eastern cities are competing with San Francisco for the trade of Arizona. Our population has more than doubled within the last six months. All kinds of industries are springing up. Tucson has over 10,000 inhabitants. Arizona about 50,000. This population opens a great market to the producers.

If you want to reach the people of this Territory advertise in the ARIZONA STAR.

The DAILY STAR will be mailed to any part of the United States for $10.00 per year, or $6.00 for six months.

The WEEKLY STAR will be mailed one year for $3.00, and six months for $2.00, to any part of the United States, post paid.

This is about one-half the price of any other journal published in Arizona, Southwestern New Mexico and Sonora.

RATES OF ADVERTISING:

Space.	1 Week.	1 Month.	3 Months.	6 Months.	1 Year.
One Inch	$ 1.50	$ 3.00	$ 8.00	$15.00	$ 25.00
Two Inches	2.50	5.50	15.00	25.00	40.00
Four Inches	4 00	8.00	25 00	45.00	80.00

The above rates are for the Daily. Daily and Weekly, 20 per cent. advance on the above; Weekly, 25 per cent. off.

L. C. HUGHES, Proprietor.

RAND, McNALLY & CO.'S
MAP PUBLICATIONS.

Rand, McNally & Co.'s Business Atlas. Price, $12.00.

Containing large scale maps of each State and Territory of the United States, the Provinces of Canada, West India Islands, etc., etc., together with a complete reference map of the World, printed in colors from plates secured by letters patent, producing the clearest typographical effect of any known engraved plates, accompanied by a new and original compilation and ready reference index, showing in detail the entire Railroad System of North America, the Express Company doing business over each road, and accurately locating Counties, Parishes, Islands, Lakes, Rivers, Mountains, etc., etc., together with all Post Offices, Railroad Stations, and Villages in the United States and Canada, with latest official census or estimated population of each. 430 pages.

Rand, McNally & Co.'s Business Atlas of the Mississippi Valley and Pacific Slope. Price, $7.50.

Including the States of Ohio, Kentucky, Tennessee and Alabama, and all States and Territories west to the Pacific Coast—a portion of our $12.00 work, containing 116 pages.

Rand, McNally & Co.'s New Railroad and County Map of the United States and Canada, mounted upon cloth, with rollers top and bottom, $15.00; or rollers at each end, "Panorama Mounting," accommodating itself to any required space, $16.00.

Compiled from the latest Government Surveys, and drawn to an accurate scale; size, 58 by 100 inches; scale, 32 miles to one inch; borders of States and Counties beautifully tinted, colors being printed from plates secured by letters patent. This work has occupied two years in compilation and engraving, at a cost of nearly $20,000; plates have been carefully corrected to date, presenting the finest work of Art of its kind. This Map is deserving of special mention as being the first map of the United States made upon a geometrical projection since the war.

Rand, McNally & Co.'s New Railroad and County Map, extending from the Atlantic Coast to Great Salt Lake, size, 58 by 80 inches, in colors, mounted upon heavy paper, rollers top and bottom, (a section of our complete United States work), a map for the people, at a popular price. Retail, $5.00.

Rand, McNally & Co.'s New Railroad and County Map of the Territories and Pacific Coast, 58 by 60 inches, in colors, mounted upon heavy paper, rollers top and bottom (a section of our complete United States work), a map for the people, at a popular price. Retail, $5.00.

Rand, McNally & Co.'s Railroad, County and Township Map of the Northwest, showing all the Railroads in red, and Rivers in blue; size, 41 by 58 inches; extending from Columbus, Ohio, to the Rocky Mountains, and from the southern boundary of Missouri to the British Possessions, north; mounted on rollers. Price, $3.00.

Rand, McNally & Co.'s New Railroad and County Map of the Northeastern States, with parts of Ontario and Quebec; size, 40 by 42 inches; scale, 17 miles to one inch; mounted upon heavy paper, rollers top and bottom. Price, $2.00.

This Map includes all of the New England States, New York, New Jersey, Pennsylvania, Maryland, Delaware, Quebec and Ontario.

Rand, McNally & Co.'s Guide Map of Chicago, with a ready reference index, showing all Parks, Boulevards, Streets, Banks, Railroad Depots, Churches, and prominent Buildings. Price, 25 cents.

Address,   **Rand, McNally & Co.,**
                        Map Publishers and Engravers, CHICAGO.
Indexed Pocket Maps of all States and Territories.

ACROSS THE CONTINENT

VIA THE

ATCHISON, TOPEKA & SANTA FE R. R.

THE GREAT SOUTHERN ROUTE

THROUGH

The Most Magnificent Mountain Scenery,
The Wonderful Mining District, and
The Most Fertile Valleys,

IN THE

WIDE WORLD.

Are you a Miner, a Tourist, a Speculator or an Invalid?

TAKE THE POPULAR ROUTE FOR WEALTH AND HEALTH

TO THE

Champion Gold and Silver Regions of the Continent.

The THROUGH PACIFIC EXPRESS with Pullman Palace Drawing Room Sleeping Cars leaves Kansas City daily for

SAN FRANCISCO.

The only **DIRECT ROUTE** to all points in

Mexico, New Mexico, Western Texas, Arizona and Southern California,

AND THE POPULAR LINE TO DENVER, PUEBLO, LEADVILLE, AND ALL POINTS IN COLORADO.

Three Daily Trains each way for all Colorado and New Mexico points.

W. F. WHITE,

General Passenger and Ticket Agent, TOPEKA, KAS.

PACIFIC COAST STEAMSHIP CO.

Steamers of this Company sail from Broadway Wharf, San Francisco, for ports in

California, Oregon, Washington

AND IDAHO TERRITORIES,

BRITISH COLUMBIA AND ALASKA,

AS FOLLOWS:

CALIFORNIA SOUTHERN COAST ROUTE.

The Steamers ANCON and ORIZABA sail every five days at 9 a. m. for San Luis Obispo, Santa Barbara, Los Angeles and San Diego, as follows: ORIZABA, 10th, 20th and 30th of each month: ANCON, 5th, 15th and 25th of each month.

The Steamer SENATOR sails every Wednesday at 8 a. m. for Santa Cruz, Monterey, San Simeon, Cayucos, Gaviota, Santa Barbara and San Buenaventura.

BRITISH COLUMBIA AND ALASKA ROUTE.

The Steamer EUREKA, carrying the United States mails, sails from Portland, Oregon, on or about the 1st of each month, for Port Townsend, W.T., Victoria and Nanaimo, B. C.; Port Wrangle, Sitka and Harrisburg, Alaska; connecting at Port Townsend with Victoria and Puget Sound Steamer leaving San Francisco the 30th of each month.

VICTORIA AND PUGET SOUND ROUTE.

The Steamers IDAHO and GEO. W. ELDER, carrying Her Britannic Majesty's and United States Mails, sail from Broadway Wharf, San Francisco, at 2 p. m. on the 10th, 20th and 30th of each month, for Victoria, B. C., Port Townsend, Seattle, Tacoma, Steilacoom and Olympia, making close connection with steamboats, etc., for Skagit River and Cassiar Mines, Nanaimo, New Westminster, Yale, Sitka, and all other important points.

NOTE.—When Sunday falls on the 10th, 20th or 30th, steamers sail from San Francisco one day earlier.

The Steamer VICTORIA sails for New Westminster and Nanaimo about every two weeks, as per advertisements in the San Francisco ALTA or GUIDE.

PORTLAND (OREGON) ROUTE.

The Oregon Railway & Navigation Company and the Pacific Coast Steamship Company dispatch one of their steamships, STATE OF CALIFORNIA, OREGON or COLUMBIA, carrying the United States Mail, and Wells, Fargo & Co.'s Express, every fifth day, at 10 a. m., for Portland and Astoria, Oregon.

EUREKA AND HUMBOLDT BAY ROUTE.

Steamer LOS ANGELES sails from Broadway Wharf on the 7th, 17th and 27th of each month. Returning, leaves Eureka at high tide on the 2d, 12th and 22d of each month.

POINT ARENA AND MENDOCINO ROUTE.

Steamer ALEX. DUNCAN sails from Broadway Wharf, San Francisco, at 3 p. m. every Monday, for Point Arena, Cuffey's Cove, Little River, Shelter Cove and Mendocino.

Rates of Fare, which include Meals and Sleeping Accommodations, are lower by this than by any other route.

Through Tickets sold at all the principal places on the coast. Stages and Railroads make close connection with Steamers for all the principal places in the interior.

For further information in regard to Tickets, call at the

TICKET OFFICE, 214 MONTGOMERY STREET,

OPPOSITE THE RUSS HOUSE.

GOODALL, PERKINS & CO., General Agents, No. 10 Market Street, San Francisco.

UNIVERSITY OF KANSAS.

The University of Kansas enters upon its sixteenth year with greatly increased facilities for affording thorough collegiate instruction. Expenses from $150 to $300.

THE COLLEGIATE DEPARTMENT

Comprises the following courses: Classical, Scientific, Modern Literature, Civil Engineering, Natural History, Chemistry and Preparatory Medical.

THE PREPARATORY DEPARTMENT

Devotes three years to the training for the Collegiate.

THE NORMAL DEPARTMENT

Embraces three courses: Classical, Scientific and Modern Literature, and is especially designed for those wishing to prepare for teaching in the higher grades.

THE LAW DEPARTMENT

Has been established three years, and is now one of the most important features of the institution. Course of two years; tuition, $25 per annum.

THE MUSICAL DEPARTMENT

Is under the charge of a competent instructor. Instruction given in piano, organ and vocal music.

For catalogue and information, address,

JAMES MARVIN, A.M., D.D.,

Chancellor, Lawrence, Kansas.

THE MONTEZUMA

—— AT ——

The Hot Springs of Las Vegas, New Mexico,

ON THE LINE OF THE

ATCHISON, TOPEKA & SANTA FE R. R.

Opened to the Public, April 15, 1882.

EVERYTHING FIRST CLASS.

For particulars as to rates, accommodations, etc., address,

W. F. WHITE,		**CLARK D. FROST,**
Gen. Pass. and Ticket Agt.,	or	Manager The Montezuma,
TOPEKA, KAS.		LAS VEGAS, N. M.

RAND, McNALLY & CO.'S

POCKET MAPS AND GUIDES

FOREIGN COUNTRIES AND CITIES.

BOUND IN CLOTH.

Afghanistan, see Persia...$	
Africa, in three sheets, two being 21x14 inches, and one 14x11 inches, showing plans of cities of Algiers and Tunis,...	.75
Alaska, 34x21 inches...	1.00
Asia, 21x14 inches. Not kept in stock.	
Australia and New Zealand, with plans of Sydney and Port Jackson, 21x14 inches......	.50
Austro-Hungarian Monarchy, with plan of Vienna, 21x14 inches...................	.50
Belgium and The Netherlands, with plan of Brussels, 21x14 inches...............	.50
British America (Dominion of Canada), 21x14 inches. Not kept in stock..........	.50
Central America, 14x11 inches...	.50
China and Japan, 21x14 inches..	.50
Cuba, 21x14 inches..	.50
Denmark, with North portion of the German Empire, comprising Schleswig, Holstein and Lauenburg, 14x11 inches..	.50
England and Wales, 21x14 inches, with Index to cities, towns, etc...............	.75
Europe, 21x14 inches...	.50
France, 21x14 inches, with plan of Paris, and Index to cities..................	.75
Germany, two sheets, 21x14 inches each, with Index to cities..................	1.00
Greece, and the Ionian Islands, 21x14 inches................................	.50
India, Indo-China and Further India, with plans of Calcutta and Bombay, 21x14 inches..	.50
Ireland, 21x14 inches, with Index to cities, towns, etc.......................	.75
Italy, 21x14 inches...	.50
Japan, in two sheets, 22x14 inches each....................................	1.00
Mexico, 21x14 inches, with Index to cities, towns, etc.......................	.50
Netherlands, see Belgium.	
New Zealand, see Australia.	
North America, showing the West India Islands and Central America. 21x14 inches. Not kept in stock.	
Oceanica, 21x14 inches...	.50
Palestine, with plats showing Environs of Jerusalem, journeyings of Christ, and sketch showing division into tribes. 21x14 inches..........................	.50
Persia and Afghanistan, 14x11 inches.......................................	.50
Portugal, see Spain.	
Russia (European), 21x14 inches..	.50
Scotland, 21x14 inches, with Index to cities, towns, etc......................	.75
South America, in two sheets, 21x14 inches each, showing plans of Bay of Rio de Janeiro, Isthmus of Panama and City of Buenos Ayres............................	.75
Spain and Portugal, with plans of Madrid and Lisbon, 21x14 inches............	.50
Sweden and Norway, 21x14 inches...	.50
Switzerland, 21x14 inches..	.50
Turkey in Asia (Asia Minor), and Transcaucasia, 21x14 inches................	.50
Turkey in Europe, 21x14 inches...	.50
World, on Mercator's Projection, 21x14 inches..............................	.50

BAEDEKER'S GUIDES.—Belgium and Holland, $2.00; The Rhine, $2.50; North Germany, $2.50; South Germany, $2.50; North Italy, $2.50; South Italy, $2.50; Central Italy, $2.50; Paris, $2.50; Switzerland, $3.00; Palestine and Syria, $7.50; Lower Egypt, $5.50.

Appleton's European Guide Book, 150 engravings, 2 volumes, Morocco, $5.00. Harper's Hand Book for Travelers in Europe and the East.—Vol. I, Great Britain, Ireland, France, Belgium, Holland, price $3.00; Vol. II, Germany, Austria, Italy, Egypt, Turkey, Greece, price $3.00; Vol. III, Switzerland, Tyrol, Denmark, Norway, Sweden, Russia, Spain, price $3.00. Standford's London Guide, $1.25; Standford's Round About London, $1.00; Bacon's London Guide, 50c. Pocket Maps of following cities: Amsterdam, Athens, Berlin, Calcutta, Canton, Constantinople, Dublin, Edinburgh, Lisbon, Liverpool, Madrid, Moscow, Rome, St. Petersburgh, Vienna and Warsaw, price 50 cents each. Sent by mail, postage prepaid, on receipt of price.

RAND, McNALLY & CO.,

Map Publishers, CHICAGO.

www.ingramcontent.com/pod-product-compliance
Lightning Source LLC
Chambersburg PA
CBHW030358270326
41926CB00009B/1159